LET THE PEOPLE RULE

Let the People Rule

HOW DIRECT DEMOCRACY CAN MEET
THE POPULIST CHALLENGE

JOHN G. MATSUSAKA

PRINCETON UNIVERSITY PRESS
PRINCETON & OXFORD

Copyright © 2020 by Princeton University Press

Published by Princeton University Press
41 William Street, Princeton, New Jersey 08540
6 Oxford Street, Woodstock, Oxfordshire OX20 1TR

press.princeton.edu

All Rights Reserved
ISBN 978-0-691-19972-6
ISBN (e-book) 978-0-691-19975-7

British Library Cataloging-in-Publication Data is available

Editorial: Bridget Flannery-McCoy and Alena Chekanov
Production Editorial: Jenny Wolkowicki
Jacket design and illustration by Karl Spurzem
Production: Erin Suydam
Publicity: James Schneider and Amy Stewart
Copyeditor: Maia Vaswani

This book has been composed in Arno Pro

Printed on acid-free paper. ∞

Printed in the United States of America

10 9 8 7 6 5 4 3 2 1

To Jia

CONTENTS

PREFACE

MORE THAN TWO CENTURIES AGO, the Founders of the United States launched an experiment to determine if ordinary people were capable of governing themselves. The results of that experiment have been immensely consequential for humankind, affirming the basic competence of common people and providing a powerful counterargument to those who would rule over others without their consent. That experiment continues to shape the modern world, and democracy has become the government of choice for free people across the globe. Yet today many people feel that something has gone wrong—that government is drifting out of their control, its strings pulled by a shadowy elite. The people with these concerns are called populists, and their growing numbers are destabilizing the trajectory of many Western democracies and sending them off into uncharted waters.

I wrote this book because I felt there was a view missing in contemporary discussions of populism and democracy: the view of the populists themselves. Public discussion of populism has been framed largely by elites who see it as an emotional reaction to changes in the world, an angry "backlash," a temper tantrum that needs to be palliated. The populists' insistent complaint that government has drifted out of the people's control has been dismissed as a rationalization or simply ignored. As the book shows, however, the populists are on to something. There is good reason to believe that government *has* gradually slipped from popular control over the past century. I wanted to bring this view into the daylight and share the evidence that lends it credibility.

Once we recognize that democracy is adrift, our entire approach to the challenge of populism changes. In the elite formulation, since the root problem is the excessive emotionality of the people, the solution is to transfer even more power from ordinary people (temperamental and irrational) to technocrats, judges, and other elites (cool headed and analytic). They would address the shortcomings of democracy by having less democracy. Yet if the loss of popular control is not feeling but fact, a different tack is called for.

ix

I argue in this book that we should fix the problem by making government *more* democratic. To restore the connection between the people and government, let the people make more of the important public decisions themselves: direct democracy.

I am acutely aware that the idea of giving the people more power might seem counterintuitive to some readers. Indeed, for those who were upset by the outcome of the Brexit referendum or who disliked recent American referendums that legalized marijuana, allowed assisted suicide, or increased the minimum wage, it may seem absurd to turn over policy decisions to ordinary, potentially uninformed citizens. Of course, some readers' intuitions may run the other way; they may find the idea of giving the people more of a voice an entirely natural extension of self-government. Either way, it is important to realize that those intuitions are simply that—intuitions. One of the book's goals is to sharpen and sometimes challenge those intuitions by exploring how referendums actually work in practice.

Having been immersed in the study of direct democracy for three decades, and having examined it closely from many different angles, I have seen its good sides and its bad sides. Public discourse, however, tends to dwell primarily on the bad. Critics often cherry-pick the rich history of direct democracy, neglecting the broader picture of its successful operation in the United States and across the globe for a century or more. These criticisms of direct democracy tap into underlying apprehensions among Americans that I suspect stem from the fact that the United States is a global outlier—one of very few countries that has never held a national referendum—making it seem more far-fetched than it actually is.

To allow interested readers to form their own opinions, the chapters that follow describe what we know about direct democracy: its fascinating history, the rich scholarly literature about its use and influence, and a variety of evidence collected specifically for this book that will be new even to specialists. I have taken pains to describe everything in nontechnical language, with technical details provided in footnotes for those readers who want to see them.

The book offers a path forward for democracy that is distinct from the ideologically driven solutions that are so common today. I have come to believe that our pervasive tendency to see the world through partisan lenses is a substantial part of our problem. The solutions advanced here resist placement on a conventional ideological spectrum; giving the people more control of policy is not a liberal or conservative position but an aspiration that spans the spectrum.

Not everyone will reach the same conclusion about the merits of direct democracy, but I hope that by the end of this book it will seem, at the very least, like an idea worth more consideration than it has been given to date. Even better, I hope some might come to see referendums as a way to meet the challenges of populism and make our aspirations for self-government more of a reality. Democracy is drifting away from popular control, but we have the tools to bring it back.

———

I have been thinking about these issues for several years, but the hard work on the book began in 2017 during a sabbatical at the University of Chicago's Stigler Center for the Study of the Economy and the State. I am grateful to Luigi Zingales, the center's director, for hosting my visit, for encouraging me to pursue the project, and gently twisting my arm to give a series of lectures in which I sketched out the framework of the book. My visit there was quite stimulating and led me to think more broadly about the questions than I originally anticipated. Discussions with faculty members and visiting scholars during my visit to the center were also important in developing my ideas.

As I wrote the book, my colleagues at the University of Southern California were immensely helpful in allowing me to test-run arguments over lunch, coffee, and dinner, and during workshops. No doubt they sometimes tired of hearing about it, but they never let on, and our wide-ranging discussions substantially sharpened the arguments. Many people informed my thinking but I want to acknowledge by name several people who provided particularly helpful comments, discussions, or written feedback: Chris Berry, Odilon Camara, Janna King, Ekkehard Köhler, Martin Levine, Anthony Orlando, Oguz Ozbas, and Yanhui Wu. I received able research assistance from Artem Joukov and Elise Matsusaka.

My editor at Princeton University Press, Bridget Flannery-McCoy, made numerous contributions to every aspect of the manuscript: organization, structure, exposition—going well beyond the call of duty. I thought I was done when I gave her the first draft, but the version here is vastly different and, in my opinion, vastly superior due to her patient questions, comments, and calls for revision—more accessible, clearer, and stripped of superfluous digressions.

Finally, my largest debt in this book is to my wife, Jia. Not only did she provide the usual moral support that spouses are supposed to provide, but she read every chapter in detail, and gave me extensive feedback. Her comments, informed by both her PhD training and her years of professional business experience, led to changes in the tone, orientation, and quality of the arguments in every chapter of the book. For her consistent support through the ups and downs, there was never any question but that I would dedicate this book to her.

Introduction

DEMOCRACY IS ordinary people governing themselves. This type of government is the best we know and has served us well for some time. Yet many today have the uneasy feeling that democracy is adrift, slowly slipping from popular control, carried by powerful undercurrents that we can only dimly perceive.

In 2016 this long-simmering anxiety came to the surface in a string of unexpected populist election victories across the world. Donald Trump was elected president of the United States on a platform promising to "drain the swamp." Democratic socialist Bernie Sanders, running on a promise to make government work for everyone—"not just the 1 percent"—came close to taking the Democratic Party nomination from establishment favorite Hillary Clinton. British voters decided to leave the European Union. Populist parties did unexpectedly well in Austria, France, the Netherlands, and Poland; by 2018, populist parties controlled the government of six European countries and through coalition agreements had a hand in governing six others.

While Trump and Sanders disagreed on just about every substantive policy, they shared a diagnosis about the root problem, and what was needed to fix it:

> Our campaign is about representing the great majority of Americans—Republicans, Democrats, Independents, Conservatives and Liberals—who read the newspaper, or turn on the TV, and don't hear anyone speaking for them. . . . I declared my campaign for the Presidency on the promise to *give our government back to the people.* (Donald Trump)[1]

> My hope is that when future historians look back and describe how our country moved forward into reversing the drift toward oligarchy, and created *a government which represents all the people and not just the few,* they will note that, to a significant degree, that effort began with the political revolution of 2016. (Bernie Sanders)[2]

Across the Atlantic, opponents of European integration sounded the same themes. The official slogan of the Brexit campaign was "take back control." As leading Brexiter Nigel Farage saw it:

> Because what the little people did, what the ordinary people did, what the people who have been oppressed over the last few years and seen their living standards go down [did]—they rejected the multinationals, they rejected the merchant banks, they rejected big politics and they said, "Actually, we want our country back, . . . *we want to be an independent self-governing, normal nation.*"[3]

All of this rhetoric is textbook populism, an appeal to "the people" to take back their government from "elites" that have captured and subverted it.[4] The identity of the elites varied with the speaker. For Trump, it was "the swamp," a shadowy combination of government officials, lobbyists, media, and special interests entrenched in Washington, DC. For Sanders, it was plutocrats and their corporate allies. In Europe, it was technocrats in Brussels and other supranational organizations. While the elites may have been different, the claim that the people were no longer in control was the same.

This populist rhetoric was not conjured out of thin air. Politicians were retailing a message that voters already believed. Over the past 70 years, voters have grown increasingly skeptical about the responsiveness of government. Figure I.1, based on the University of Michigan's long-running American National Election Studies (ANES) opinion survey, illustrates this trend. Since 1952, the ANES has asked people whether they agreed or disagreed with the statement "People like me have no say in government."[5] The figure shows the percentage of people who *disagreed* with the statement—and while there is some volatility, the downward trend is unmistakable.

In 1952, only a small fraction of Americans felt left out by government; 87 percent of college-educated Americans disagreed with the statement, as did 65 percent of high-school–educated Americans. Since then, public opinion has soured considerably. As of 2016, the worst year yet, only 35 percent of college-educated Americans and 25 percent of high-school–educated American disagreed. We are now in a situation where a large majority of Americans—both more and less educated—believe they have no say in government.

Disaffection is also high in Europe. A 2017 Gallup poll of the 27 European Union member states found that 57 percent of people had "no confidence" in their national government.[6] Although Europe lacks a long-standing survey like the ANES tracking public confidence in government, a major study of opinion in OECD (Organisation for Economic Co-operation and Development)

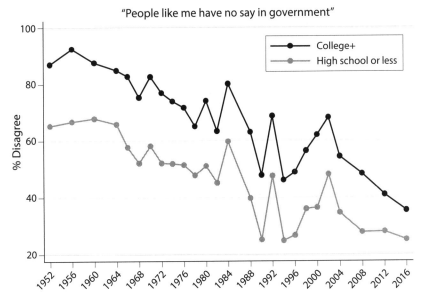

FIGURE I.1. Public Opinion on Government Responsiveness

countries combining a variety of different surveys concluded that "citizens in nearly all advanced industrial democracies [have become] increasingly skeptical toward politicians, political parties, and political institutions" since the 1960s or 1970s (depending on the country).[7]

———

What explains the long downward slide in public confidence? Why do so many people feel they have lost control of the government?

Two possible explanations dominate public debate.[8] The "economics view" is that people are frustrated by the government's failure to shield them from economic dislocation caused by globalization, automation, and the changing demand for skills in the emerging information and technology industries. Looking at the United States, advocates of this view argue that the government has alienated ordinary Americans by catering to the economic winners—large financial institutions and big high-tech firms—especially during the financial crisis, when it bailed out big banks and corporations while watching impassively as ordinary people lost their jobs and homes.

The "cultural view" is that people feel threatened by social and cultural changes associated with globalization and immigration, which they see as undermining their traditional beliefs and ways of life. The people do not see government as striving to stem the inflow of new people and ideas; to the contrary, they see it as actively promoting open borders, cultural change, and the importation of global social values.

The debate between these two views is the subject of a rapidly growing, empirically sophisticated literature spanning economics, political science, and sociology. To assess the competing arguments, researchers look for statistical connections between support for populist candidates and a voter's exposure to economic or cultural "shocks." For example, if a study shows that people who recently lost their jobs were more likely to vote for Trump, it supports the economics view; if it shows that people in communities with an influx of immigrants were more likely to vote for Brexit, it supports the cultural view.

Both explanations enjoy some empirical support, but the literature shows no sign of converging to a consensus view, and neither explanation seems to account for the broader reality shown in figure I.1. The decline in public confidence is a long-running phenomenon, requiring a long-run explanation; it cannot be attributed primarily to recent economic shocks, such as the Great Recession, or recent surges in immigration. Moreover, both views see populism as a phenomenon involving less-skilled and less-educated citizens, which makes them hard to square with the fact that trust has deteriorated among both more- and less-educated people. If we want to understand the growth of populist sentiment, we need causes that have been at work for nearly a century, and that affect citizens at all levels of education.

One impediment to understanding, it seems to me, is the way this debate has been framed. When considering potential explanations, the one professed by the populists themselves has been largely ignored. The populists, as voiced by the politicians who represent them, say they are frustrated because the government is drifting out of their control and into the hands of elites. Yet contemporary discussion usually treats their words as a façade behind which hides the "true" explanation. The idea that the connection between the people and the government might be fraying, making the system less democratic, is dismissed out of hand.

The first goal of this book is to take the populist argument on its own terms, and seriously consider the possibility that government might well be slipping from popular control. Investigating this possibility leads down a variety of disciplinary paths, into the terrain of political science, economics, history, and law, and involves examining published evidence as well as new data I have assembled specifically for this book. What emerges is a picture of the evolution of government over the past 100 years that lends support to populist claims:

stretching back a century, government in fact has become less responsive and less accountable to the people.

A particularly intriguing part of the story is that loss of popular control came as an unintended consequence of a series of sensible changes in the structure of government. Disconnection has its roots in an increasingly complex world characterized by rapid technological change, globalization, and immense governments that citizens expect to address every important social and economic issue. To deal with these complications, governments have become increasingly reliant on experts to design and implement public policies.

The heart of government was once the small group of elected legislators that passed the laws; it is now the immense technocratic bureaucracy that produces the flow of regulations that constitute most of what we call "law" today. The rise of the "administrative state," which I chronicle in chapter 1, has tilted the playing field in favor of corporations, industry groups, and other organized interests with the resources to monitor and influence bureaucratic decisions, while simultaneously making it difficult for ordinary citizens to understand and participate in the policy process. It has also empowered the unelected technocrats within the bureaucracies, giving them greater scope to pursue their personal policy interests.

We cannot "cure" the problem simply by rewinding history and rolling back the administrative state. The factors driving the loss of control—growth of the administrative state and reliance on experts—were necessary responses to the growing complexity of the world; reverting government to a simple preindustrial form seems impossible, and would be unwise in any case. To find a solution, we need to think in terms of *augmenting* existing institutions—adding tools that allow more popular control—while maintaining a central role for technocratic expertise.

———

Nothing would bring policy more directly under popular control than allowing the people to choose the policies themselves. This can be accomplished by cutting out the middlemen that cause the disconnection in the first place, and holding votes on policy issues: in other words, referendums.

Referendums are the best-known form of "direct democracy," a term that contrasts with "representative democracy" where the people's role is restricted to choosing their representatives. Referendums take many forms, from advisory votes called by governments (such as Brexit), to votes required by law (such as Ireland's vote on a constitutional amendment legalizing abortion), to votes on proposals drafted by citizens themselves (such as California's famous "initiatives"). All of these referendums are implemented through "ballot propositions" that give voters the option to indicate their position on a proposed law.

The second goal of this book is to breathe new life into the old idea of using direct democracy to address the problem of democratic drift. During the Populist and Progressive eras a century ago, direct democracy featured prominently in public discussions. It was widely supported by civic leaders, journalists, academics, and leading politicians of both parties—including presidents Theodore Roosevelt (Republican) and Woodrow Wilson (Democrat)—as a way to restore popular control and curtail the power of special interests. From 1880 to 1920, states, cities, and towns across the country incorporated referendum procedures into their governing practices. As a result, the United States now makes extensive use of direct democracy at the state and local levels, more so than any other country except for Switzerland.

At the state level, for example, voters approve amendments to their state constitutions, vote on bond issues, repeal existing laws by petition referendum, and propose and approve new laws via the initiative process. At the local level, school districts in New York State hold votes on their annual budgets; cities and counties in California require voter approval for tax increases; and cities and towns in Alaska, Arkansas, Kentucky, Ohio, Pennsylvania, and Texas vote on whether to permit liquor sales. All told, over 99 percent of Americans vote directly on laws in their state or local governments from time to time.

The Populist and Progressive movements ran out of steam before referendums reached the national level, when the world plunged into the Great Depression and then World War II. This left the country with a rich culture of direct democracy at the state and local levels and a complete dearth of referendums at the national level. The direct democracy deficit at the national level is not for lack of public interest: according to a 2017 Pew Research Center survey, two-thirds of Americans back the idea of "voting directly on major national issues to decide what becomes law," and other surveys show that a majority in every American state favors letting citizens propose and approve state laws by initiative.[9]

The United States today finds itself as one of a dwindling group of democracies in the undemocratic position of never having held a national vote on a policy issue.[10] Elsewhere, countries are increasingly utilizing referendums as a way to gauge public opinion on important policy issues. Prominent recent examples were the United Kingdom's 2016 vote to leave the European Union, Colombia's

2016 vote against a peace treaty with the FARC militia,[11] and Ireland's 2015 vote to legalize same-sex marriage and 2018 vote to legalize abortion. The idea of voting on important national issues enjoys majority support in all regions of the world: Europe (70 percent), Asia (67 percent), Africa (64 percent), Latin America (62 percent), and the Middle East (60 percent). Since 1980, a majority of countries in all regions have held at least one national referendum, with the proportion of countries reaching 90 percent in Europe, Latin America, and Africa.[12] Some of these referendums were held by authoritarian regimes and cannot be considered genuine exercises in democracy, but it nevertheless remains the case that many democracies are consulting their people directly on important national issues.

All of this suggests that expanding the use of direct democracy does not require a heroic leap of faith. People are used to voting on policy issues, and we have a rich history across the globe that provides lessons in how to do it right. Explaining more concretely how this might be done so as to reduce democratic drift, and how to capture the potential benefits while mitigating the risks, is the third and final goal of this book.

———

Giving people more control over policy decisions is the main attraction of direct democracy, but not the only one. A comparison of abortion policy in the United States and Italy points out another potential benefit.

Abortion is one of the most divisive issues in the United States—yet often lost in the polarized debates is the fact that ordinary Americans take a centrist view on the issue. Unlike those on the extreme left who assert that abortion should be permitted in all cases, most Americans believe that abortion should be prohibited in some circumstances, such as to select the sex of the child; and unlike those on the extreme right who believe that abortion should be banned in all circumstances, most Americans believe that there are situations in which it should be allowed, such as rape or when the health of the mother is at risk.[13] As such, abortion has the appearance of a "normal" policy issue that could be resolved through standard democratic processes. A sizable moderate group would be amenable to development of nuanced policies that balance a woman's right to choose against the value of prenatal life.

The United States appeared to be heading down the path of adopting nuanced policies in the 1960s and early 1970s, as public opinion evolved and individual states grappled with the issue. Abortion had been largely outlawed throughout the country in the late nineteenth century. In 1967, Colorado became the first state to reconsider, legalizing abortion in cases of rape, incest, or danger to the woman's health, followed by California, Oregon, and North Carolina. The state of Washington legalized early-pregnancy abortions by referendum in 1970. The country seemed to be heading toward an equilibrium that would allow abortion in some circumstances and restrict it in others, with the lines drawn based on each state's distinct values, roughly consistent with public opinion.

The political process, however, was short-circuited by the Supreme Court's *Roe v. Wade* decision in 1973. In that decision, the court declared that abortion was a "fundamental right" that could not be restricted in the first trimester, could be limited in the second trimester for "reasonable" health reasons, and could be prohibited entirely in the third trimester. As a matter of legal reasoning, the decision has been criticized as lacking a grounding in the text of the Constitution; more relevant for this discussion is the fact that it overrode the country's democratic processes with a judicial mandate. The court has been forced to return to the issue again and again over subsequent years to extend and elaborate its original decision, becoming the nation's de facto abortion-policy maker.

The backlash against *Roe v. Wade* was swift. It catalyzed the pro-life movement, leading to the formation of interest groups such as the Moral Majority; legislators repeatedly tried to chip away at the right, and there were even isolated cases of bombings of abortion clinics. As time passed, the controversy spilled over to the Supreme Court nomination process, where a nominee's position on abortion became an unstated litmus test for both parties.

The battle has gone on for more than 40 years, with no armistice in sight. Abortion has become one of the most divisive and emotional issues in American politics, and a leading cause of polarization in politics. Instead of letting the states work out the issue as public opinion gradually evolved, nine unelected officials imposed a uniform policy on the entire country. "Abortion is a cause and symbol of the ruination of American politics," observed celebrated political journalist Howard Fineman. "It was the first shot in a culture war that has turned the two-party system into a fractured mess."[14]

It did not have to be this way; there was an alternative path in which the court left the issue to be worked out through the democratic process. "It's not that the judgement was wrong, but it moved too far, too fast," reflected liberal Supreme Court justice Ruth Bader Ginsburg, a strong supporter of abortion rights, who at the time of the decision was directing the American Civil Liberties

Union's Women's Rights Project. "My criticism of *Roe* is that it seemed to have stopped the momentum that was on the side of change."[15]

A counterexample to the American experience is Italy, a predominantly Catholic country with laws influenced by the values of the Catholic Church. As in the United States, abortion had been illegal in Italy for decades when public opinion began to shift toward a more permissive approach in the 1960s. In 1978, the parliament approved a law that legalized abortion, under a formula similar to the one adopted in *Roe v. Wade*. Political groups on the left and right organized to challenge the law, using the country's petition referendum process to call a national vote in 1981. The left-wing Radical Party proposed to strike language in the law that limited abortion access, in effect liberalizing abortion law; the right-wing Christian Democrats proposed to repeal the core of the law, in effect making abortion illegal except when the health of the mother was endangered. Voters soundly rejected both proposals, the first by a margin of 12 percent to 88 percent, and the second by a margin of 32 percent to 68 percent. The "compromise" policy incorporated in the original law thus prevailed.

This appeared to settle the issue: since then abortion has receded as a point of contention in Italian politics. In contrast to the United States, Italy did not see the emergence of powerful interest groups dedicated to removing or defending abortion rights, nor did abortion policy become the locus of corrosive political polarization. Parties rarely seek electoral advantage by taking positions on the issue, and voters do not choose candidates hoping they will appoint judges to influence abortion law. It seems that most Italians, whether or not they agreed with the referendum outcome, recognized the decision's legitimacy, and it brought a semblance of closure to the issue.

While some Americans believe that abortion is too contentious to resolve through the democratic process, the European experience suggests otherwise. Indeed, precisely the reverse may be true: the US Supreme Court may have *created* contentiousness by short-circuiting the democratic process. As the *Economist* pointed out, "It would be hard to design a way of legalizing abortion that could be better calculated to stir up controversy. . . . By going down the legislative road, the Europeans managed to neutralize the debate; by relying on the hammer-blow of a Supreme Court decision, the Americans institutionalized it."[16]

That Italy, a heavily Catholic country, voted to legalize abortion allays the fear that religious voters (or other majority groups) will trample individual rights if the issue is turned over to a popular vote. Referendum votes in Ireland, another Catholic nation, that legalized abortion (2018) and same-sex marriage

(2015) reinforce this point. Referendum voters are more thoughtful and sophisticated than most people realize.

———

The idea of addressing democratic drift by giving the people more power runs against an alternative view that would give the people *less* power and turn over more decision making to nonelected technocrats. In his book *Technocracy in America*, Parag Khanna goes so far as to hold up Singapore, a one-party authoritarian state with a reputation for technocratic efficiency, as a role model, asserting that "America needs less of its own version of democracy—much less."[17] Variations on this theme—usually coupled with skepticism about partisan politics and the capabilities of ordinary voters—are increasingly common in public discussions of democracy.[18]

A few months after the 2016 elections, I attended a conference of economists, lawyers, government officials, journalists, and activists. The conference was about competition policy, but the issue on everyone's mind was how to understand Brexit and Trump's win. The keynote speaker was an eminent scholar with a distinguished public service record. His remarks traced the populist backlash to the failure of elites over the past generation to understand and respond to the economic concerns of less-educated workers who have been buffeted by globalization, automation, and the transition to a knowledge-based economy. After diagnosing the problem, he offered a solution: elites in the policy community should do a better job of listening to and understanding the concerns of ordinary people.

I found it a remarkable blind spot that he did not mention the other possibility: giving the people more of a voice in decisions. His operating assumption, which I suspect was shared by most people in the room, was that elites would continue to monopolize policy decisions. The only question was how they should do it better.

While a worthy aspiration, expecting more responsive behavior from elites does not seem like a realistic approach to solving democratic drift. For one thing, we have reason to believe that political elites misunderstand the preferences of the people they ostensibly represent. A recent survey of empirical research concludes that "political elites often make systematic and self-serving errors about voter preferences."[19]

Moreover, policy elites are a culturally distinct group—highly educated, white-collar professionals clustered in the coastal cities—compared with

Americans living in "flyover country." In a study of policy preferences, political scientist Morris Fiorina found: "Not only is the political class more extreme in its positions . . . but its priorities do not mirror those of the larger public."[20] Even if elites were able to accurately perceive the interests and values of the rest of the country, to reflect those views would require them to suppress and act against their own preferences.

Prioritizing the views of the general public over one's own opinion would be difficult for an open-minded person, but is likely to be especially challenging for political elites because survey evidence tells us that they do not respect the judgment of ordinary people. A Pew Research Center survey asked government officials if Americans "know enough about issues to form wise opinions about what should be done." A total of 47 percent of Congress members answered *no*; 77 percent of presidential appointees answered *no*, and an amazing 81 percent of civil servants answered *no*.[21]

It seems to me that relying on elites to be more conscientious and attentive to popular concerns comes close to hoping that men will be angels, which James Madison famously warned Americans two centuries ago was not a sound basis for government.[22] More generally, the speaker's analysis reflects a common mindset among elites: that they should remain in control but perform better. I want to explore the other possibility, the one that speaker missed: that shifting power to the people is a viable alternative to ever-increasing technocracy.

———

The book is organized in four parts. In part I, I look closely at the disconnection between ordinary people and policy, and describe the changes in American government over the past century that have contributed to a loss of popular control. I explain the rise of the administrative state, which has shifted policy decisions from elected legislators to unelected technocrats in the bureaucracies, the concurrent shift in policy making to unelected judges, and the tendency of legislators to vote without regard to the preferences of their constituents.

Part II introduces a potential solution: direct democracy. I describe how direct democracy is currently used in the United States and Europe—where it is most prevalent—as well as other regions of the world where it is thriving. I also correct some common misconceptions about referendums, especially that referendums represent a novel and untested practice and that they lead to chaotic and turbulent policies. I then turn to the anomaly of the United States, which almost alone among advanced nations has never held a national referendum.

I trace this back to misunderstandings about democracy during the founding era, and show how (often in response to populist surges) each succeeding generation of Americans has expanded the scope of democracy. Greater use of referendums would follow the time-tested path of updating American democracy to meet the needs of the times.

In part III, I explore the pros and cons of direct democracy more systematically. I start by outlining a menu of concrete reform proposals, some easy to implement (national advisory votes) and others extremely difficult (allowing voters to initiate and approve constitutional amendments). To flesh out how direct democracy works in practice, I tell the story of two prominent and controversial ballot measures, California's Proposition 13 and the United Kingdom's Brexit referendum. With these cases in mind, I then lay out potential benefits associated with referendums as well as potential downsides. I give special attention to three issues that are particular causes of concern: Are voters up to the task of making important decisions? Will interest groups hijack the process? Does direct democracy threaten minority rights?

Part IV turns to the practicalities of making direct democracy work. Voters do not want to micromanage government; they only want to participate in select issues of particular importance. Corralling insights from previous chapters, I present a simple framework that highlights which issues should be put to a referendum and which should be left to representatives and bureaucrats. And because holding a referendum the wrong way can cause more problems than it solves (Brexit comes to mind), I draw together a set of practical suggestions for the proper design and execution of a referendum. Together, the chapters in part IV aim to show how we can make the most of direct democracy.

————

The success of populist candidates and parties is an alarm sounding with increasing insistence across the globe. Whatever one thinks of the populist agenda, it is finding a receptive audience. That so many people believe government is failing to represent them should concern us all.

The spread of populism is causing some to lose faith in government by the people. A growing collection of books and articles argues that the way to save democracy is to make it less democratic. Ordinary people do not appreciate the benefits they are receiving from existing policies, the argument goes, and their temperamentality is politically destabilizing; our best hope is to turn over more decisions to technocrats whose disinterested expertise provides a more reliable means to advance the public good.

This book argues that we should not give up so easily on the idea of ordinary people governing themselves—instead, we should double down on democracy and give the people even more control. Previous generations of Americans did exactly this when they faced periods of rising populist sentiment, broadening democracy by extending suffrage to include persons without property, African Americans, Asian Americans, and women; replacing appointed with elected governors and senators; opening up candidate nominations to all voters; utilizing referendums at the state and local levels; and more.

Referendums are a natural next step in the development of American democracy, and offer a direct way to address core populist concerns. People around the world say they would like to vote more often on important national issues, and the evidence shows they are capable of doing so effectively.

I find it remarkable that the United States, the country that pioneered democracy and proved that a government created and controlled by ordinary people could succeed, has never allowed its citizens to vote on a single national issue. While almost every other nation holds referendums to decide matters of national importance, ordinary Americans continue to be kept at a distance from the public issues that most affect their lives. I do not fully understand why this is the case. To be sure, those with power seldom give it up voluntarily, so there may be a self-interest among today's elite to retain its influence. But I like to think there is more to it, that many people have not recognized the opportunity that is available. The broadest goal of this book is to rectify this apparent knowledge gap in the hope that it will enhance public discussions about how to manage the challenges that animate populist sentiment. Our democracy is adrift, but there is a way to put it back on course.

PART I

Democracy Adrift

1

Disconnected by the Administrative State

IN A 2017 SPEECH, Supreme Court Justice Samuel Alito remarked that:

> the vast majority of federal law is . . . made in a way that is never mentioned in the Constitution. It is promulgated by unelected executive branch officials in the form of federal regulations. . . . [T]he result has been a massive shift of lawmaking from the elected representatives of the people to unelected bureaucrats.[1]

Justice Alito was referring to a phenomenon much discussed by law and public-administration experts, now commonly referred to as the "rise of the administrative state." The rise of the administrative state is a primary cause of the disconnection between public opinion and policy, and a growing concern across the political spectrum.[2]

To understand this disconnection, we need to start with a picture of how laws are made in the federal government (the states use the same process, with minor variations). The federal government consists of three branches: the legislative (Congress, which includes the House of Representatives and the Senate), the executive (the president and federal agencies like the Environmental Protection Agency [EPA] or the Food and Drug Administration [FDA]), and the judicial (the Supreme Court and other lower courts). The people directly elect the members of Congress and—through the convoluted Electoral College system—select the president. Judges are appointed by the president with the Senate's concurrence.

As originally envisioned in the Constitution, Congress would pass the laws (subject to a possible presidential veto that Congress could override with enough support), the president would administer the laws, and the courts would referee when disagreements arose in connection with the laws. For example, Congress would set the law determining the tariff rate on tea imports, the president (through customs officials that he appointed and managed) would collect the tariff revenue when the goods arrived at a port, and the courts would adjudicate disputes, such as when an importer and a customs official disagreed about whether the product imported met the definition of tea. Under this system, the laws are controlled by the people through their selection of members of Congress.

As the government has expanded, the president's agents—those charged to help the president administer the laws—have multiplied. They are now scattered throughout numerous agencies, each of which focuses on enforcing a particular set of laws. The EPA monitors pollution and air and water quality; the FDA oversees the safety of new medical products. As these agencies have grown, the nature of their work has changed. Executive-branch employees, once tasked to administer the laws, are now empowered to make the laws. For instance, Congress has ceased setting tariff rates and given the power instead to the executive branch. This shift of lawmaking authority from the legislative to the executive branch constitutes the most important change in policy making from the founding of the nation to today.[3]

We have come to call this immense government bureaucracy with lawmaking power the administrative state. It is the central feature of modern government in every advanced democracy.[4] The next task is to understand how and why the administrative agencies became the center of policy making.

Origins of the Administrative State

For the first hundred years, the government ran essentially according to the original plan. Congress formulated and passed the laws, the president administered them, and the courts adjudicated disputes. The executive branch was small, with only a few cabinet-level agencies: initially just the Departments of War, the Navy, State, and the Treasury, later supplemented with the Departments of the Interior, Justice, and Post Office.

In 1887, Congress created the first independent regulatory agency, the Interstate Commerce Commission (ICC), to regulate railroad rates and other railroad business practices. The move was a response to pressure from farmers and commercial shippers, who felt overcharged and exploited by railroads, and from the railroads themselves, who felt that competition had reached a ruinous level.

In setting up the ICC, Congress departed from its past practices in two important ways. First, instead of specifying rates itself, Congress simply stated that rates must be "reasonable and just" and left it up to the Commission to flesh out the details. Delegating this responsibility had significant advantages: it allowed experts to shape regulatory decisions and enabled more rapid adaptation to shifting market conditions than if Congress had played a hand's-on role.[5] Second, Congress gave the ICC some degree of independence from the president. Unlike traditional executive departments, where the head served at the president's pleasure, ICC commissioners could be removed by the president only because of "inefficiency, neglect of duty, or malfeasance in office," not over policy differences.[6]

The ICC was followed by a host of new agencies over the subsequent half century. During the Progressive Era, the FDA (originally Bureau of Chemistry) was set up to safeguard the purity of food and drugs, the Federal Trade Commission was created to promote fair trade practices and competition, the Federal Reserve System was empowered to regulate the banking system, and the Federal Communications Commission (originally Federal Radio Commission) was created to oversee radio and other telecommunications. The New Deal witnessed the creation of the Securities and Exchange Commission (SEC) to regulate securities markets and the National Labor Relations Board to regulate collective bargaining and prevent unfair labor practices. As with the ICC, these agencies often were set up as partially independent of the president.

These new agencies signaled an expansion of the government's responsibilities. Unlike traditional departments that were designed to carry out the government's business (such as collecting taxes, delivering the mail, or national defense), the new agencies were built to protect consumers and workers from economic forces that arose in the wake of industrialization, urbanization, and the emergence of what has been called a "consumer culture." That Congress acted by creating agencies instead of regulating directly reflected a growing recognition that regulatory problems and solutions were complex enough to require expert engagement. Congress could state its broad goals in the enabling legislation, leaving it to those with technical expertise—"technocrats"—to develop the detailed implementation rules that Congress had neither the expertise nor time to produce on its own. These agencies can thus be seen as a response to the growing complexity of the American economy, as well as the expanding scope of the problems that government chose to address. In addition to creating these new agencies, Congress delegated more and more responsibilities to existing agencies (more on this below). The end result was that by the end of the 1930s, the locus of government decision making had shifted from Congress to the agencies.

After World War II came to an end, Congress took a close look at the sprawling administrative state it had constructed in a piecemeal fashion, and was not entirely happy with what it saw. The public had also soured on administrative agencies after exposure to the inefficiencies and arbitrariness of wartime agencies. In an attempt to rein in administrative discretion, Congress passed (by unanimous vote in both houses) the Administrative Procedure Act (APA) of 1946, now seen as "the fundamental charter of the U. S. administrative state."[7] The APA brought a host of changes: it imposed complex procedures by which agencies were to propose and promulgate regulations, required transparency in the regulatory process, mandated an opportunity for public comment on proposed regulations, and provided a role for judges to oversee agency decisions (elaborated over time through a series of court decisions). Otherwise, it left agencies with substantial discretion to set policy.

Another wave of agency building took place in the 1960s and early 1970s as the country confronted a new set of economic and social problems, culminating in the presidency of Richard Nixon. Increased public concern with the damage caused by industrial pollution to the environment and public health led to the creation of the EPA in 1970. The emergence of an automobile culture led to creation of the National Highway Transportation Safety Administration to monitor motor-vehicle safety, also in 1970. Growing concern over workplace injuries and deaths led to the Occupational Safety and Health Administration (OSHA) in 1971. The proliferation of consumer products that were not covered by existing agencies (that is, products other than food, drugs, alcohol, tobacco, guns, and cars) prompted creation of the Consumer Product Safety Commission in 1972.

The new century brought new crises, met once again with new agencies. After the terrorist attack on September 11, 2001, in an effort to provide a more coordinated approach to public safety inside the country, Congress created the Department of Homeland Security by combining 22 separate agencies into a single department. The Consumer Financial Protection Bureau, the newest agency, was created in 2010 in response to the financial crisis three years earlier to protect consumers from unfair practices by financial institutions. These agencies, like those that came before, reflected Congress's desire to frame basic policy approaches and directions for regulation, while leaving the implementation details to experts.

A Picture of the Administrative State Today

As of 2019, there were somewhere between 70 and 117 separate federal agencies, depending on how one defines an agency.[8] Those agencies collectively employed about 1.4 million workers, not counting the Department of Defense (with more than 700,000 employees) and the Postal Service (about 500,000 employees). By way of comparison, in 1900 there were about 10 federal agencies with 15,000 civilian employees.

Agencies administer the laws, in part by taking enforcement actions, and in part by issuing rules and regulations. In 2016 alone, more than 97,000 pages were added to the *Federal Register*—the federal government's official journal—including 3,853 final rules and 2,391 proposed rules. The president also issued various executive orders and memorandums. In addition to rules and regulations, agencies often issue advisory letters (e.g., the SEC's so-called "no-action letters" in response to requests from companies). Although these rules are not "laws" in the sense of acts passed by the legislature, most of them have the force of law, so for all practical purposes are equivalent to laws. The volume of laws that emerges from executive agencies every year dwarfs the amount produced by the Congress.

A close look at a few important issues that are now largely governed by executive agencies (or the executive directly) illustrates how decision-making authority has moved from Congress to the agencies.

Environment

The nation's environment is protected by a series of laws enforced primarily by the EPA, but also by the Department of the Interior and Department of Agriculture. The EPA, an independent agency whose head is appointed by and can be removed by the president, was established in 1970 on the recommendation of President Richard Nixon, as mentioned above.

Stripped down to its essentials, environmental regulation has two components: (1) a list of "contaminants" that are considered unhealthy, and (2) a set of standards governing emissions of the unhealthy contaminants—how much can be emitted, where, and under what conditions. Congress, in principle, could make both determinations. For example, it could declare that arsenic is harmful to health, and prohibit coal mines from releasing more than a certain amount into nearby streams. Yet these sorts of determinations are complex. To determine how much (say) arsenic in drinking water is harmful to human health requires scientific knowledge concerning water systems, air systems, geology, chemistry, human health, industrial processes and technologies, and so forth. Rather than make these decisions itself, Congress has delegated them to the EPA.[9]

The EPA's authority comes from a series of laws concerning air, water, and land pollution. The Clean Air Act of 1970, considered the nation's first substantive environmental statute, instructs the EPA administrator to reduce air pollution that may "endanger public health or welfare," but gives the administrator substantial discretion on how to go about this mission. To emphasize the delegation of authority, the act states that the Administrator is to identify pollution sources that "in his judgment" cause air pollution, and once he decides what counts as air pollution, he shall limit those emissions "as he deems appropriate."[10] Similarly, the Clean Water Act (the primary federal statute governing water quality) and the Safe Drinking Water Act call for the EPA to identify contaminants and set limits for emission of contaminants into navigable waters, ground waters, underground waters, and drinking waters that "in the judgement of the Administrator" would protect the public's health.[11]

All three acts run on for thousands of words, specifying in varying degrees of detail the sort of things that the EPA shall regulate, the processes by which it shall arrive at its regulations, and the sort of regulations that can be considered. But despite the details, the acts ultimately give the EPA administrator broad discretion over implementation: the EPA defines what is to be considered a pollutant and what remedies are adequate. Congress has essentially told the EPA to protect the environment, and left it up to the agency to determine exactly what that means and how to do it—in effect delegating a substantial portion of its lawmaking power to the EPA.

The scope of that power is incredibly broad: the number of activities that impact the air, water, and land is virtually unlimited. The charge to provide safe drinking water alone potentially extends from rules concerning drinking fountains in schools to purification standards in municipal water-treatment plants to emissions from coal mines near mountain streams.

Because so much lawmaking power is concentrated in the hands of a single administrator appointed by the president, policy can swing dramatically with a change in presidential administration—even if public opinion remains stable. For example, in 2015 President Barack Obama's EPA adopted the Clean Power Plan, which mandated a 32 percent reduction in greenhouse gas emissions at power plants by 2030, compared with 2005 levels. The Clean Power Plan was considered Obama's signature climate-change policy and hailed by supporters as a "landmark" law, but decried by opponents as unfairly requiring low- and middle-income workers to bear most of the costs of pollution abatement. In 2017, immediately after taking office, President Trump issued an executive order calling for the EPA to reconsider the plan, and the administrator repealed it in 2019. Both the decision to adopt and the decision to repeal were made under discretionary authority granted to the administrator by the Clean Air Act; they were not driven by swings in public opinion but by changes in partisan control of the government.[12]

Business Competition

The first big businesses—railroads and mining and manufacturing companies— appeared in the late nineteenth century, and by the early twentieth century corporations had come to dominate the economy. Public concern over the power of these large organizations—both their political power and their market power in relation to workers, suppliers, and customers—grew in tandem with industrialization. Congress attempted to restrain them through the Sherman Antitrust Act of 1890, which banned "every contract, combination in the form of trust or otherwise, or conspiracy, in restraint of trade or commerce," but enforcement was ineffective (with a few exceptions, such as the breakup of Standard Oil in 1911). The problem was in part that enforcement relied on the enthusiasm of the president, which waxed and waned, and in part that courts interpreted the act's vague language in ways that favored business.

In 1914, Congress tried a new approach, creating the Federal Trade Commission (FTC) and passing a new antitrust law, the Clayton Antitrust Act. The FTC was established as an independent commission governed by five commissioners appointed by the president for seven-year terms, who could be removed only for cause. The FTC was empowered to prevent "unfair methods of competition" (a concept it was left to define) and given broad powers to investigate individual firms.

By delegating the power to define "competition" and decide what business practices were uncompetitive, Congress in effect turned over to the FTC (and Department of Justice) its power to regulate competition throughout the American economy. This was deliberate: a Senate committee report on the Federal Trade Commission Act explained that:

> The committee gave careful consideration to the question as to whether it would attempt to define the many and variable unfair practices which prevail

in commerce and to forbid [them] or whether it would, by a general declaration condemning unfair practices, leave it to the commission to determine
what practices were unfair. It concluded that the latter course would be
better

—because it would be too complex to try to define all present and future unfair
practices.[13]

In the following century, American antitrust policy veered dramatically, taking a muscular approach toward regulation from the 1940s through the 1970s
before becoming more hands-off in the 1980s under the influence of Chicago
School free-market thinking.[14] The government's position shifted substantially
on a number of business practices—mergers, predatory pricing, resale price
maintenance, tie-in sales—yet none of the changes were caused by acts of Congress, which has been largely silent on competition policy over the past century.
Instead, the policy changes were driven by changing views inside the two responsible agencies, the FTC and the Department of Justice (and to some extent the federal courts).

International Trade

In addition to delegating authority to independent agencies, Congress turned
over its powers to the president. The US Constitution explicitly assigns trade
policy to Congress: "The Congress shall have the power to lay and collect taxes,
duties, imposts and excises, [and] to regulate commerce with foreign nations."[15]
Yet we often observe the president setting tariffs, establishing quotas, and imposing penalties for unfair trade practices, such as President Trump's 24 percent
"countervailing duty" on Canadian softwood lumber imports in 2017, or President Ronald Reagan's imposition of Japanese auto import quotas in 1981.

It was not always this way. For the first 150 years, Congress was in full control of trade policy.[16] Tariff bills were among the most important pieces of
legislation that Congress considered, and battles over tariff rates could become
national issues, such as with the "Tariff of Abominations" (1928), a protection-
ist measure designed to help Northern industry that infuriated the South, and
the Smoot-Hawley Tariff (1930), considered by some economists to have contributed to the Great Depression. In 1930, however, Congress began to delegate
significant trade responsibility to the president. The Tariff Act of 1930 established that:

Whenever the President shall find as a fact that any foreign country places
any burden or disadvantage upon the commerce of the United States by any

of the unequal impositions or discriminations aforesaid, he shall, when he finds that the public interest will be served thereby, by proclamation specify and declare new or additional rate or rates of duty as he shall determine will offset such burden or disadvantage.[17]

Congress renewed and gradually expanded the president's authority in subsequent trade laws: the Trade Expansion Act of 1962 allowed the president to take trade actions "he deems necessary" for national security; the Trade Act of 1974 authorized the president to impose surcharges and quotas; the North American Free Trade Act of 1993 conferred authority to modify or continue any tariff; and the Bipartisan Congressional Trade Priorities and Accountability Act of 2015 allowed the president to retaliate against a foreign country's unfair trade practices by entering into trade agreements with other countries.[18] The cumulative effect of these congressional actions is to give the president a free hand to increase and reduce tariffs, apply surcharges, and impose import quotas.

Presidents have not been shy about using these powers. Even President Reagan, who was generally seen as a free trader, used the delegated powers to tighten sugar quotas, restrict certain textile imports, impose a duty on Japanese motorcycle imports, raise tariffs on Canadian lumber and cedar shingles, extend quotas on imported clothespins, impose a 100 percent tax on selected Japanese electronics, and negotiate quotas on Japanese auto imports and global steel imports—all without explicit involvement of Congress.[19] A study of presidential proclamations, executive orders, and memoranda found 345 unilateral trade modifications by presidents from 1917 to 2006, or about 4 per year.[20]

Presidents have also unilaterally expanded their powers when it comes to treaties with other nations, which the Constitution clearly intends to be a joint responsibility of the president and the Senate.[21] For much of American history, the president would negotiate a treaty, sometimes including senators in the negotiating team, and then submit the final draft to the Senate for approval.[22]

Presidents now conclude most international agreements using executive agreements instead of treaties. The difference is that while executive agreements and treaties are equally binding under international law, executive agreements do not require Senate approval. Since the end of World War II, 94 percent of international agreements have taken the form of executive agreements. An analysis of the presidents from Harry Truman to Barack Obama found that the ratio of executive agreements to treaties fell from the already high ratio of 9:1 under Truman to 32:1 under Obama. The most plausible reason for this shift is presidents' impatience with Senate resistance to their diplomatic initiatives: "You can't pass a treaty anymore," complained John Kerry, Obama's secretary of state.[23]

President Obama, in particular, submitted, "by far, the fewest treaties for ratification by any modern president." Two of his signature diplomatic accomplishments—the Paris Agreement on Climate Change and the Iran Nuclear Agreement—were concluded unilaterally without the advice and consent of the Senate. President Trump unilaterally withdrew from both arrangements. This state of affairs is troubling to some observers because it undermines US credibility as an international partner. More to the point of this book, it is another example of how the executive branch is making important national decisions largely decoupled from public opinion and democratic accountability.[24]

National Parks

In April 2006, shortly after watching a PBS documentary by Jean-Jacques Cousteau on endangered marine environments at a private White House screening, President George W. Bush announced the creation of a vast new national marine preserve covering the Northwestern Hawaiian Islands. The new preserve, named the Papahānaumokuākea Marine National Monument, covered 140,000 square miles of ocean islands, an area 100 times larger than Yosemite National Park and larger than 46 of the 50 states. Fishing, development, and other human activities were banned within the preserve's limits. President Bush acted unilaterally, without any formal involvement of the Congress. Again, this is surprising on the face of it since the US Constitution clearly grants these powers to Congress, not the president: "The Congress shall have the power to dispose of and make all needful rules and regulations respecting the territory or other property belonging to the United States."[25]

For the first century of US history, Congress used its authority over public lands to create national parks, such as Yosemite, established in 1864.[26] Things changed in 1906 when Congress passed the Antiquities Act, giving the president unilateral power to create national parks (called "national monuments"). The act was a response to looting at prehistoric ruins in the West, and intended to protect "historic landmarks, historic and prehistoric structures, and other objects of historic or scientific interest" more quickly than the cumbersome congressional process of creating a national park. President Theodore Roosevelt immediately used his new authority to create Devil's Tower National Monument in Wyoming in 1906, followed by creation of 17 others before he left office in 1909. In total, presidents have designated 129 national monuments, more than twice the number of national parks created by Congress (59).

The president's power to set aside federal land is substantial. In the Antiquities Act, Congress attempted to limit the scope of the president's power by stating that monuments must be "confined to the smallest area compatible with proper care and management of the objects to be protected," but courts have held that the president has essentially unlimited discretion to determine the nature and size of the protected area. President Bush was able to create Papahānaumokuākea despite opposition from fishermen and Hawaiians themselves. President Obama added 24 more national monuments, and increased Papahānaumokuākea by 442,781 square miles. The expansion of Papahānaumokuākea brought the total area of the monument to 582,681 miles, larger than the country of Germany. All of this was done with the stroke of the pen, without the involvement of Congress or the people.

———

There are many more examples like these that illustrate the same point: the transfer of power to the president and executive branch agencies and the growth of the administrative state is significant and largely a result of deliberate decisions by Congress to delegate its power. One recent study found that of 442 major laws passed by Congress since 1947, 99.1 percent of them delegated power to one or more executive agencies.[27]

This trend shows no signs of abating. The two signature pieces of legislation during the Obama administration both contained extensive delegation of rule-making power to agencies. The Dodd-Frank Act of 2010, a response to the financial crisis that was intended to reform the country's regulation of financial institutions, contains 330 provisions that expressly require or permit rule making by various agencies, including the SEC, Federal Reserve Board, Commodity Futures Trading Commission, and Consumer Financial Protection Bureau. The *New York Times* described the law as "basically a 2,000-page missive to federal agencies, instructing regulators to address subjects ranging from derivatives trading to document retention. But it is notably short on specifics, giving regulators significant power to determine its impact."[28] As of 2017, 280 rules had been issued, with more than 100 rules still to be determined.

Similarly, the Patient Protection and Affordable Care Act of 2010 ("Obamacare") that sought to reform the nation's health-care system, contained more than 40 provisions that required or permitted rule making by agencies. The

Congressional Research Service described that law as "a particularly notewor-thy example of congressional delegation of rulemaking authority to federal agencies" and *CQ Weekly* noted that "most prominent among the complaints from critics of the overhaul is the degree of discretion handed to Health and Human Services Secretary Kathleen Sebelius and to multiple divisions in her department."[29]

The Challenge of Controlling
the Administrative State

Although the rise of the administrative state is largely a rational response to the growing complexity of the problems that the public wants to have addressed, some less benign forces may be at work as well. As mentioned above in the discussion of treaties, executive-branch officials have also arrogated powers that properly belong to Congress, without the consent of Congress. A particularly blatant attempt to use executive power to make policy was President Obama's "We Can't Wait" initiative in 2011 that called on his administration to use ex-ecutive orders and administrative rules to advance his policy goals. Obama justi-fied the initiative as a response to "congressional gridlock," saying, "we can't wait for . . . Congress to do its job."[30]

There is also a line of argument that Congress sometimes delegates not for efficiency, but to shift blame to the agencies. According to this story, the Clean Air Act allowed Congress to take credit for improving air quality, while still being able to blame the EPA for the burdens of regulation imposed on some pollut-ers. A related argument is that Congress sometimes delegates simply to avoid having to make politically difficult decisions.

Regardless of the reasons for the growth of the administrative state, its domi-nance in American government is indisputable. The locus of policy making now resides in administrative agencies, not the elected Congress.

Yet even if the administrative state is essential for modern governance, as I believe it is, it is a problem for American democracy. The administrative state disconnects policy and popular control because it gives the public only the most indirect role in choosing the policies. The technocrats who make the rules are not elected, the rule-making process is opaque, and the public has no power to influence their decisions. Ben Sasse, senator from Nebraska, explained the citizen's predicament:

> There's nobody in Nebraska . . . there's nobody in Minnesota or Delaware who elected the Deputy Assistant Administrator of Plant Quarantine at the

USDA. And yet, if the Deputy Assistant Administrator of Plant Quarantine does something that makes Nebraskans' lives really difficult—which happens to farmers and ranchers in Nebraska—who do they protest to?[31]

Of course, there is a sense in which the people formally remain in control. The people elect the president, and the president supervises the agencies, so there is a line of accountability running from technocrats to the public. In principle, Nebraskans unhappy with a decision made by the deputy assistant administrator of plant quarantine could vote at the next presidential election for a candidate who will intervene with the deputy assistant.

It is worth a few words to make precise why this formal accountability does not give the people any meaningful control. First, 34 agencies are nominally "independent" agencies, including the Central Intelligence Agency, EPA, Federal Communications Commission, FTC, and the Federal Reserve Board. These agencies are governed by commissioners whose terms may extend beyond the president's term, and the president's authority to remove them is limited.

Second, most technocrats are civil servants. In a typical agency, the top few managers are political appointees, and the very topmost must be confirmed by the Senate. Below the top group of political appointees, the rest are permanent employees. They remain in place even when the president changes, and generally enjoy civil-service protections, meaning they cannot be summarily dismissed, replaced, demoted, and so on, and their pay is set according to schedules determined by Congress. The president and top managers have a limited number of levers they can pull to affect their behavior.

Third, the president is only one person and, as a practical matter, has neither the time nor energy to actively supervise more than a small fraction of executive-branch activity. In corporations, consultants advise the CEO to have no more than 10 direct reports to avoid the risk of becoming overloaded. The US president, in contrast, oversees something in the range of 70 to 117 agencies. Each of these agencies makes decisions every day, issuing rules, regulations, and advisory opinions throughout the year. No matter how attentive the president is to popular opinion, there is no way he or she can channel that information to the agencies on an operational basis.

Fourth, the president is unlikely to know the electorate's preferences on most issues. The presidential election conveys little information about the public's preferences. If there was only one policy issue, the election outcome would function like a referendum on that issue, but with literally hundreds of issues in play, the electorate's choice of one candidate over another is not a sufficiently fine-grained signal to reveal its opinion on any particular issue. If I favor the Democrat's position on social issues and the Republican's position on fiscal issues, how should I vote, and how can the winner know those were my preferences? A candidate election reveals only that voters preferred one candidate over the others—it leaves their specific policy preferences open to conjecture.[32]

Agency decisions, even if not "controlled" by the public, could still be aligned with the public's preferences if the decision makers chose the policies that the people wanted. Indeed, that was the hope of the progressives who constructed the administrative state. They reasoned that by empowering neutral, nonpolitical experts and charging them to make unbiased decisions based on data and scientific principles, agencies would choose the policies that the people wanted, instead of the policies favored by the politically powerful. While an admirable goal, experience has revealed several obstacles standing in the way of the progressive aspiration.

One is that technocrats are not likely to be unbiased or impartial arbiters of the facts. Rather, they are likely to have strong personal preferences about policies related to their agency's mandate. In an open letter protesting President Trump's environmental policies, an anonymous EPA employee wrote: "My colleagues and I . . . got into this work because we believe it is our duty to protect people and the planet we live on for future generations."[33] The sort of person who would seek a career in the EPA may develop what Justice Stephen Breyer calls "tunnel vision," a narrow focus on environmental goals at the expense of other valid policy goals, such as job preservation in mining and manufacturing industries.[34] If technocrats begin with strong and narrow policy views, they will find it difficult to step back and serve as neutral evaluators of the evidence.

Political scientists Sean Gailmard and John Patty provided a theoretical grounding for this idea, developing a model showing that because civil-service rules fix workers' pay and protect them from being fired, the only way to give them incentives is to allow them to influence policy decisions. They argue this form of "compensation" attracts people with strong preferences about the policy, making it inevitable that agencies will be staffed by policy "zealots."[35]

Because workers sort into agencies that have missions aligned with their preferences, over time agencies develop identifiable ideological orientations. Using surveys of experts and surveys of employees, researchers have found that the Department of Defense, Department of Commerce, and Office of National Drug Control Policy tend to be conservative; OSHA, the Department of Health and Human Services, and the Equal Employment Opportunity Commission tend to be liberal; and the FTC and Office of Government Ethics are moderate.[36]

Another source of disconnection is that technocrats share a socioeconomic background that sets them apart from many of their fellow citizens and likely gives them a different worldview. They are often highly educated—more than half of the EPA's 15,000 employees are scientists, engineers, or environmental protection specialists; they work in white-collar offices, not in factories, farms, mines, or with their hands; and they reside in the coastal urban centers, primarily Washington, DC.[37] Because of their shared values within group, and differences from those outside the group, some see technocrats as a distinct social class. Congress's delegation of power to the agencies, then, has not only reduced popular control, but also empowered a class of people whose preferences and priorities may differ from those of the general public.

The Challenge of Capture by Interest Groups

The administrative state breaks the connection between policy and the people in one other particularly important way: by enhancing the power of organized interest groups (this is an important issue, and one I examine at length in chapter 15). "Rulemaking and regulatory review are, virtually by their nature, wonky and involve esoteric processes that rely upon knowledge of existing laws and regulations," observed a journalist focused on regulation and technology.[38] This makes it almost impossible to interact with an agency without retaining lawyers or experts—a state of affairs that favors large corporations, trade and professional groups, unions, and other groups or individuals with ample resources. A recent study found that 73 percent of the lobbyists focused on administrative agencies were employed by business and occupational groups, concluding that "business groups dominate administrative lobbying at least as much as they do legislative lobbying."[39]

Interest groups are not necessarily an affliction of democracy. All of us have interests, and all of us are members of various groups that advocate for their members' interests. Such groups play an important, and perhaps necessary, role in democracy, prodding decision makers to take into account the concerns of the different groups in society.[40] The problem is not with the existence of interest groups, but with the disproportionate power that some hold, especially those representing concentrated economic interests such as corporations and unions. The ability of these groups to hijack regulatory decisions contributes to the public's disconnection from public policy.

Congress took some steps to alleviate this problem in the APA by requiring that proposed rules must be publicized and the public must be allowed to offer feedback before they go into effect. This was intended to bring decisions out of the back rooms and make it easier for ordinary citizens to be involved. There is some evidence that this so-called "notice-and-comment" procedure helps Congress to monitor agency decisions, because it hears from citizens about rules they don't like, so they can then intervene.[41] But the notice-and-comment process itself remains dominated by organized interests.

The influence of interest groups on agency decisions is so pervasive that scholars have formalized it and given it a name: "capture theory."[42] According to capture theory, no one has a stronger interest in monitoring and trying to influence a regulatory agency than the groups being regulated. As these groups invest time, effort, and money in gaining influence, they come to gain effective control of the agency itself.

The classic example is the ICC, which was originally set up to regulate the railroads for the protection of farmers and merchants but soon came to be controlled by railroad interests. In addition to allowing the railroads to maintain high prices, the ICC took a variety of other railroad-friendly actions such as prohibiting price *decreases* to prevent railroads from competing with one another and, when trucking became a viable competitor, imposing tight limits on the entry of trucking companies that would compete with railroads.[43] By the 1970s, the ICC had come under sustained criticism from the both the Left and the Right for being inefficient and corrupt, as well as under the thumb of the railroads. Congress began to roll back its powers, and finally closed it down in 1995.

———

The US Constitution set up American democracy with the idea that the people would govern by selecting members of Congress who would make the laws. A tectonic shift has occurred since the founding, with the locus of lawmaking shifting from Congress to unelected technocrats in the administrative agencies, leaving the people with few levers to control policy decisions. As troubling as this is, the problem is compounded by a second source of disconnection, the shift of a substantial amount of policy making to unelected federal judges, who are arguably even more removed from popular control than executive-branch officials. The next chapter describes the disconnection associated with judges and explains how it happened.

2

Disconnected by Courts

JUDGES ARE NOT SUPPOSED to make laws, so on the face of it they should not be one of the factors causing democracy to drift from popular control. Chief Justice John Roberts characterized judges as "umpires" whose job is simply to call balls and strikes.[1] Their charge, when it comes to the review of laws and regulations, is to interpret and ensure these policies are consistent with foundational documents such as the US Constitution.

Yet in the process of review, judges can end up making policy by striking down a law or vacating a rule or regulation. When the US Supreme Court declared a right to abortion in its 1973 *Roe v. Wade* decision, it swept away decades of state laws restricting abortion. Similarly, in a series of decisions on campaign finance—most recently *Citizens United v. FEC* in 2010—the Supreme Court nullified numerous laws limiting contributions and spending. Neither abortion nor campaign finance is mentioned in the Constitution, so the court's decisions involve the creation of substantive new policies.

Judges also set policy when Congress relies on courts to flesh out the meaning of statutes. Antitrust is a leading example, discussed in the previous chapter, where the law has been shaped more by judges (and the agencies) than by Congress. Congress prohibited "restraint of trade" and business practices that "substantially lessen competition," but left it to judges to put flesh on these concepts. They have done this through rulings on specific cases.[2]

The role of judges in making policy has grown over time, especially since the 1960s. Figure 2.1 provides an illustration, plotting the number of Supreme Court decisions nullifying a federal or state law each decade from the founding of the republic through 2017.[3] The court played virtually no policy role during the country's first 100 years, then became more active after the Civil War and more active still during the Progressive Era and Great Depression. The biggest jump in the court's policy-making activity occurred in the 1960s. That burst of

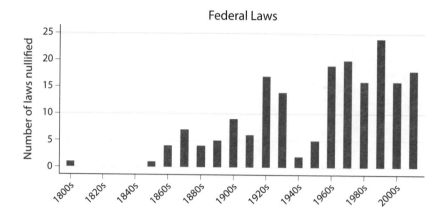

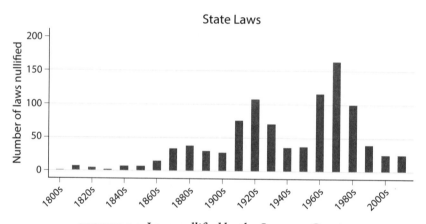

FIGURE 2.1. Laws nullified by the Supreme Court

activity featured important civil rights decisions, as the country finally moved to guarantee equality before the law for all citizens regardless of race. The court's involvement in national law has continued at a high level to the present. Whereas in the first century of the republic, one could reasonably assume that an act of Congress would go into effect, nowadays one expects that any act of significance will be challenged in court, and its fate ultimately will be determined by judges.[4]

The importance of the Supreme Court today is also illustrated by the amount of attention paid to the identity of its members. Being appointed to the Supreme Court has always been a high honor, but until recently was not seen as pivotal for public policy. Media coverage of Supreme Court nominations has exploded in recent years, going from almost nonexistent, to significant in the 1960s, to immense beginning in the mid-1980s.[5] Reflecting the court's growing importance, the Senate confirmation process has become more thorough and demanding. After the president sends a nomination to the Senate, senators interview the nominee, the nominee testifies before a Senate subcommittee, the subcommittee votes, and the Senate as a whole votes; the entire process typically takes two or three months. It was not always this way: prior to Harlan Stone in 1925, no nominee testified before the Senate (the innovation was greeted with outrage by the media at the time), and confirmation hearings did not become routine until the 1950s.[6]

The stakes are now so high that in 2016 the Senate refused even to vote on President Obama's nomination of Merrick Garland for eight months, gambling that a Republican would take the White House in the November election and a more agreeable nominee would be selected. Even President Trump's relatively uncontroversial nomination of Neil Gorsuch in January 2017 was not confirmed by a friendly Senate until April of that year, after 20 hours of testimony by the nominee.[7] By way of comparison, in 1910 President William Taft sent three Supreme Court nominations to the Senate on a single day: the nominee for chief justice was confirmed on the same day and nominees for associate justice were confirmed three days later.[8]

The policy-making role of the Supreme Court has grown so much that it spills over into other elections. In exit polls during the 2016 presidential election, 21 percent of voters said that the president's choice of Supreme Court justices was *the* most important factor in their voting decision, and another 48 percent indicated that it was an important factor—meaning that 69 percent of voters considered it an important or the most important factor.[9] Because the vote margin between Hillary Clinton and Donald Trump was only a few percentage points, it is not a stretch to say that the country may have selected its chief executive not based on who could do the best job as president, but based on what it would mean for control of the Supreme Court!

Why the Influence of Judges Is Growing

The reasons for the growing importance of the Supreme Court are subject to debate. Some argue that activist judges are acting "willfully," grabbing power unlawfully and encroaching on legislative prerogatives in order to advance their personal policy views. There may be an element of truth to that—a large literature shows that judges' decisions are influenced by their personal ideologies—but it seems unlikely that their basic disposition and character have changed dramatically over time. The transformation is more plausibly attributed to changes in external conditions. One such change, discussed in the previous chapter, is the growing complexity of government and the issues it seeks to resolve. Just as the need for experts has led to more decisions being delegated to officials with technical expertise in the agencies, it has also led to a larger role for judges in sorting out the complexities of the law and monitoring the actions of the experts in the bureaucracies.

Another external factor is the ossification of the US Constitution, which has become almost impossible to amend and adapt to modern conditions. The first 10 amendments (the Bill of Rights) were adopted in 1791, just three years after the Constitution became the law of the land; three amendments were ratified in the nineteenth century; and six more during the Progressive and New Deal eras. Since the end of World War II, there have been only six amendments, most on relatively minor or technical issues such as the timing of congressional salary changes, abolition of poll taxes, and filling a vacancy in the Office of the Vice President. The most recent amendment, which required congressional pay increases to be delayed until after the subsequent election, was ratified in 1992—203 years after it was proposed.

The dearth of amendments is not always recognized as the anomaly that it is; consider that the 50 American states continually amend and update their constitutions, and that as a group the states have approved 330 amendments in the period from 2010 to 2015 alone.[10] Most other nations frequently update their constitutions as well. The lack of federal amendments is not due to a lack of important issues that ought to be addressed or a lack of changing conditions in the world, but to the onerous amendment procedures set down in article V of the Constitution. A constitutional amendment requires approval of two-thirds of the members of both chambers of Congress as well as three-quarters of the states, a hurdle that has become increasingly difficult to surmount.

One consequence of having an unamendable Constitution is that it makes Supreme Court justices "superlegislators"—they can change the country's basic laws and there is no practical way to appeal or reverse their decisions. The problem is compounded by the fact that, unlike regular legislators, the justices are not elected and are largely beyond control of the people. This situation creates a serious tension within American democracy, as noted by Abraham Lincoln in his first inaugural address in 1861: "[I]f the policy of the government upon vital questions affecting the whole people is to be irrevocably fixed by decisions of the Supreme Court . . . the people will have ceased to be their own rulers, having to that extent practically resigned their Government into the hands of that eminent tribunal."[11]

The absence of updates to the Constitution has left federal judges in an awkward position. They are forced to resolve modern issues based on text that was written in 1787, a text that does not anticipate many of the controversies that arise today. The question in *Citizens United*—whether the government could prohibit a group from advertising and broadcasting a documentary critical of presidential candidate Hillary Clinton in the weeks before an election—was decided based on an interpretation of the First Amendment's prohibition of laws "abridging the freedom of speech." When the First Amendment was approved, the country was a century away from the invention of moving pictures and recorded sound, let alone the broadcast, cable, and satellite communications that the government sought to restrict; deciding whether the text applies to those forms of communication is fundamentally conjectural.

Of course, judges are not forced to update the Constitution themselves. They could take a literal ("plain-meaning") approach and refuse to invoke the Constitution to strike down laws when the text does not speak to the issue at hand. If this led to a decision that the country found to be outdated or unjust, it would be up to Congress to amend the Constitution and bring it into alignment with current sentiment. In effect, this judicial stance would force the Constitution to be updated through democratic channels. While this approach may resonate with our democratic sensibilities, it also feels like an abdication of judicial responsibility since the Congress is unlikely to act in practice. Judges may consider it necessary and just to update the text themselves, under the rationale that no one else will step up and do it otherwise.

In practice, the court has developed a body of doctrine ("legalism") specifically designed, in part, to update the text to deal with unanticipated issues—by, for example, attempting to infer the intentions of those who wrote it. These rules aim to turn the act of judging into a technical exercise, essentially an application of logic and legal rules. But as Judge Richard Posner, a distinguished legal scholar who served as a federal judge for 36 years, observed: "Many of the cases that arise in our dauntingly complex, uncertainty-riven legal system—featuring an antique constitution, an overlay of federal on state law, weak political parties, cumbersome and undisciplined legislatures, and executive-legislative tugs-of-war . . . —cannot be decided by the straightforward application of a preexisting rule."[12] The upshot is that whether they like it or not, federal judges have been drawn increasingly into the business of functioning as legislators and making substantive policy decisions.

The Challenge of Lawmaking by Judges

The shift in policy-making authority from Congress to courts contributes to the disconnection by moving decisions from the most to the least democratic branch. Federal judges are appointed, not elected, and they serve for life. Their decisions, by design, are disconnected from public opinion. As the Constitution is de facto updated by judges over time, it becomes a document that reflects the core values of a small group of unelected judges and not necessarily the values of the American people at large.

This is particularly troubling for democracy because judges themselves are increasingly a class apart from ordinary Americans in terms of their life experiences, values, and political preferences. Until the early twentieth century, it was customary for presidents to nominate Supreme Court justices to ensure representation of all regions of the country. But as of 2019, seven of the nine members grew up in metropolitan New York or Washington, a region with just over 10 percent of the country's population. Over the past 30 years, the court has had only one member who grew up in the South (Clarence Thomas)— dramatically underrepresenting a region that is home to 38 percent of the country's population.

An even more remarkable indication of their distinctiveness is the fact that as of 2019, all nine justices on the Supreme Court studied at either Harvard or Yale; which has been the case since 2006 with the appointment of Samuel Alito. This trend has been under way since the 1970s, and even before Harvard and Yale achieved complete dominance, judges were drawn disproportionately from those who attended a small number of elite universities.

The fact that federal judges are increasingly unlike the general population matters because, when legalistic methods fail to prescribe a clear outcome in a case, judges are forced to introduce their personal beliefs and intuitions to reach a decision. Judge Posner lists a variety of factors that lead to the formation of a judge's beliefs and intuitions: upbringing, education, salient life experiences, occupational experiences, and personal characteristics such as race, sex, and ethnicity.[13] Because of their atypical life histories, judges are likely to have intuitions and values and thus make decisions that sometimes differ from what the general public would prefer.

Although judges may be culturally and socially homogeneous, they are not ideological clones; court decisions often reveal sharp divisions along the conservative–liberal spectrum. But while judges represent viewpoints across the ideological spectrum, they may be unrepresentative on issues that do not line up along a conventional left–right continuum—particularly issues related to the relative power of elites versus the general public. We might expect judges to be less amenable to "populist" reforms, for example, such as term limits for elected officials and judges, or expansion of direct democracy.

One reason judges have become a class apart from the general population is because the act of judging is increasingly viewed as a technocratic exercise rather than an application of common sense, fairness, and personal experience. For the country's first 150 years, judges were drawn from various walks of life—some were former politicians, some were lawyers in private practice, some worked in the executive branch, some came from academia. In the 1950s a strong predisposition toward appointing professional judges began to emerge and quickly became a general rule: since 1971 only one Supreme Court justice has been appointed without prior judicial experience.[14] Of the nine current justices, eight were previously federal judges on a circuit court of appeals. By way of comparison, *none* of the chief justices during the nineteenth century had previously served as a judge in any way; nor had John Marshall, the most important chief justice of the founding era; nor had Earl Warren, perhaps the most renowned chief justice of the twentieth century.

Whether or not judging is a neutral, "scientific" activity that requires technical knowledge to correctly make decisions is debatable; according to Felix Frankfurter, reflecting on his 18 years of service on the Supreme Court, "the correlation between prior judicial experience and fitness for the functions of the Supreme Court is zero."[15] Posner and others argue that the task of an appellate judge is inherently nontechnical, taking issue with the idea that judicial decisions flow from objective application of rules, independent of a judge's beliefs and intuitions.[16]

———

Given the enormous complexity of the law and government, a system of technocratic judges has its advantages. But it also creates problems: policy making by judges with educational, career, and life experiences substantially different from the general public is likely to produce policies that differ from the preferences of the people at large. In this way, the expanding role of judges amplifies the disconnection between the people and policy that is created by the administrative state.

The next chapter considers the final and most democratic link in the policy chain: the legislators elected by the people. Legislator do appear to be connected to their constituents, but even this link is weaker than might be expected.

3

Disconnected by Legislatures?

ACCORDING TO opinion surveys, people are more frustrated with legislatures than any other branch of government—and so, not surprisingly, it's in this area on which reformers focus most of their energy. We have already seen that democratic drift originates in part from the shift in power to technocrats in the agencies and courts, so making legislatures more responsive can only address part of the problem. Nevertheless, given the huge amount of reform activity concentrated here, it is worth examining the issues and the potential to enhance popular control of policy through the legislative channel.

In the American system, legislators are designed to be the main link between the people and the government. The legislature was called the "popular branch" in *The Federalist Papers*, reflecting its intimate connection with the people, and elections were intended to be the glue that held them together.[1] Accordingly, much reform activity focuses specifically on elections, with the goal of making them more competitive. The premise is that representatives who are at risk of losing their seats will be more attentive to public concerns than those who are so entrenched that they cannot be beaten at the polls. The reforms that flow from this premise include: redistricting that creates competitive districts, public funding of campaigns and restrictions on large campaign contributions to level the playing field, open primaries that allow more challengers, and term limits that prevent incumbents from becoming entrenched.

Thinking about these issues leads to several questions: How connected in fact are legislators to their constituents? To the extent they are disconnected, what is the reason? And finally, will more competitive elections and restrictions on campaign contributions improve matters? This chapter considers these questions one by one, using a detailed new data set on legislator votes to venture answers. The evidence shows that representation is alive and well, albeit far from ideal, but casts doubt on the potential for improvement from the most popular reform ideas.

How Disconnected Are Legislators from Their Constituents?

The best-known theoretical proposition concerning legislators is the median voter theorem, which holds that competition between candidates for votes causes their positions to converge to the policy preferred by the median voter.[2] Roughly speaking, one can think of it as saying that candidate positions converge to the middle of the policy spectrum, to a position that the majority of voters supports. In a world in which this theorem holds, citizen preferences are represented and incorporated into policy decisions in a meaningful sense. Unfortunately, a large body of empirical research shows that the median voter theorem does not describe the actual behavior of legislators. Consider the simple fact that US senators from the same state often vote differently even though they represent the same constituents and therefore have the same median voter.

With theory inconclusive here, we must turn to data for some guidance. The starting point for empirical inquiry is identification of whether a legislator's vote does or does not reflect constituent preferences. With such information in hand, we can assess how often legislators follow constituent preferences, and isolate the circumstances where they go astray. However, it is surprisingly difficult to determine whether a legislator's vote matches what his or her constituents want, because of the scarcity of reliable information about constituent preferences. While there are many opinion surveys at the national level and occasional surveys for states and cities, few have opinion data at the level of *legislative districts*.

A way around this problem is to concentrate on a set of issues for which we have very accurate information about constituent preferences. Twenty-three American states allow citizens to challenge, by petition, state laws approved by the legislature and governor. By collecting enough signatures from fellow citizens, a petitioner can force a referendum in which voters approve or repeal the law. The key feature of these elections for the present purposes is that we observe a legislator's vote on the original law ("roll-call vote") as well as his or her constituents' vote on the same law when the referendum is held. By direct comparison, we can assess whether or not a legislator's vote was aligned ("congruent") with majority opinion in his or her district.

This chapter examines 3,555 roll-call votes associated with 28 referendums held between 2000 and 2016. Because these issues were only a small subset of the policies considered by legislators, we should be cautious about generalizing from them; their virtue is bringing the connection between legislators and constituents into sharp focus on those votes.

The referendums took place in nine states: Alaska, California, Maine, Maryland, Michigan, North Dakota, Ohio, South Dakota, and Washington. These states represent a mix of urban and rural, and include both "blue" and "red" states in terms of partisan orientation: Republicans typically controlled Alaska, Michigan, North Dakota, Ohio, and South Dakota; Democrats usually controlled California, Maine, Maryland, and Washington.

The laws covered fiscal, political, and social issues, and included high-profile topics of national interest such as same-sex marriage and the minimum wage, as well as issues of mainly local interest such as Alaska's law permitting aerial hunting of wolves and North Dakota's law allowing the state university to stop using the name "Fighting Sioux" for its mascot. The ideological orientation of the laws was also mixed, with some proposing to move policy in a progressive direction (e.g., allowing same-sex marriage or granting tuition to illegal immigrants) and others proposing to move policy in a conservative direction (e.g., allowing charter schools or limiting collective bargaining by public employees).[3]

A legislator's vote on a law is said to be "congruent" with district opinion if it matched the majority vote in his or her district, as revealed in the referendum election (for short, I will sometimes refer to the majority opinion in the district as "the district's opinion"). Figure 3.1 lists each law and shows the percentage of roll-call votes that were congruent with majority opinion. For all laws together, congruence was 65 percent, meaning that about two-thirds of legislators' votes were aligned with the preferences of a majority of people in their district. The lowest congruence was on South Dakota's 2015 law reforming the candidate nomination process (23 percent), California's 2013 law allowing tribal gaming (28 percent), and South Dakota's 2015 law creating a subminimum wage for youth (31 percent). Voters repealed all three laws, indicated by the dashed lines in the figure. The highest congruence was on California's health insurance law of 2003 (92 percent), which, counterintuitively, was also repealed. Whether 65 percent is a high or low number is to some degree in the eye of the beholder; the next chapter considers the question of how much congruence is enough, but clearly legislators often follow their own counsel.

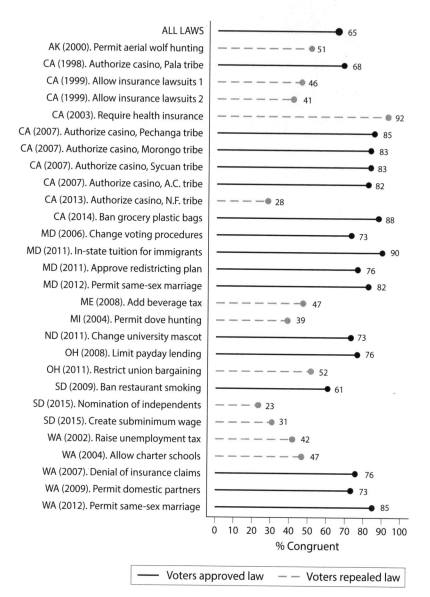

	% Congruent
ALL LAWS	65
AK (2000). Permit aerial wolf hunting	51
CA (1998). Authorize casino, Pala tribe	68
CA (1999). Allow insurance lawsuits 1	46
CA (1999). Allow insurance lawsuits 2	41
CA (2003). Require health insurance	92
CA (2007). Authorize casino, Pechanga tribe	85
CA (2007). Authorize casino, Morongo tribe	83
CA (2007). Authorize casino, Sycuan tribe	83
CA (2007). Authorize casino, A.C. tribe	82
CA (2013). Authorize casino, N.F. tribe	28
CA (2014). Ban grocery plastic bags	88
MD (2006). Change voting procedures	73
MD (2011). In-state tuition for immigrants	90
MD (2011). Approve redistricting plan	76
MD (2012). Permit same-sex marriage	82
ME (2008). Add beverage tax	47
MI (2004). Permit dove hunting	39
ND (2011). Change university mascot	73
OH (2008). Limit payday lending	76
OH (2011). Restrict union bargaining	52
SD (2009). Ban restaurant smoking	61
SD (2015). Nomination of independents	23
SD (2015). Create subminimum wage	31
WA (2002). Raise unemployment tax	42
WA (2004). Allow charter schools	47
WA (2007). Denial of insurance claims	76
WA (2009). Permit domestic partners	73
WA (2012). Permit same-sex marriage	85

——— Voters approved law　　－ － Voters repealed law

FIGURE 3.1. Congruence between legislator votes and district opinion

Why Do Legislators Sometimes Ignore
Constituent Preferences?

The overall congruence of 65 percent indicates that legislators usually voted in accord with their districts' preferences. How we think about representation, and how best to reform it, depends on the reason for the 35 percent of roll-call votes that were cast contrary to district opinion. There are two broad possibilities: either they were conscious decisions to ignore majority opinion, or they were "honest mistakes." Faced with hundreds of votes during a legislative session, and with thousands of constituents to represent, legislators can be forgiven if they occasionally misjudge constituent opinion.[4]

The possibility of honest mistakes is especially plausible in districts where opinion is evenly divided, say, with a 51–49 split on an issue. Determining the majority position is likely to be difficult in a situation like this. This suggests the possibility of assessing the importance of honest mistakes by focusing on districts where opinion was "one-sided," say 55–45. Honest mistakes should be rare in these districts because majority opinion is easy to determine. Looking at only such one-sided situations, which account for 83 percent of the 3,555 total votes, congruence is 67 percent, essentially unchanged, casting doubt on the idea that honest mistakes are the main explanation for noncongruent votes.

The legislative votes examined here are unusual in that they were challenged by a referendum. We might wonder if congruence was lower on these issues than it would be on "regular" issues; indeed, perhaps low congruence is the reason they were challenged in the first place. While possible, the story is difficult to square with the observation that voters backed most of these laws when they went to referendums—the laws were not inherently unpopular with the majority of voters.

Alaska's 2000 law on aerial wolf hunting is a good illustration. The law was approved by sizable majorities in both the Senate (14 to 5) and House (27 to 11), yet it was repealed in the referendum, with a majority of voters rejecting it in 29 of 40 house districts. Congruence was only 53 percent in the House and 47 percent in the Senate. Could legislators have been unaware that their constituents objected to this form of wolf hunting? This seems doubtful; the law in question overrode an existing ban on precisely this form of wolf hunting that voters had approved by initiative only three years earlier! Legislators had a clear and explicit statement of voter preferences on this issue that they chose to ignore. They may or may not have had a good reason for ignoring constituent opinion, but it was not a mistake based on misunderstanding what voters wanted.

Another possibility is that legislators are more likely to adhere to constituent preferences when it comes to issues that receive more public attention. To get a sense of this, we can divide issues according to the amount of media attention they received in the days surrounding the legislature's vote—"high" means covered on the front page of the state's top-circulating newspaper, "medium" means covered on a page other than the front, and "low" means not covered at all. As expected, congruence was higher when the media were watching: it was 71 percent for high-attention issues, 62 percent for medium-attention issues, and 56 percent for low-attention issues. Still, media coverage was not a panacea; even for the most publicized issues, legislators voted against constituent preferences 29 percent of the time.

Why, then, did legislators vote against constituent opinion more than one-third of the time on these issues? The most likely explanation seems to be that legislators were following their own personal policy preferences even though they conflicted with constituent opinion.

Figure 3.2 provides the basis for this conclusion by showing how legislators voted when their personal preferences agreed and disagreed with constituent opinion. For this exercise, each legislator was classified as being a conservative or liberal, and each district was classified as preferring a conservative or liberal outcome on each issue.[5] The top-left panel shows that when a legislator was conservative and the district favored the conservative outcome, the legislator voted conservative 87 percent of the time; and the bottom-right panel shows that when the legislator and district both wanted the liberal outcome, the legislator voted liberal 91 percent of the time. Not surprisingly, congruence was high when legislators agreed with their constituents. In contrast, when a legislator was conservative and the district favored the liberal outcome, the legislator voted conservative 79 percent of the time. Similarly, when a legislator was liberal and the district preferred the conservative outcome, the legislator voted liberal 64 percent of the time. In short, legislators had a pronounced tendency to vote in accord with their own policy preferences, regardless of district opinion.

This evidence conforms to what is called the "trustee" view of representation: legislators do not simply parrot the preferences of their constituents but rather exercise their own judgment to decide the best course of action, apparently heavily informed by their ideology. These 3,555 roll-call votes were congruent with district opinion most of the time not because legislators sought

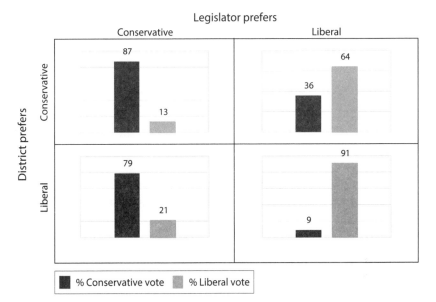

FIGURE 3.2. Legislator votes and their relation to district
and legislator preferences

to follow district preferences but because districts tended to elect legislators whose ideologies matched district preferences. The conclusion for these particular issues, that legislators tended to vote based on their ideologies, is consistent with a variety of other evidence in economics and political science.[6]

Will More Competition and Less Campaign Money Increase Connection?

With this picture of legislators in mind, we can now consider whether certain reforms might help address democratic drift. Most proposals fit into one of two broad categories: those designed to increase electoral competition, and those designed to take money out of politics. The premise of both types of proposal is that they will make legislators more responsive to the public, or more "congruent," in the language of this chapter. We can explore these premises using the same roll-call/referendum-voting data.

Making elections more competitive seems like a natural target for reform because most legislators have little or no competition. For the state legislators we have been examining, 14 percent ran unopposed and 21 percent received over 80 percent of votes, meaning there was only token opposition. This is typical

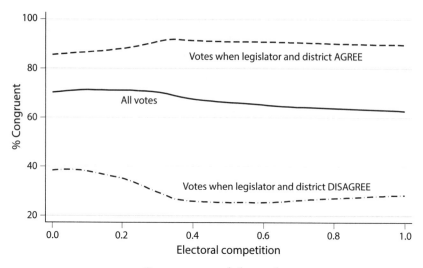

FIGURE 3.3. Congruence and electoral competition

for legislative races in the United States. Scholars have documented a long-running decline in competition for national and subnational elections. Reformers hope to increase competition by drawing districts that are more competitive, opening primary elections to independent voters, providing public funding for challengers, and so on.[7]

Consider first whether legislators are more likely to vote in accord with constituent opinion when competition increases. Figure 3.3 shows the relation between congruence and competition, using the vote margin as the measure of competition.[8] Vote margin is the percentage difference between the votes received by the winner and the loser; numbers are rescaled (reversed) so that 0 represents a candidate running unopposed and 1 represents a district in which the top two candidates exactly split the vote. The main takeaway is that congruence is *not* higher when competition is higher—in fact, the relation goes the other way. While this might seem surprising at first glance, there is a reasonable explanation: in the least competitive districts, legislators are very likely to be ideologically aligned with their constituents, so when they vote according to their ideologies, this happens to be congruent with district preferences most of the time. In contrast, in competitive districts, ideological legislators are more likely to be out of step with voters on some issues because constituent opinion is about evenly divided.

Does competition matter more in cases where the legislator and district disagree? The hope of reformers is that a tough re-election battle will make a legislator more attentive to district opinion. But figure 3.3 shows the opposite—in cases of disagreement, congruence is *lower* when competition is greater.

The upshot is that there is not a direct line between competitive districts and congruence. The evidence here suggests that there may even be a virtue in noncompetitive districts: when most voters hold the same views, they are likely to get a representative who shares their views, and thus reflects their preferences in the legislature. In a highly competitive district, roughly half of the voters end up with a representative opposed to their views. This raises questions about reforms that are intended to increase competition, such as Missouri's 2018 redistricting law that required state legislative districts to be "competitive" between the two major parties. Creating competitive districts does not guarantee more congruence, and could even make representation worse by increasing the number of citizens who are represented by a legislator who opposes their views.[9]

Now consider the idea of increasing congruence by reducing the influence of money in campaigns. The concern is that campaign contributions may function as bribes, making legislators more beholden to their contributors than to the residents of their districts. By taking money out of politics, reformers hope that legislators will be free to follow the preferences of their constituents instead of listening to big contributors.

To get a sense of the importance of campaign contributions, we can compare congruence with the amount of contributions. If legislators neglect constituent opinion because they are doing the bidding of big contributors, we might expect to observe that legislators who raised a lot of money cast fewer congruent votes than those who raised little money.[10]

As figure 3.4 shows, there is no relation between congruence and the contributions raised by a legislator.[11] Legislators who raised very little money were no more likely to vote in accordance with district opinion than legislators who raised a lot of money. When legislators disagreed with district opinion, congruence was actually higher among those legislators who raised a lot of money. This puzzling pattern might arise because constituents are more likely to provide campaign contributions and other support for legislators who cast congruent votes.

The evidence from figures 3.3 and 3.4 isn't enough to conclude that competition and campaign contributions have *no* effect on how responsive legislators are to district opinion—but it does suggest that these factors might not be as dominant as some reformers believe.[12] A number of other studies in economics, law, and political science raise similar doubts about the potential of reforms that pull these levers.[13]

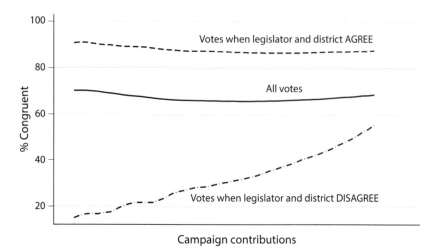

FIGURE 3.4 Congruence and campaign contributions

The main reason for noncongruence appears to be that legislators generally follow their ideological predispositions, independently of district opinion. This suggests that reforming elections to make them more competitive and remove money from politics is unlikely to repair the disconnection between policy and public opinion in a significant way.

The Challenge of Polarization and Population Growth

In some respects, the picture for legislators is fairly benign—legislators usually reflect constituent interests in the short run, and almost always do so in the long run because voters eventually replace misaligned incumbents with representatives sharing their values. The key to strengthening the connection between the people and legislators may be simply to select legislators who share voter preferences.

Yet finding such legislators may be harder given another trend—increasing political polarization. Polarization is one of the most discussed and troubling facts about American politics in the twenty-first century. Across a variety of measures—for example, how far apart the parties are from each other or how many committed conservatives and progressives there are compared to moderates—it is clear that polarization has been growing since the 1970s.[14] Because of this polarization, elections today often present voters with a choice between an extremist on the left and an extremist on the right; centrist candidates who might appeal to the moderate majority are scarce in a polarized world. If legislators vote their ideologies once in office, as the evidence above suggests, giving voters a choice between two extreme candidates means they end up with one of two extreme policy outcomes. When people prefer more centrist policies, they may find that outcomes are disconnected from their preferences.

It is also possible that polarization is in part a *consequence* of democratic drift. The gradual shift in power out of Congress and into the agencies and courts itself may have contributed to polarization in Congress. As legislators became less involved in making substantive policy decisions, they have less of a need to come together, find common ground, and make policy. Moderates are no longer needed, and the path to electoral victory lies in staking out extreme, non-compromising positions. In this way, extremists come to replace centrists in the legislature, and polarization grows.

Population growth probably also contributes to legislative drift for the simple reason that it is more difficult to represent a large group than a small one. A small group is more likely to be homogeneous, and it is easier to meet its members individually and learn their preferences and values. When the country was founded, each of the 65 congressmen represented an average of 57,169 people—and even then, critics argued that this was too large a group to allow popular control. Seats were added over time until 1929, when Congress capped the number at 435. Of course, the population continued to grow; by 2019, each member of the House represented about 750,000 people. According to one study, the United States has the highest ratio of people per seat in its lower house among the 35 nations in the OECD—and by a large amount; the runner-up, Japan, has one lawmaker per 272,000 citizens.[15] Similarly, the average number of constituents for a senator has grown from about 150,000 to 3 million since the founding, and, of course, the president represents 327 million people, well above the 4 million when George Washington was president. It seems inevitable that representatives will grow more distant as their number of constituents increases.

———

We can draw a few conclusions by pulling together the strands of evidence in this chapter. There appears to be a meaningful connection between the people and their representatives, at least at the state level. That connection is mainly brought about by voters selecting legislators who share their values, not by legislators suppressing their ideological preferences in deference to constitu-ent opinion. We lack comparable data for Congress, but if similar underlying forces are at work, congruence is probably lower for Congress. Unlike state legislators, who turn over fairly often because of term limits or to run for an-other office, members of Congress stay in office for a long time. Because voters seldom replace their representatives to bring in more ideologically compatible persons, Congress members can drift out of alignment with their constituents' preferences over time.

Unfortunately, there is reason to doubt that current reform proposals will make much of a dent in the problem. The main proposals—to increase electoral competition and reduce the amount of money in campaigns—sound good but don't appear to be very effective in giving the people more control. Moreover, the broader issue is that disconnection is not fundamentally a problem with legislatures; it stems from the shift in decision-making authority to unelected technocrats and judges. Even if legislators were made fully responsive to con-stituent preferences, most policy decisions would remain outside the control of the people.

These chapters have shown the existence of a disconnect between people and policy. Before getting to the book's main proposal—to address drift by mak-ing more use of direct democracy—we need to look at one more issue: whether the disconnect is large enough to require action. There isn't a crystal-clear answer, but the next chapter reports some evidence suggesting that the amount of disconnection is substantial. The chapter then wraps up the discus-sion of democratic drift by considering some conceptual counterarguments that drift is not necessarily a problem that needs to be solved.

4

How Disconnected
Is Government?

WITHOUT DOUBT, the structure of American government has evolved over the past century in ways that increase the distance between ordinary people and policy decisions. Some are deeply frustrated by this, but is it really that bad? If the disconnection is modest overall, perhaps we should simply accept it as the price we pay for having a complex, technically sophisticated government.

Putting a number on the amount of drift is challenging, but we can get a sense of the magnitude by piecing together evidence from several scholarly studies—and the resulting picture is grim. As this chapter shows, the disconnect between policy and public preferences appears to be substantial.

The most direct evidence comes from two studies of policy making in the American states, summarized in figure 4.1. These studies pick an issue, such as whether or not an estate tax was levied, and compare the policy choice to the preference of the state's citizens. (Finding state-level public opinion data on specific policies is the main obstacle to conducting such studies.)[1] As in the previous chapter, a policy was defined to be "congruent" if it conformed to the preference of the majority of people, otherwise it was "noncongruent."[2] Since each instance of a noncongruent policy was a case of disconnection—the majority did not get the policy it wanted—the prevalence of noncongruent policies is a measure of policy drift.

I conducted one of these studies, focusing on 10 policies for which opinion data were available in the ANES.[3] The policies included three concerning abortion (late term, parental consent, public funding) and one each involving the death penalty, English as an official language, the estate tax, gay rights in

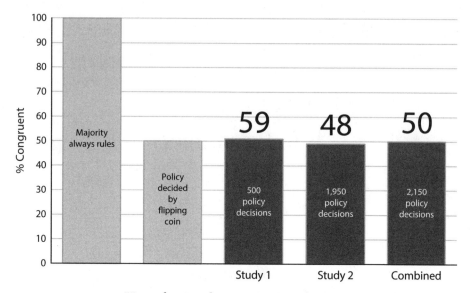

FIGURE 4.1 How often is policy congruent with majority opinion?

employment, same-sex marriage, school prayer, and term limits. Altogether, there were 500 separate policy decisions to evaluate.

If the majority always ruled, congruence would be 100 percent; yet for the 10 policies the ANES tracks, states adopted the outcome preferred by the majority in only 59 percent of cases. At first glance, this might seem like a healthy number: most of the time policies were congruent. But to put it in perspective, note that congruence would be 50 percent if policies were chosen by flipping a coin without any attempt to align them with citizens' preferences. A 59 percent congruence rate is only 9 percent greater than if policy were chosen randomly. Perfect congruence is too much to hope for, but 9 percent better than pure randomization seems disappointing.

One might object that these calculations use public opinion of all citizens, not just those who vote. Is policy more responsive to the preferences of voters? To investigate this possibility, I also calculated congruence using preferences of the majority of citizens who actually vote in each state—and found that congruence was 58 percent, essentially the same.

Another possibility is that the political system does not reflect the simple majority view counting everyone equally, but also factors in intensity of preferences. On any given issue, some people care strongly about the outcome while others do not care much one way or the other. Perhaps policy choices respond more to the views of those with strong preferences because they are more likely to make a campaign contribution, call their representative, blog about the issue, and so on. To investigate this possibility, I calculated the congruence of policy with the preferences of those who said they held their opinion "strongly." Congruence was 60 percent, still about the same.

A second study, by political scientists Jeffrey Lax and Justin Phillips, extended the analysis to 39 policies across the 50 states.[4] They were able to cover so many different policies by using a new statistical method that allowed them to extract state-specific opinion data from national surveys. In addition to most of the policies considered in my study, they examined issues related to affirmative action, assisted suicide, campaign finance, charter schools, gambling, guns, hate crimes, health insurance, immigration, marijuana, and school vouchers, among others—and found that policy choices were congruent with majority opinion only 48 percent of the time, a remarkably low level that Lax and Phillips labeled a "democratic deficit."

Combining the two studies by deleting overlapping issues leaves 44 issues across the 50 states—a grand total of 2,150 separate policy decisions. Congruence across these policy decisions was exactly 50 percent. The connection between public opinion and policy was observationally equivalent to a political system where policies are chosen by flipping coins.[5]

Related evidence shows a similar breakdown for the federal government. Political scientists Martin Gilens and Benjamin Page examined 1,779 policy issues, focusing on whether policy changes favored by a majority of people were adopted in the following four years.[6] They found that narrow majorities got the change they wanted only 30 percent of the time, and even large majorities (greater than 80 percent) got the change they wanted only 43 percent of the time.

It is important to recognize that the evidence in figure 4.1 and from Gilens and Page is based on controversial, high-profile issues—since pollsters only ask about contentious issues—and is therefore not representative of the full set of government policies. A majority of Americans in every state believe that murder should be illegal, and every state has adopted a congruent policy on that issue. So congruence over all government policies is surely higher than 50 percent. Having said that, it is still remarkable how little connection there is between public opinion and policy on prominent issues. It would be nice to have more evidence, but everything so far points not only to a disconnection, but to a big one. When citizens complain about policy makers ignoring their preferences, they are not making it up.[7]

———

To some, this lack of popular control is a desirable feature of democracy, not a "bug." Doubt about the competence of ordinary voters is the foundation of a flourishing literature arguing that the problem with modern democracy is that the people have too much power. "Democracies end when they are too democratic," Andrew Sullivan declared in the *New Yorker* in 2016.[8] From this perspective, low congruence might be desirable because it shows that representatives are exercising their own (allegedly superior) judgment when choosing policies rather than catering to popular sentiment.

There is something to this argument—sometimes ordinary people are uninformed about public matters and would be better off delegating those decisions to their representatives or experts in the bureaucracy—but it should not be taken too far. Democracy theorists believe that representatives should consult their consciences when setting public policy, and be willing to act against constituent preferences when convinced the public good requires it. However, overruling the public should be a rare exception, not the rule. When running for a seat in the Illinois legislature in 1836, Abraham Lincoln pledged:

> If elected, I shall consider the whole people of Sangamon my constituents, as well those that oppose as those that support me. While acting as their representative I shall be governed by their will on all subjects upon which I have the means of knowing what their will is, and upon all others I shall do what my own judgment teaches me will best advance their interest.[9]

When congruence is 50 percent, overruling the people is not a rare exception.

A democracy in which the people's views are routinely overruled by political elites is at risk of becoming unstable over time. Political institutions that habitually allow elites to substitute their policy preferences for those of the majority will lose legitimacy, and create a fertile ground for demagogues to challenge the institutions themselves. The American colonists exploded into an armed revolt because they were frustrated at being governed by a parliament in London that did not have their interests at heart. This is an extreme case, of course, but it is not a stretch to imagine frustrated voters turning to leaders who would like to undermine the system rather than work within it. In some countries, such leaders have managed to concentrate power in themselves in order to fight "the interests" on behalf of the people. If voters come to believe that democracy is no longer by and for the people, then they may search for alternatives to democracy.[10]

Democracy is predicated on the idea that the people usually are the best judges of their own interests; a government in which most decisions are made by a narrow elite, without regard to majority opinion, is not a democracy. Even James Madison, the architect of the US Constitution, and as far from a populist as you can get, was careful to remind the readers of *The Federalist Papers* that while government officials might occasionally ignore popular opinion, "the cool and deliberate sense of the community ought, in all governments, and actually will, in all free governments, ultimately prevail over the views of its rulers."[11]

———

This brings us to the central question: Given that policy often fails to reflect the preferences of the majority, how can the system be reformed to let the people rule? One line of thinking is to try to make technocrats, judges, and elected officials more responsive to the public. As discussed in preceding chapters, I believe this would be a tall order to deliver. Fortunately, there is a simpler approach. Instead of trying to make the middlemen—technocrats, judges, legislators—more responsive, we could cut them out of decisions that the people are capable of deciding on their own. That is, we could let the people decide important issues using referendums. The next part of the book begins to explore this idea, describing the experiences of nations, states, and cities that have used referendums, and showing that it is a less radical step than some believe.

PART II

Referendums Past and Present

5

Direct Democracy Defined

PART I SHOWS that ordinary people believe government is drifting out of their control—and that their belief has a basis in fact. As governments have evolved to meet the challenges of an increasingly complex world, they have turned over more and more decisions to unelected experts, weakening the link between the people and policy decisions. Democratic drift is worrisome because it threatens our aspirations for self-government, and if left to fester could undermine support for democratic institutions. This leads to the question of what steps can be taken to halt or reverse the drift. Direct democracy—asking the people to vote on important public issues—is a natural idea to consider, or at least to include on the list of possibilities, yet it is seldom mentioned in today's policy discussions.

The discounting of direct democracy stems in part from confusion over basic facts. A recent Brookings study analyzing the "legitimacy crisis" of the administrative state dismissed referendums as a solution on the grounds that "citizens are neither willing nor able to take on this job."[1] Nothing could be further from the truth: as consistently shown by opinion surveys, the public is eager to participate in deciding important issues. A 2017 Pew Research Center survey, to take a recent example, found that two-thirds of Americans (and two-thirds of people around the world) were in favor of citizens voting "directly on major national issues."[2] And when countries do hold referendums, public interest is high and voters flock to the polls, as witnessed by record or near-record turnout in recent referendums in the United Kingdom (Brexit), Greece (debt bailout terms), and Ireland (abortion).

There is also confusion about the place of direct democracy in American government. David Broder, the unofficial dean of the Washington press corps, began his book *Democracy Derailed* by describing referendums as "a new form of government [that] is spreading in the United States." He went on to call it "alien" and "an import," and said it threatened to "subvert the American system of government."[3] Broder is not alone in believing that direct democracy is a new and exotic foreign import that is in tension with the principles of American democracy, but this, too, is incorrect: as will be shown, direct democracy is neither new nor exotic nor alien to American political traditions. Referendums have been part of American democracy since the birth of the country and are widely used across the nation, except at the national level. Far from being an alien contaminant of "authentic" American government, direct democracy has been an integral feature from the beginning.

Misconceptions promulgated by pundits have in some sense polluted the waters, creating an undeserved bias against direct democracy that interferes with attempts to form an objective picture. If we hope to properly assess direct democracy, we need to start by clearing away the misconceptions to make sure we are seeing the picture without distortions. That is the purpose of part II of this book, which describes the landscape of direct democracy in the United States (chapter 6), Europe (chapter 7), and elsewhere in the world (chapter 8). These chapters review the history of direct democracy, its dispersion and evolution, and the various forms it takes, and attempt to dispel some of the more popular misunderstandings.

———

A few definitions before proceeding:

Direct democracy is any form of democracy in which the people vote on policies, rather than voting on candidates who themselves choose the policies. One can think of direct democracy as an alternative to representative democracy, although the two forms usually coexist. The ancient Greeks and Romans gathered in assemblies and voted in person, which still happens in some small American and Swiss towns, but that is feasible only in small communities. Nowadays direct democracy takes place through **ballot propositions** or **ballot measures**: citizens go to the polls and indicate approval or disapproval on a ballot.

Propositions can be placed in one of two broad categories, based on the origin of the proposal: in a **referendum**, the proposal originates with the government; in an **initiative** the proposal comes from the citizens themselves.[4] Referendums can be subdivided into three types:

Advisory referendum. A vote on a government proposal, called by the government, not required by law, and the government is not bound to abide by the outcome. Recent advisory referendums include Brexit in the UK and the peace agreement with FARC militia in Colombia, both in 2016.

Mandatory referendum.[5] A vote on a government proposal, required by law, the outcome is binding. For example, American states and many nations require voter approval for constitutional amendments, and Swiss cantons require voter approval for new spending programs.

Petition (or popular) referendum.[6] A vote on repealing an existing law, called by citizen petition. Citizens trigger a referendum by collecting a specified number of signatures from fellow citizens. In 2016, California voters decided whether to repeal a law banning plastic bags in grocery stores (voters kept the law); and South Dakota voters considered a law exempting workers younger than 18 from the minimum wage (repealed). In Italy, petitioners attempted unsuccessfully to repeal laws that legalized divorce (1974) and abortion (1981).

With an initiative, citizens write the law themselves, and trigger an election by collecting signatures. Initiatives allow citizens to bring up issues that the government might prefer to ignore, such as marijuana legalization, expanded animal rights, legislator term limits, and tax cuts, in recent years.

The procedural rules for direct democracy vary across jurisdictions. Some important distinctions pertain to:

Subject matter. Votes on certain topics may be required or may be prohibited. Some American states require a vote on constitutional amendments, on bond issues, or on tax increases. The Swiss constitution requires a vote on international treaties. In terms of restrictions, Massachusetts has one of the most detailed lists, prohibiting measures related to religion, judges, courts, freedom of the press, freedom of speech, freedom of elections, peaceable assembly, and jury trials, among other things.[7]

Approval conditions. The normal rule is that a proposal passes if it receives 50 percent plus one vote in favor, but there are interesting variants: Nevada requires an initiative constitutional amendment to pass in two successive elections, Florida requires 60 percent approval for constitutional amendments, and Minnesota requires affirmative votes equal to 50 percent of all ballots cast.

Amendment or repeal. In most cases, legislatures are permitted to amend or repeal a referendum through standard legislative procedures, but some states make it more difficult. Arkansas, Michigan, and Washington require legislative supermajorities to amend, and California flat-out prohibits the legislature from amending initiatives without voter approval.

Petition procedures. A key procedural rule for initiatives and petition referendums is the number of signatures required to qualify for the ballot. Practices vary widely: for constitutional amendments, California requires signatures equal to 8 percent of the votes cast in the previous gubernatorial election, which translates into 997,139 signatures for 2019–22; North Dakota requires signatures equal to only 2 percent of the state's population, roughly 27,000 signatures. The signature requirement is a major influence on the number of proposals that qualify for the ballot.[8] Petition rules sometimes require signatures to be distributed geographically, as for the European Citizens' Initiative, which requires 1,000,000 signatures in total, with a minimum number from at least seven countries (for example, 55,500 from France; 72,000 from Germany; 4,500 from Estonia).

Implementation and enforcement. Ballot propositions that nullify existing laws are self-executing because no further action is required. Propositions that create new law, on the other hand, need to be implemented by the executive branch, and sometimes require the legislature to provide supporting legislation. In the not uncommon case where sitting officials disagree with a law approved by the voters, they may drag their feet or simply refuse to implement it. A case in point is Utah, where voters approved a constitutional amendment allowing initiatives in 1900, but the legislature failed to create the implementing law for petitioning until after World War II, essentially nullifying the will of the voters for 50 years.[9] While no one has calculated the actual rates of implementation, political scientists Elisabeth Gerber, Arthur Lupia, Mat McCubbins, and Rod Kiewiet concluded from a series of case studies that complete and faithful implementation occurs less than one would hope.[10] In any event, the threat of unfaithful implementation appears to be inherent to direct democracy since it is hard to imagine how the people in any collective capacity could enforce the laws on their own; reliance on other government officials to implement is unavoidable.

Finally, a terminological point that I mention only because experience has taught me it will concern some readers: In the English language, the plural of referendum is sometimes expressed as "referendums" and sometimes as "referenda." I use "referendums" following the practice of most specialists and the recommendation of the *Oxford English Dictionary*. The rationale is that because "referendum" is not a Latin noun—it is a modern invention inspired by a Latin word—there is no reason to use Latin rules to form its plural.

———

With these terminological points out of the way, the following chapters turn to how direct democracy has actually been used, over time and around the world.

6

Direct Democracy in the United States

WHILE THE UNITED STATES has never held a national referendum, it nonetheless has a rich history of direct democracy—among the richest in the world—thanks to its state and local governments. Direct democracy has been around since the country's birth, a fact not always recognized, and virtually every American voter participates in referendum elections on a regular basis through initiatives, constitutional amendments, bond issues, charter amendments, and other propositions. Referendums are a standard part of the toolkit of American democracy. This chapter describes direct democracy's deep roots in the country's political culture, its origin and expansion across the continent, and its widespread use today.

Direct Democracy at the Beginning

Once the Constitutional Convention concluded in 1787, each state was left to decide whether or not to ratify the proposed constitution and join the union. Most of them convened a state convention to decide, but Rhode Island held a vote of the people instead. In a real sense, then, it can be said that direct democracy was part of the country's government from the moment of its birth (notwithstanding that Rhode Island voters rejected the new constitution, 237 votes in favor versus 2,708 votes against, with the state only joining the union two years later through a constitutional convention).

Rhode Island's vote typified the primary use of direct democracy in the early republic—to ratify and modify constitutions. The first step in setting up the new country after declaring independence in 1776 had been for each colony to adopt a constitution to replace its colonial charter. Two states did this by referendum:

Massachusetts voters adopted a constitution in 1780, one that remains in force today, after rejecting an initial proposal two years earlier; and New Hampshire voters adopted a constitution in 1783 after turning down proposals in 1779 and 1781. The other states adopted their new constitutions through self-ratifying conventions—not because they viewed this as a more proper approach (indeed, many towns instructed their convention delegates in writing to refer the document back to the people for approval), but because it would have been impractical to hold a statewide vote while the colonies were in a state of war, with much of their territory occupied by British troops.

After the war ended in 1783, ratification by popular vote became the norm. New states followed the examples of Massachusetts and New Hampshire, starting with Maine in 1819, then Tennessee in 1834, Michigan in 1835, and Florida in 1838. Popular ratification became mandatory for new states starting with Minnesota in 1857, when Congress required it as part of the enabling act for admission to the union. Existing states also increasingly sought voter approval when they created new constitutions, beginning with New Hampshire in 1792, followed by Connecticut in 1818, New York in 1821, Virginia in 1829, Georgia in 1833, and North Carolina in 1835. By the middle of the nineteenth century, the notion that state constitutions should be approved by the people was essentially uncontested and has remained that way to the present, except for a few anomalous cases in the South during the Civil War and post-Reconstruction periods.[1]

The process of amending state constitutions followed a similar path. The idea of popular approval of amendments can be found as early as Thomas Jefferson's draft constitution for Virginia in 1776, and New Hampshire's rejected 1779 constitution contained such a provision, but none of the original state constitutions called for a referendum on amendments. Things began to change as the new nation found its footing and the democratic ethos spread. Connecticut moved first—its 1818 constitution required voter approval for amendments (as well as approval of each house in two successive legislative sessions, the second by a two-thirds majority). Other states soon fell in line: Alabama and Maine required referendums on amendments in 1819, New York in 1821, Massachusetts in 1822. As experience proved that the people could effectively safeguard their liberties at the polls, popular ratification became the norm by midcentury, and today every state except Delaware requires a vote of the people for constitutional amendments.[2]

The embrace of direct democracy in the early republic may seem paradoxical given the Founders' well-known skepticism about lawmaking by ordinary people, which they embedded in the Constitution (more on this in chapter 9). But in fact it drew on long-standing traditions of self-government in the colonies, such as the use of town meetings to make collective decisions. The practice of trial before juries, included in the US Constitution's Bill of Rights and in each of the original state constitutions, also testifies to early Americans' confidence in the judgment of ordinary people. In continental Europe, trials were decided by judges appointed by the state. Britain allowed jury trials, but juries could decide only questions of fact; questions of law were reserved for judges. The Americans, in contrast, empowered juries to make findings of law as well as fact, reflecting their confidence in their fellow citizens, and as a buttress against lawless behavior by government officials.[3]

Voting on constitutions involved the people directly with the most fundamental issues of democracy: the structure and powers of government and the rights of the people. As it became widely accepted that the citizenry could and should make such decisions, it was only a small conceptual step to broaden the scope of their involvement to encompass nonconstitutional issues. As the nineteenth century progressed, the states extended direct democracy in a variety of ways, sometimes idiosyncratically, but some common directions emerged.[4]

Issuing State Debt

In the 1810s states began to borrow in order to fund railroads, public works projects like canals, and to capitalize banks. Many of these investments were dubious economic propositions from the start, and corruption in the allocation of money only made matters worse. The recessions of 1837 and 1839, among the most severe in the young nation's history, brought to light the questionable borrowing practices of many state governments, and several states slid into bankruptcy. Michigan and Indiana were the first to default, in the spring of 1841, followed by Arkansas, Illinois, Maryland, Mississippi, and Pennsylvania over the next year.

This financial mismanagement by state governments prompted a search for preventative mechanisms, and thoughts turned toward using the people as a backstop. Rhode Island was the pioneer; its 1842 constitution required voter approval for state borrowing in excess of $50,000, except in emergencies such as repelling an invasion or putting down an insurrection. Illinois, Iowa, Michigan, New Jersey, and New York followed suit in the 1840s, along with seven other states before the end of the century.[5]

New York's debt referendum requirement emerged from a constitutional convention that was called specifically to address the state's alarming debt growth. The state's wildly successful investment in the Erie Canal (constructed 1817–25)—which produced enough toll revenue to cover operating costs and repay its $7.9 million cost while spurring economic growth throughout the region—prompted state and local governments to launch a plethora of new canal projects. By 1846, it was evident that too many canals were being built that were not economically viable, and that much of the new construction was being used to grant political favors. The convention considered the possibility of an absolute cap on the total amount of debt, but when that was deemed too inflexible, a compromise was reached to require voter approval of new debt issues.[6]

Chartering Banks

In the early republic, most banks were chartered and capitalized by the states in the hope that they would finance projects that benefited the public. The financial panics of the late 1830s revealed that bank loans were extended for political purposes, leaving taxpayers on the hook when the loans could not be repaid and triggering debt crises in several states. The search for ways to prevent creation of corrupt banks led Iowa in 1846 to require voter approval before the state could charter a bank. Similar requirements were adopted in Illinois and Wisconsin in 1848, Michigan in 1850, and Ohio in 1851.

Location of State Capital

The choice of where to site a state's capital attracted significant interest from the public, but especially from land speculators who stood to win or lose fortunes depending on the decision. With its obvious potential for corruption, and legislators' hesitancy to take a side on such a hot-button issue, some states opted to turn over the decision to voters. Texas was the first state to require a popular vote on the location of the state capital in its constitution of 1845. It held a referendum in 1850 that resulted in the choice of Austin, settling a long-running contest with Houston. California held an advisory vote on the location of its state capital in 1850. Mandatory referendums on proposals to relocate or determine the location of the state capital were incorporated into the constitutions of Oregon (1857), Kansas (1859), Pennsylvania (1873), Colorado (1876), Montana (1889), South Dakota (1889), and Washington (1889).[7]

The Dramatic Expansion of Direct Democracy in the Populist and Progressive Eras

The scope of direct democracy expanded most dramatically during the Populist and Progressive eras that ran from about 1880 to 1920. The biggest innovation was the initiative and petition referendum, which for the first time empowered ordinary people to determine what issues went on the ballot, breaking the legislature's monopoly over the policy agenda. Direct democracy spoke directly to the populists' and progressives' central concern: the power of interest groups that they believed had captured their governments. "If we felt we had genuine representative government in our state legislatures," commented then-governor of New Jersey Woodrow Wilson, "no one would propose the initiative and referendum."[8] The reformers were particularly disturbed by the huge industrial corporations that had recently emerged, the political bosses they believed answered to the corporations, and the urban machines that organized new immigrants in the cities.

South Dakota, a sparsely populated frontier state best known at the time for its bloody conflict with Indian tribes, was the first to adopt the initiative and petition referendum. The Populist Party gained control of the governor's office and state legislature in 1896, and immediately proposed a constitutional amendment providing for these tools at both the state and municipal levels. Voters turned the party out of office in 1898, but approved its initiative and referendum amendment by a vote of 23,816 to 16,483. Looking back, a leading reformer in the state explained their motivation:

> Our experience was that the railroad and allied corporations controlled the political machines of both political parties, and thru them our conventions and legislatures. We were discouraged by the failure of our representatives to do the will of the people even when promised in platform pledges. . . . We were helpless and almost hopeless until . . . the initiative, referendum, and imperative mandate (recall).[9]

Utah was the next state to adopt in 1900, followed by Oregon in 1902. Oregon became the first state to actually use the new tools in 1904, when voters approved three initiatives: a statute providing for direct election of US senators, a statute providing a local option for liquor regulation, and a constitutional amendment authorizing the legislature to regulate the office of the state printer. Other states followed in quick succession, adopting either the initiative or the petition referendum, or both. By 1918, 22 states provided one or the other.[10]

At the same time that states were adopting the initiative and petition referendum, so too were cities. Sometimes the processes became available to cities en masse through an amendment to the state constitution, as in California and South Dakota. In other cases, cities adopted the processes individually through their charters. San Francisco and Vallejo in California were the first cities to incorporate initiative and referendum rights into their charters in 1898, followed by Los Angeles in 1900 (prior to California's statewide amendment). While we don't have data on the exact number of cities that adopted the initiative and referendum during this period, a partial survey indicates that by 1910, 38 of 51 medium-to-large cities allowed initiative charter amendments, including Dallas and Houston in Texas, Chattanooga and Memphis in Tennessee, Spokane and Tacoma in Washington, and Pontiac in Michigan, and 10 states provided initiative rights to all or almost all cities in the state.[11]

After the Progressive Era ended around 1920, the pace of reform slowed. Four more states, and an unknown number of cities adopted the initiative process over the subsequent decades, but the basic landscape of direct democracy in the United States had achieved the form it takes today.

A Closer Look at the Initiative Process

While referendums are by far the most common form of direct democracy, the initiative process commands the headlines, and since its arrival in the 1890s has been the dominant force shaping popular perceptions of direct democracy in the country. It is also the most controversial form of direct democracy. Given its influence, the initiative bears a close examination, especially so we can sweep away some prominent misconceptions.

Today, 24 states allow initiatives, shown in figure 6.1 with their date of adoption.[12] Most states adopting the initiative did so during the Progressive Era, with Alaska, Wyoming, Florida, and Mississippi coming later. Other states have come close to adopting but fallen short—most recently Rhode Island in 1996, where the people voted in favor of adoption in an advisory referendum, but the legislature declined to take action. The initiative is most common in the West, where it is available in almost every state west of the Mississippi River, but it is also present in all the other regions of the country, South (Arkansas, Florida, Mississippi), Northeast (Maine, Massachusetts), and Midwest (Michigan, Ohio).

Figure 6.2 shows the percentage of American cities that allow initiatives either for ordinances or charter amendments. Again, almost all cities in the West

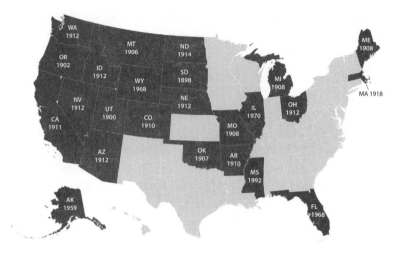

FIGURE 6.1. States with the initiative (showing year of adoption)

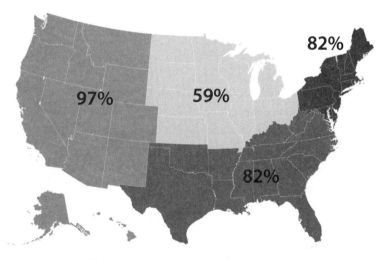

FIGURE 6.2. Percentage of cities with the initiative, by region

provide for initiatives, but the process is common in every region, never dipping below 59 percent availability. Focusing only on the 1,500 largest cities, 82 percent permit initiatives. Table 6.1 lists the direct democracy provisions of the 10 largest cities. All but one of them allow initiatives and all but one (Chicago) require referendums on certain issues, such as bond issues or tax increases.[13]

TABLE 6.1 Direct Democracy in the Largest American Cities

City	Initiative	Petition Referendum	Mandatory Referendum Topics
New York	Yes	No	Bidding for public contracts rules Bonds Charter amendments City council form City planning commission powers Elective office elections, terms, powers, creation Government salaries Mayor's veto power and succession Public notice and hearing rules Public utility franchises Sale or lease of government property Transfer of powers of agency heads
Los Angeles	Yes	Yes	Bonds Charter amendments City engagement in commercial enterprises Railroad grade crossing plans Sale of excess water and water rights Sale of public utilities Sale or grant of tidelands Tax increases
Chicago	No	No	...
Houston	Yes	Yes	Bonds Charter amendments Zoning laws
Phoenix	Yes	Yes	Bonds Charter amendments Land grant for stadium Nonroutine expenditure
Philadelphia	Yes	No	Bonds Charter amendments
San Antonio	Yes	Yes	Bonds Charter amendments
San Diego	Yes	Yes	Bonds Major public projects conferring private benefits Retirement benefit increases Tax increases
Dallas	Yes	Yes	Bonds Charter amendments Public utility purchases
San Jose	Yes	Yes	Agreements for long-term use of public parks Bonds Retirement benefit increases Tax increases

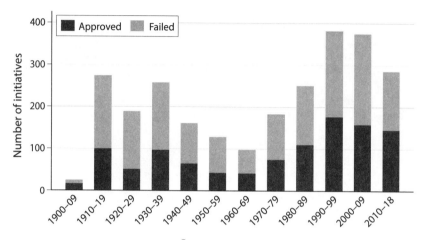

FIGURE 6.3. State initiatives over time

Figure 6.3 provides a snapshot of initiative use over time, showing the number of state initiatives on the ballot and approved by decade (recall that the first state initiatives appeared in Oregon in 1904). Initiative use has waxed and waned over time. There was a burst of lawmaking by initiative in the decades immediately after adoption, fueled by a pent-up demand for policies that rural-dominated legislatures had been able to block before, such as redistricting, the eight-hour workday, workers' compensation, and public education. Initiative use fell off after the Great Depression and remained low through the 1960s. A new surge began in the late 1970s triggered by California's Proposition 13, which cut property taxes and set off a nationwide tax revolt (this groundbreaking proposition is covered more detail in chapter 12). Initiative activity peaked in the 1990s, and while it fell a bit in the most recent decade, it has remained at historically elevated levels.[14]

Through 2018, a total of 2,609 statewide initiatives have reached the ballot, with 41 percent of them passing. Figure 6.4 shows the numbers by state. Twenty-four states have voted on at least one initiative; California has been the most active with 379, closely followed by Oregon with 373. Other active states are Colorado (236), North Dakota (197), Washington (187), and Arizona (177).

Table 6.2 lists the most common initiative topics during each decade. Many of the central policy debates over the past century, from social issues to fiscal issues to election reform, have been addressed by initiative. While topics vary over time, there is no obvious ideological slant; plenty of initiatives can be

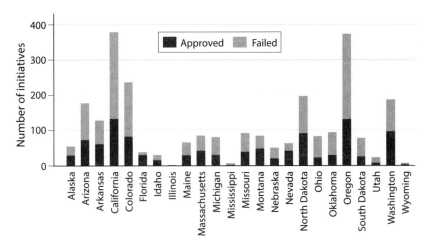

FIGURE 6.4. State initiatives by state, 1904–2018

TABLE 6.2 Prominent Initiative Topics by Decade

1900–1909	Alcohol regulation and local option
1910–19	Alcohol prohibition and regulation Government debt Women's suffrage Direct primary elections Eight-hour workday
1920–29	Public education Taxes (income, property, vehicle)
1930–39	Repeal of alcohol prohibition Taxes and tax limits (income, property, vehicles) Old-age pensions and welfare
1940–49	Alcohol regulation and local option Public schools Labor unions Taxes (income, property, vehicles) Old-age pensions and welfare
1950–59	Gambling Labor unions Old-age pensions and welfare
1960–69	Public education Redistricting
1970–79	Campaign regulation Nuclear power Recycling Taxes and tax limits (income, property, sales)

Continued on next page

TABLE 6.2 Continued

1980–89	Public funding of abortion
	Nuclear power and ban on nuclear weapons
	Gambling and state lottery
	Taxes and tax limits (income, property, sales)
1990–99	Hunting and fishing
	Campaign regulation
	Discrimination and racial preferences
	Environment
	Gambling and state lottery
	Tax referendums and taxes and tax limits (income, property, sales, tobacco)
	Term limits
2000–2009	Medical marijuana
	Public schools
	Gambling
	Minimum wage
	Limits on political activity of labor unions
	Eminent domain
	Same-sex marriage
	Smoking ban
	Taxes (income, tobacco, vehicle)
2010–18	Animal rights
	Marijuana legalization
	Minimum wage
	Taxes (income, sales, tobacco)

found on both left-wing and right-wing topics. This is easy to explain: the initiative process is the last resort for groups that feel shut out of the legislature, so liberal initiatives appear when the legislature is controlled by conservatives, and conservative initiatives appear when the legislature is controlled by liberals.

Even though initiatives command the most attention, legislative referendums are by far more common. Consider the number and approval rate for propositions over the past two decades, broken down in figure 6.5 into initiatives, petition referendums, and legislative proposals.[15] There were 2,580 propositions in all during this time period, or 123 per year on average.

Legislative propositions comprised 69 percent of all ballot measures, meaning that in practice citizens are usually voting on proposals advanced by the legislature. The small number of petition referendums (70) compared with initiatives (726) can be explained by activists preferring to overwrite a

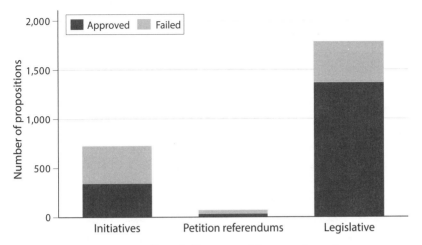

FIGURE 6.5. State ballot propositions, 1998–2018

law they dislike instead of simply repealing it. Voters approved 77 percent of legislative propositions, much higher than the 47 percent approval rate for initiatives.

Clearing Up Some Misconceptions

This overview of direct democracy in the United States gives a sense of how deeply referendums are embedded in the country's political culture, and dispels a few misconceptions that sometimes find their way into public discussions. Direct democracy is not a recent invention; it has been part of American democracy since the birth of the country. Every state but Delaware uses referendums to decide its most fundamental issues—the provisions of the state constitution—and states have been doing this for more than two centuries. Even the "novel" initiative process has been in use for more than a century, making it older than the federal income tax, universal women's suffrage, and social security. It is also evident that direct democracy is not an isolated practice confined to a select region of the country, contrary to the view that it is a California-specific aberration. It is common across the country at both the state and local levels. The notion that direct democracy is in some way alien to American political culture because the United States is "a republic and not a democracy," as some tendentiously claim, does not square with the basic facts of American history and the country's democratic practices.

The prevalence of direct democracy raises a question that gets to the heart of this book's argument: If direct democracy is a (partial) cure for democratic drift, why are Americans so dismayed by their government?

The answer in part has to do with the difference between the national and state governments: Americans lack trust primarily in the national government, where direct democracy is entirely absent, not in their state or local governments where direct democracy is widely used. Measured by the percentage of respondents who say they have a great deal or fair amount of "trust and confidence" in government, trust in the national government over the past decade averaged 41 percent, compared with 59 percent for state governments and 71 percent for local governments.[16] This is not to say that trust is higher in state and local governments just because they use direct democracy—although there is reason to believe it is a contributing factor—but rather that it is not a contradiction to see popular dissatisfaction with the national government and at the same time widespread use of direct democracy at the state and local levels.

———

By walking through the basic facts about direct democracy in the United States, I have tried to sweep away some misconceptions and lay the foundation for an assessment of possible reforms. The next chapter does the same for direct democracy in Europe, where the practice has enjoyed the most extensive use. Its wealth of historical examples offers lessons about when referendums can help and when they can be misused.

7

Direct Democracy in Europe

EUROPE HAS THE HIGHEST concentration of democracies in the world. Most of them are prosperous and stable, with distinct political cultures that stretch back centuries. Yet, like the United States, many are grappling with surging populist movements, each of which is colored by issues of local importance, but all of them aiming to give the people more control over governments they believe have been captured by elites. Unlike the United States, Europe has been actively experimenting with direct democracy and exploring options to expand its use. Europe thus offers a different but complementary set of experiences from which to form a picture and draw lessons about the possibilities and perils of direct democracy.

Populism and Democracy in Europe

Populism has surged in Europe over the past two decades. From 1998 to 2018 the vote share of populist parties in parliamentary elections more than tripled, from 7 percent to 25 percent, based on election results in 31 countries. According to one reporter, "2018 was the year populism went mainstream and beyond the United States and Britain"—populist parties took control in Italy (Five Star Movement and the League), Austria (Freedom Party), and the Czech Republic (ANO Party), and made inroads into Germany, where Alternative for Germany entered the Bundestag with 94 seats, becoming the largest opposition party. Populists continued to rule in Hungary, where Prime Minister Viktor Orbán's Fidesz party secured a third term, Greece (Syriza), and Poland (Law and Justice Party), and had a hand in governing through formal or informal coalitions with mainstream parties in Bulgaria, Denmark, Finland, Latvia, the Netherlands, and Norway. Even when populist parties are too small to take power, they can draw enough support from the main parties to influence politics, and their electoral strength has pushed some major parties to become more populist, particularly those on the center right. "Europe's populists are waltzing into the mainstream" is how the *Economist* put it in 2018.[1]

Populism springs from different sources in each country, but dissatisfaction with European integration is part of the story almost everywhere. This is not surprising because although integration has provided Europeans with many benefits, it has done so at the cost of reducing local control over policy. Membership in the European Union (EU) means giving up control of national borders; member countries must accept any and all immigrants from the other member countries, as long as the immigrants are working, seeking work, or self-sufficient. EU members must also permit these immigrants to vote and run for office in local elections, even if they are not citizens. In order to maintain the EU's free trade zone, member countries also turn over much of their power to regulate business activity to the European Commission. And the EU's strict limits on government deficits constrain the members' ability to manage their fiscal policies, taxes, and spending.

The design of the central EU government apparatus, which is largely free from popular control, amplifies the sense of lost power. Europeans elect representatives to the European Parliament, but most decision authority resides in the European Commission and other agencies like the European Central Bank. Political scientist Sheri Berman observed:

> The EU is a technocracy not a democracy. It was designed as a protected sphere of policymaking, free from direct democratic pressures. . . . Critical decisions made by unelected EU technocrats are made without any direct input from citizens who also, of course, lack the ability to throw technocrats out of office if their decisions prove unpopular or counterproductive.[2]

As the scope of EU activities has expanded, more citizens have come to believe that national sovereignty has been surrendered to distant and unresponsive supranational bodies. A recent survey found that 62 percent of Europeans believe the EU "does not understand the needs of its citizens."[3]

Loss of control due to European integration intersects with the continuing growth of the administrative state within each country, compounding frustrations. For similar reasons as in the United States—namely, an increasingly complex economic and social policy environment—European nations developed administrative agencies that are now the locus for much of their policy making.

Popular frustration came to a head in France in late 2018 with the *gilets jaunes* protest movement, named after the distinctive fluorescent yellow vests worn by demonstrators, who blocked roads and occupied traffic circles. The movement was sparked by a new diesel tax but mushroomed into a general protest against the pro-business policies of President Emmanuel Macron and the technocratic establishment in general. Macron, himself a technocrat, acknowledged the root issue in a TV interview, where he admitted a failure "to reconcile the French people with its leaders."[4] Macron canceled the diesel tax, and as the protests ground on, expressed an openness to holding national referendums and allowing citizen initiatives so the people could have a direct hand in policy decisions.

Europe would seem to be fertile ground for direct democracy—educated electorates, frustration with current politics, durable democratic traditions—and indeed Europeans express strong support for referendums in opinion surveys. A 2017 Pew Research Center poll of 10 European nations found 72 percent support overall for voting on "major national issues to decide what becomes law," with support ranging from a low of 56 percent in the Netherlands to a high of 80 percent in Poland (figure 7.1).[5] And not just support but use of the tools is widespread; a recent survey found that 44 European nations use referendums, and 18 allow citizen initiatives.[6]

The confluence of sovereignty issues with European integration has prompted over 50 referendums related to the European Union, starting in the 1970s in Denmark, France, Norway, Ireland, and the United Kingdom. Most of these referendums were sponsored by pro-EU elites as a way to override opposition to integration, and for the most part that strategy worked. Exceptions are Norway and Switzerland, which declined via referendum to pursue membership in the EU. Recently, however, voters in member countries have become more skeptical of proposals calling for closer integration; the UK's controversial Brexit referendum in 2016 is the best-known example (discussed at length in chapter 12), but it was preceded by votes against closer union in France, Ireland, and the Netherlands. Another notable referendum occurred in Greece in 2015, when voters chose not to accept the terms of the international community's debt-relief program.[7]

Of course, EU leaders are aware of the underlying tensions between their enterprise and popular attachment to self-government. One potentially far-reaching response was the development of the European Citizens' Initiative (ECI). The Treaty of Lisbon, which established the constitutional structure for the EU in 2007, declares that citizens have the right to petition the European

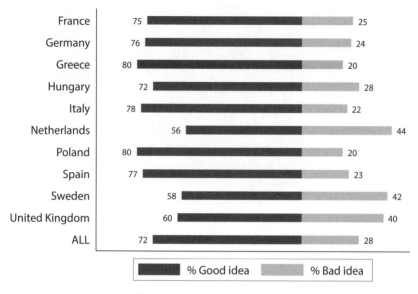

FIGURE 7.1. Public opinion about voting on national issues

Parliament and calls for creation of an initiative process.[8] After several years of discussion, the European Commission developed the ECI as an initiative process, which is a step—albeit a small one—forward. The ECI allows a citizen group that collects one million signatures representing nationals of at least one-quarter of the member states to submit a proposal to the European Commission. However, the Commission is not required to approve or even vote on the proposal, and there is no provision for submitting it to a vote of the people.

To date, three proposals have met the signature requirement—one calling for a halt to animal vivisection, one declaring a right to life starting at conception, and one declaring a basic human right to water and sanitation—and in each case the Commission has responded by adopting an official communication but taking no legislative action. While the ECI in its current form gives the people no real power, democracy tends to create a demand for more democracy, so it may turn out to be a forerunner to something more significant down the line.[9]

Referendums by Autocrats

Europe was the site of one of the earliest nationwide referendums, in 1793, when over 90 percent of French voters approved a new republican constitution in the midst of the French Revolution. Many nations went on to experiment with direct democracy, and following World War II European democracies gradually introduced provisions for referendums on constitutional amendments.

However, the path of experimentation has left behind a checkered history. The recurring use of referendums by authoritarian governments, not to advance democracy but to give their regimes an air of legitimacy, is the dark side of direct democracy. Direct democracy's reputation has been tarnished more than a few times by association with despotic rulers. Two cases in particular cast a shadow over popular perceptions of referendums: Napoleon and Hitler.

On July 14, 1789, a crowd of commoners and mutinous troops stormed the Bastille fortress and prison in Paris, setting off the French Revolution. After 10 years of bloody turmoil that saw the rise and fall of a series of republican governments, the relentless use of the guillotine to settle political disputes, and the execution of the king and queen, General Napoleon Bonaparte staged a coup, assuming dictatorial powers. Napoleon held a series of plebiscites to legitimize his gradual accretion of power—in 1799 to create the dictatorship ("Consulate"), in 1802 to become consul for life, and in 1804 to become hereditary emperor. These referendums were entirely window dressing: they merely formalized powers that Napoleon had already acquired through control of the army.

Napoleon's actions were textbook examples of the cynical way autocrats sometimes use referendums. He suppressed the press—by the second referendum Napoleon had shut down 60 of 73 newspapers, prohibited creation of new newspapers, and instituted censorship. The people were not free to cast their vote as they chose: one general is said to have told his troops that "they were free to vote for or against the new empire, but that the first soldier to register a negative vote would be taken out and shot."[10] The vote counting, supervised by Napoleon's brother who served as interior minister, was corrupt (none of the referendums received less than 99.8 percent in favor) and the outcomes were foregone conclusions; Napoleon once even declared a law to be in force weeks before the voting had concluded.

The other notorious case is Germany under Adolf Hitler and the Nazi Party. At the conclusion of World War I, the kaiser abdicated and Germany became a democratic republic under the Weimar Constitution. Weimar democracy (1919–33) was highly unstable, with the legislature (Reichstag) fragmented into numerous polarized parties, none of which could secure a majority.[11] In 1932, in the midst of a severe worldwide depression, the Nazi Party became the largest bloc in the Reichstag with 37 percent of the vote, and Adolf Hitler was appointed chancellor.

The decisive step in Germany's transition from a democracy to an autocracy occurred in March 1933 when the Reichstag passed an Enabling Act that gave Hitler's cabinet the power to enact laws without consent of the Reichstag and without regard to the constitution. This is sometimes described as a democracy voting itself out of existence, but it is better seen as a coup because the vote was illegitimate: in order to secure the necessary two-thirds majority, the Nazis arrested deputies representing the 81 Communist Party delegates and prevented other opponents from attending. A few months after the Enabling Act, the government passed a law declaring the country to be a one-party state under the Nazi Party. Hitler's consolidation of power was completed in 1934 upon the death of President Paul von Hindenburg, when the cabinet gave Hitler all of the presidential powers, in addition to his existing powers as chancellor. He was then an absolute dictator, and took the title *Führer* (leader).

Hitler's government held four national referendums. The first, in 1933, asked voters if they wished to leave the League of Nations, in effect exiting from the humiliating Versailles system that had been imposed on Germany by the victorious allies after World War I. It passed with 95 percent in favor, in an election that seemed reasonably free. The second referendum was held in 1934 on whether to give Hitler the powers of chancellor and president, and make him *Führer*. This was purely symbolic since the cabinet had already granted him these powers and the title. In an election featuring widespread voter intimidation and fraud, and with the media controlled by the Nazi Party, the official vote was 96 percent in favor. In 1936 and again in 1938, referendums were held asking voters to automatically appoint the full list of Nazi candidates to the Reichstag instead of going through the process of actual elections. The official vote totals, again from elections regarded as fraudulent, were 99.0 percent and 99.7 percent, respectively, in favor.

There are plenty of other examples of cynical and manipulative referendums by authoritarian regimes. Dictators often find it useful to drape their regimes with the mantle of legitimacy that a popular vote confers. This makes the point that holding a referendum is not in and of itself a good thing; for a referendum to advance the public good, certain conditions must hold. At a minimum, the people must be able to express their opinions freely, the election must be free from voter intimidation, votes must be counted honestly, and there must be a free press to cover the issues, none of which applied under Napoleon and Hitler. The more general lesson is that a country cannot simply call for a vote of the people and just assume it will produce good public policy; attention must be paid to the design and context of the referendum. I expand on this point later when discussing Brexit, a referendum that was poorly designed, and devote all of chapter 18 to "best practices" for referendums.

At the same time, we should be careful not to draw the wrong lessons from these episodes. It is sometimes suggested that these examples show that referendums are dangerous because the people may use them to vote away their own democratic rights. The argument is that by affirming the dictatorial powers of Napoleon and Hitler, the people voluntarily chose to extinguish their democracies. Yet Napoleon and Hitler had both acquired dictatorial powers de facto prior to calling referendums. The referendums merely formalized political reality; they did not create it.

Success Stories

Fortunately, success stories are much more common than cynical referendums by dictators. Many nations have managed to use direct democracy productively, customizing it to suit their unique political environments. Three countries provide particularly interesting illustrations of different paths that can be followed.

Switzerland

The Swiss republic is the world's preeminent practitioner of direct democracy. The Swiss use direct democracy at every level (national, cantonal, and municipal); they use it often, holding three to four national elections a year; and they have been doing so for centuries. Swiss communes (towns) have held voting assemblies, *Landsgemeinde*, going back to the Middle Ages. Those practices were incorporated into the Swiss constitution of 1848, and extended throughout the late nineteenth century, with a provision for national initiatives added in 1891.

Today, at the national level, voter approval is required for constitutional amendments, collective security agreements, and membership in supranational communities; petition referendums are allowed to challenge all laws passed by the national parliament, as well as international treaties and membership in international organizations; and voters are allowed to propose and approve constitutional amendments by initiative. At the subnational level, all cantons allow initiatives and most require referendums on new spending programs.[12]

Not only does Switzerland provide a full menu of direct democracy tools, it does not hesitate to use them. According to a list provided by the Swiss Federal Chancellery, 641 national referendums have been held through 2018,

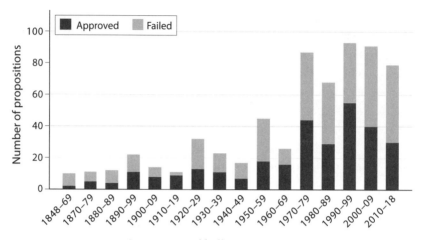

FIGURE 7.2. Swiss national ballot propositions, 1848–2018

47 percent of which were approved. Figure 7.2, showing decade-by-decade totals, reveals a surge in the number of measures beginning in the 1970s, mirror-
ing the pattern for the United States.[13]

Swiss referendums cover a breathtaking array of topics. The first national initiative, approved in 1893, prohibited the slaughter of cattle without stunning
them first. This initiative illustrates the complexities of direct democracy: it is
on its face an animal-welfare law, and still today defended by animal rights activists, but Jewish groups consider it anti-Semitic since it prohibits ritual
slaughter under kosher rules. Recent propositions have asked voters if they
wished to: limit immigration by establishing quotas (approved), guarantee every
citizen a minimum income (failed); expel foreigners who commit a crime
(failed); end public funding of abortion (failed); reduce the sales tax (VAT)
in restaurants (failed); require shareholder votes on executive compensation
(approved); abolish compulsory military service (failed); ban construction of
minarets (approved); and eliminate funding for the Swiss Broadcasting Corporation (failed).

Switzerland's hyperdemocracy provides an antidote to the claim that direct
democracy is inherently turbulent, bloody, and chaotic because the people cannot regulate their passions. The Swiss have been governing themselves by referendum for centuries—in the process creating a prosperous and largely peaceful society that bears no relation to the anarchy that critics of direct democracy
claim should result.

Italy

In Italy, direct democracy takes the unusual form of the petition referendum, called the *referendum abrogativo,* by which voters can strike a law from the books, no matter how long ago it was adopted (as long as it is at least one year old). The referendum was provided in the country's 1948 constitution, but the implementing legislation was delayed until 1970. Petitioners must collect the signatures of 500,000 people in order to call a vote. An important feature of the process is that repealing requires approval by a majority of voters, but, in addition, at least 50 percent of the electorate must participate. This latter condition is often determinative, as opponents simply stay home on election day.

The first referendum, held in 1974, proposed to repeal a law allowing married couples to divorce; it was rejected with 59 percent against. From then through to 2018, the country has held 67 national referendums, repealing 24 laws. Among the more controversial referendums were proposals related to legal abortion (not repealed), expanded nuclear power (repealed), assignment of parliamentary seats to coalitions of parties (not repealed), and allowing offshore oil drilling (not repealed).

Italy also provides direct democracy in the form of mandatory referendums on constitutional amendments if they do not receive a two-thirds vote in parliament. Three amendments have gone to the voters in this way, with one approved—a measure to decentralize power from the national to local governments—and two rejected. Italy also held an advisory vote in 1989 in which 88 percent approved of membership in the European Union.

Direct democracy has received growing attention in the country since the populist Five Star Movement received the most votes in the 2018 election and entered the government. Direct democracy is one of the movement's core principles, closely linked to its vision of using the internet to transform democracy by allowing the people a more direct role in political decisions (universal internet access is one of the "five stars" that give the movement its name). The party chooses its parliamentary candidates through an online vote of registered members, and holds online votes to discuss and approve its legislative proposals, such as a 2014 vote in which it decided to support same-sex marriage. Among the new government's first plans was to revise the quorum rules that have enervated the referendum process, causing many citizens to sit out referendum elections.[14] Symbolizing the importance of the issue, the new government named Riccardo Fraccaro the minister for parliamentary relations and direct democracy, the first time any nation in the world created a cabinet-level position focused on direct democracy.

Ireland

Direct democracy appears in Ireland through the requirement that all constitutional amendments be approved by a vote of the people after passing both houses of the parliament. The referendum requirement is part of the Irish constitution, ratified by a vote of the people in 1937; through 2018, 36 amendment referendums had been held, with 30 amendments approved. Many proposed amendments have involved social issues, and they have gradually moved the largely Catholic country in a progressive direction. Divorce was legalized in 1996; the death penalty was banned in 2002; same-sex marriage was legalized in 2015 (the first time a country had done this by national vote); and after a string of antiabortion elections, abortion was legalized in 2018. There have also been several referendums relating to European integration.

———

Europe provides interesting examples of the various forms direct democracy can take, when it can work, and when it might be harmful. Several nations have experienced referendums called by authoritarian regimes in an effort to legitimize their rule. These referendums were held under conditions in which citizens were unable to cast a free and fair vote, and they provide lessons on how not to use direct democracy. On the more positive side, other European nations have had successful experiences with direct democracy over long stretches of time. The forms of successful direct democracy vary by country, highlighting that the practice is not one-size-fits-all, but something that can and should be customized to a country's unique political culture and history. The next chapter completes this tour of direct democracy around the world by describing the use of referendums in other regions where we might not expect it would take hold.

8

Direct Democracy in
Unexpected Places

SO FAR WE'VE CONSIDERED direct democracy in industrialized Western nations—but referendums can be found across the world, including in some unexpected places. According to data collected by the Sweden-based International Institute for Democracy and Electoral Assistance, between 1980 and 2018 the percentage of countries that held at least one national referendum was 96 percent in Europe, but also a sizable 64 percent in Asia, 72 percent in Latin America, 88 percent in Africa, and 82 percent in Oceania.[1] These numbers don't tell the whole story—Africa is not the hotbed for direct democracy that this percentage suggests—but they illustrate that referendums are part of the democratic toolkit for most countries across the globe.

One reason that so many countries turn to referendums, at least occasionally, is because their citizens want them. Figure 8.1 shows the percentage of people who support holding referendums on important national issues according to a Pew Research Center survey from 2017. The figure lists countries according to GDP per capita, from highest (Australia) to lowest (Tanzania); there is no obvious difference in approval between rich and poor countries.[2] The countries could be grouped instead by population, region, or form of government, and the same nonpattern would appear: whether a country has a large population (India, Indonesia) or small population (Israel, Lebanon); whether it is in Africa, Asia, or Latin America; and whether it is a well-functioning democracy (Japan, South Korea) or an autocracy (Vietnam), the people generally favor the idea of voting on important national issues.

This chapter does not attempt comprehensive coverage of referendums across the globe—several surveys along those lines are already available—but instead looks at a few interesting and informative cases from outside the United

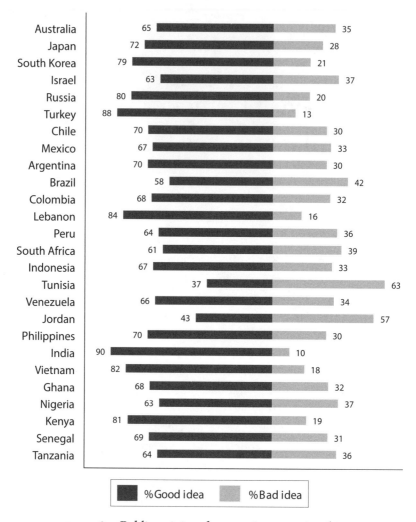

FIGURE 8.1. Public opinion about voting on national issues

States and Europe to round out the picture of direct democracy.[3] While all referendums have common elements, countries are experimenting with variations of the basic idea, customizing the practice to meet their local needs.

Taiwan: Blazing a Trail in Asia

It was once fashionable to claim that Asian culture was incompatible with democracy. But in the second half of the twentieth century, one Asian nation after another threw off its authoritarian and colonial past and became a functioning democracy—including Japan, South Korea, Taiwan, and India. Even so, the region remains home to some of the world's most prominent autocracies, especially China, North Korea, and Vietnam, and democracy's roots are shallow. Given this, it would not be surprising if the region's democracies were conservative about the amount of popular participation they allow, but several are exploring direct democracy in limited forms.

Taiwan is perhaps the most interesting case. It has been a fully functioning democracy only since 1996, but boasts the most citizen-friendly direct democracy rules in the region and is on the leading edge worldwide in some respects. That it has been able to push to the frontiers of democracy while under the shadow of an implacable, existential threat from mainland China makes it even more remarkable.

The modern history of Taiwan dates to 1949, when communist forces took control of the mainland and declared the People's Republic of China (PRC), and the remnants of the Nationalist government fled to the island of Taiwan, claiming to be the legitimate government of China in exile. The PRC maintains that Taiwan is a renegade province, but the island has been self-governing, as the Republic of China, and functionally an independent country since 1949.

The Kuomintang Party (KMT) ruled the island under martial law until 1987, at which point Taiwan began a successful transition to democracy. Free elections took place for the Legislative Yuan (parliament) in the 1990s, and direct elections for the president were held starting in 1996. With the presidential election of Chen Shui-bian of the opposition Democratic Progressive Party (DPP) in 2000, and his peaceful assumption of power, the country's transition to a full-fledged democracy was complete. Corruption remains a political problem, but elections are generally considered to be fair and media are free to criticize the government and politicians.

The 1947 Republic of China constitution provides for both initiatives and referendums, but the government was slow to create the implementing legislation. Not until 2003, under pressure from President Chen, did the KMT-controlled legislature begrudgingly adopt a Referendum Act that permitted national initiatives and referendums. The act circumscribed the direct democracy processes in several ways, leading democracy advocates to call it a "birdcage law." It allowed the president to call national referendums, but set a steep signature requirement—5 percent of the electorate—for initiatives. The biggest impediment was a requirement of at least 50 percent turnout for a law to be approved, allowing opponents to defeat proposals by boycotting the election. The law also allowed the government-controlled Referendum Review Committee to reject proposals before they went to a vote.

From 2003 through 2018, only six national referendums were held under the act, all of them presidential proposals. Two questions involved relations with mainland China (2004), one pertained to property acquired by the KMT (2008), one concerned corruption in politics (2008), and two involved United Nations membership (2008). A majority voted in favor of all six questions, but due to strategic abstention by the opposition, none met the turnout requirement. No initiatives qualified for the ballot; the attempts either failed to collect enough signatures or were rejected by the Referendum Review Committee.

In 2017, with both the presidency and legislature under DPP control, Taiwan adopted a much more user-friendly referendum law that "returns the power to the people," according to President Tsai Ing-wen.[4] The signature requirement for initiatives was cut from 5 percent to 1.5 percent, the Referendum Review Committee lost its power to reject proposals, and the turnout rate required for the election to count was cut from 50 percent to 25 percent. Some important restrictions remain, such as a prohibition on proposals relating to the budget and national sovereignty, and a limit of 100 words for proposals, which prohibits sponsors from making their proposals concrete. The biggest limitation may be related to implementation; because questions are stated as general principles and not laws, the legislature is required to draft and approve the actual law—and it is unclear what happens if the legislature fails to act, and who decides if its implementation is faithful to what the voters approved.

As soon as the new Referendum Act went into effect in 2018, citizen groups and political parties launched petition drives to advance their favored policies. Ten initiatives came before the voters in November 2018, spanning a wide array of issues. Voters showed an inclination to make changes, but in small steps. On three proposals relating to marriage, voters declined to legalize same-sex marriage, but they did approve same-sex civil unions. On four environmental issues, voters agreed to reduce output from thermal power plants and prohibit new coal-fired power plants, but also reversed a government decision to shut down existing nuclear power plants. Voters also approved the continuation of a ban on food products from Japan's Fukushima nuclear disaster area. In international relations, voters rejected a proposal for Taiwanese athletes to compete in the Olympics using the name "Taiwan" instead of "Chinese Taipei," a change that would have provoked the PRC.

Taiwan's transition from an authoritarian state to a path-breaking pioneer in self-governance in just over 20 years is breathtaking. Swiss-Swedish direct democracy advocate Bruno Kaufmann calls Taiwan's 2017 Referendum Act "one of the best direct democracy laws worldwide." This may be too strong—especially if the act turns out to be mainly advisory in nature—but it certainly puts Taiwan at the forefront of direct democracy. Another commendable development is that the process is administered in a way that helps citizens take advantage of their rights: among other things, the electoral commission assists proponents in collecting signatures by allowing for electronic signatures and by holding a public hearing and offering advice. The Referendum Act extends similar direct democracy provisions to the local and regional levels, on top of existing requirements to hold local referendums on matters concerning the siting of nuclear waste and casinos. Moreover, since 2005 Taiwan requires popular approval of constitutional amendments.[5]

Smaller Steps: Japan, South Korea, and the Philippines

Japan and South Korea—two other (for the most part) successful postwar democracies—have also made use of direct democracy, but in a more limited way. Both countries were ruled by emperors and warlords for centuries and had almost no experience with democracy until it was imposed on them by occupying American military forces at the end of World War II.[6] Japan moved seamlessly forward under a democratic regime, albeit one dominated by a single party, while South Korea struggled through a cycle of weak democracies and military dictatorship until civilian rule was conclusively established in 1987.

Both countries require a national referendum to amend their constitutions, and South Korea permits the president to call a national referendum on matters related to diplomacy, national defense, and unification. South Korea has amended its constitution 10 times; Japan, never.[7] Japanese prime minister Shinzo Abe, in office 2006–7 and since 2012, has repeatedly called for an amendment to article 9 of the constitution that prohibits the country from maintaining a standing military, hoping to add a clear statement of the country's right to arm in self-defense.

While both countries make little use of direct democracy at the national level, they use it more often at the local level. In Japan, more than 30 cities have adopted their own referendum laws and, according to the country's Local Autonomy Law, residents are allowed to initiate proposals if their city does not otherwise provide a referendum law. Recent referendums have addressed nuclear power plants, dam construction, and industrial waste management, among other things.[8]

South Korea allows initiatives under its Local Autonomy Act of 2000. Citizens are allowed to propose ordinances by petition, which the government can adopt, ignore, or send to a vote of the people, and governments are authorized to call for referendums at their discretion. Even before the act was passed, some local governments held referendums to resolve territorial issues, such as the consolidation of the cities Yeosu and Yeocheon in 1997, and a few similar referendums have been held since then. By far the most popular subject for initiatives, comprising more than half of the total, is proposals to provide free lunches to school children.[9]

The Philippines is another Asian country with extensive direct democracy provisions, but it rarely uses them. Its democratic experience has followed a worn path: under American influence, it adopted the forms of democracy upon independence in 1946, but succumbed to a dictatorship from 1972 to 1986. The country did approve its current constitution by referendum in 1987, and it contains extensive provisions for direct democracy. Initiatives and petition referendums are permitted at the national and local levels—citizens can even initiate constitutional amendments—and national referendums are required for constitutional amendments and to allow foreign military bases, troops, or facilities. Yet despite this rich menu of options, the country has not held a national vote since the constitution was adopted, and direct democracy is seldom used at the local level either; this may be a vestige of a series of plebiscites held by the dictator Ferdinand Marcos in the 1970s to legitimize his rule and martial law that made the public distrustful of such tools.

Uruguay and the Latin American Experience

Democracy's history in Latin America is patchy, a story of unstable governments cycling between civilian rule and military dictatorships. Uruguay, a small country of 3.5 million people on the Atlantic coast of South America, is no different in that regard—its most recent military regime ended in 1985—but it is atypical in its enduring attachment to direct democracy. In 1934, when only a few nations were using direct democracy, it adopted a constitution that required mandatory referendums on constitutional amendments and provided initiative and petition referendum rights. The somewhat anomalous appearance of direct democracy in Uruguay at this early date was partly due to the efforts of its former president, José Batlle y Ordóñez, who championed the holding of national referendums starting in 1917. Batlle drew his inspiration from a visit to Switzerland, where he came away impressed after seeing direct democracy at work firsthand.

Since the end of military rule, Uruguay has held 17 national referendums, with many used to resolve high-profile issues. The end of the military dictatorship itself was hastened when voters rejected a new constitution proposed by the government in 1980 that would have extended military rule and reduced the power of the legislature and political parties. The government had called the election expecting voters to bless its continued control; its rejection by 57 percent of voters revealed the government's lack of popular support and prompted a return to civilian rule a few years later.

A petition referendum triggered another important election in 1989. As part of the arrangement to end military rule, the civilian political leaders earlier had passed an act granting amnesty for political and military abuses under the military regime. The referendum proposed to repeal the act, potentially destabilizing the new political equilibrium, but voters declined to repeal the amnesty law, with 56 percent opposed.

Another consequential election was triggered by a petition referendum in 1992. The proposal this time was to repeal the government's plan to privatize state-owned companies, part of a general policy to liberalize the economy and reduce the role of the government, which accounted for 40 percent of GDP. The repeal campaign was led by labor unions representing workers in the companies that were to be privatized. Voters delivered a smashing rebuke to the government, with 73 percent in favor of revoking the law. This election outcome was widely discussed throughout the region, and interpreted as a warning sign for the "Washington Consensus," which favored development through privatization. Voters reinforced the message in 2003, when they used another referendum to repeal a law that would have ended the monopoly of the state-owned ANCAP oil company, this time with 64 percent in favor. And they put an accent on the point in 2004 when 65 percent approved an initiative that established a constitutional right to safe drinking water and declared that only public entities could be authorized to provide water services.[10]

Direct democracy has been at the center of several of the most consequential public decisions in Uruguay over the past 40 years. At critical forks in the road, the country has turned to the people to decide which branch to take. In some cases, the voters have supported the government's choices, and in others they have rejected the government's plans. By preventing policy from going down a path opposed by a large majority of people, direct democracy kept policy more connected to popular preferences, and by doing so, may have contributed to Uruguay's reputation as the most democratic nation in Latin America, and among the most democratic nations in the world.[11]

———

Uruguay provides a rare example of a referendum backfiring on an authoritarian regime. An equally surprising example comes from Chile, a country that rarely uses direct democracy. In 1988, longtime dictator Augusto Pinochet held a vote on a new constitution that would have extended his rule another eight years. Voters had approved previous referendums legitimizing Pinochet's rule in 1978 and 1980, so many expected the same outcome in 1988. Unlike other authoritarian regimes, the government legalized political parties, allowed opponents to organize, and gave them access to media during the campaign. To the surprise of many observers, voters rejected the proposal by a decisive 56–44 margin. The election outcome brought pressure that led to the return of civilian rule one year later. This suggests that even referendums held by authoritarian regimes can sometimes be useful conduits of public opinion if the elections are conducted in an environment where opponents are free to organize and campaign.

The most prominent examples of direct democracy come from wealthy, industrialized nations; Uruguay fits the picture in a relative sense as one of the wealthier countries in South America, ranking behind only Chile in income per capita. Bolivia offers an interesting point of contrast, as the poorest country in Latin America and one of the poorest in the world.

Bolivia first provided for national referendums in 2002. Current law requires voter approval for constitutional amendments, allows amendments to be proposed by the government or by initiative, and allows treaties to be challenged by petition referendum. Although the signature requirement for constitutional initiatives is an onerous 20 percent of the electorate, a coalition of civic and business groups collected enough signatures to call a referendum in 2006 on the issue of local autonomy (voters rejected the proposal). Prior to that, in 2004, the government called a referendum on its privatization plans for the gas industry, which voters decisively rejected.

In 2016, Bolivian voters narrowly rejected a proposed constitutional amendment by populist president Evo Morales that would have allowed him to serve a fourth term. Later that year, Morales signaled that he intended to run for a fourth term anyway, awakening concerns about the stability of Bolivian democracy. In 2017 the country's Constitutional Court, packed with Morales supporters, cleared a legal path for him by declaring the constitution's term-limits provision to be in violation of an international human rights treaty, a ruling that many legal experts considered dubious.[12] If Morales in effect nullifies the referendum results, it will call into question the legitimacy of the country's referendum process and raise doubts about its democracy more generally.

Mexico is relatively new to the direct democracy game. In 2014 it adopted the Federal Law of Popular Consultation that allowed national votes on issues proposed by the president, Congress, or citizen petition. To qualify, an initiative requires signatures of 2 percent of registered voters. The law prohibits referendums on issues that would restrict constitutional rights; alter the Aztec nation's institutional identity; or pertain to taxes, spending, or national security. Several months after the act was approved, leftist parties submitted signatures to call a referendum on the government's plan to allow competition in the oil and gas industry, breaking the 75-year monopoly of the state-run PEMEX oil company. Their proposal was invalidated by the Mexican Supreme Court because it impacted a forbidden topic, the government budget. The country had yet to hold a referendum under the law by the middle of 2019.

In 2018, Mexicans elected left-wing populist Andrés Manuel López Obrador president. His campaign alleged widespread corruption in government, and pledged to hold nationwide votes to solicit public opinion (*consultas*) on important public issues. Shortly before taking office, the incoming government arranged unofficial *consultas* on several government investment projects. Turnout was low—only 1 million in a country with 90 million eligible voters—but 70 percent voted to cancel construction of a controversial new airport in Mexico City, favored by elites as a step toward modernizing the country, and a majority voted in favor of 10 projects supported by López Obrador. The president's commitment to popular consultation is in the spirit of direct democracy, but the low turnout and irregular nature of these elections raise concerns about their legitimacy and whether they may be cynical public relations maneuvers.

———

This chapter shines light on only a few corners of the globe. In its brevity it omits numerous other exercises of direct democracy, some of great importance, such as South Africa's 1992 referendum that ended apartheid, Canada's referendum on independence for the French-speaking province of Quebec, and national referendums in Australia and New Zealand.

The purpose is to give a broader sense of how direct democracy is used across the globe, in part to break away from the more familiar (to most readers) cases from the industrialized Western democracies of the United States and Europe that occupy most of this book. As can be seen, nations across the globe are experimenting with different forms of direct democracy, searching for formulas that fit with their political cultures. Many are using referendums to address important issues, ensuring that policies do not veer too far from the preferences of the majority, and they appear to be having some success.

Given how widely referendums are used by countries around the world, it is a curiosity that the United States has never held one at the national level. Understanding why this is the case is important when thinking about potential reforms, and is the subject of the next chapter.

9

The American Anomaly

THAT THE UNITED STATES has never held a national vote on an issue is a strange anomaly. The country that first demonstrated the feasibility of popular government is now one of a tiny group that has never consulted its people by referendum. This begs for an explanation. Why has the country that pioneered democracy fallen so far behind the democracy frontier?

The American case is particularly puzzling because we can immediately rule out several potential explanations. It is certainly not because Americans don't want to vote on issues; as mentioned above, 67 percent of Americans support the idea of national referendums.[1] Nor can it be claimed that Americans are less competent to decide important issues than the citizens of dozens of other democracies across the globe that hold referendums. Nor is it the case that direct democracy is alien to American political culture: as shown in previous chapters, Americans have been voting on state and local issues for over two centuries. And, of course, it is not the case that the country lacks important issues that need to be resolved!

The explanation is at once more prosaic and more complicated. It starts with the fact that the US Constitution did not provide for direct democracy, and the Founders explicitly condemned direct participation by the people. The veneration Americans hold for the Constitution and the Founders and the sensible desire not to fix something that isn't obviously broken have combined to inhibit innovation and lock in past practices, even if they are increasingly anachronistic and out of touch with the spirit of the times.

This is only half of an answer, though, because it does not explain why the Founders were so hostile to popular participation in the first place. This chapter explains their reasons. It is important to understand them because although the Founders got some things wrong (slavery, most obviously), they got many things right. We would like to know if omitting direct democracy was one of the things they got right, or one of their mistakes.

The Founders came to their skepticism about direct democracy in two ways: through their reading of ancient historians (reinforced by recent political developments in the country), from which they concluded that popular rule inevitably led to political turmoil and tyranny, and, more pragmatically, because conditions on the ground made representative democracy much more natural than direct democracy at the time. Both arguments lack force today: modern research suggests that ancient democracies actually performed well, and while direct democracy might have been undesirable in the preindustrial world of the eighteenth century, the conditions that made it so no longer prevail in the twenty-first century.

Why the Founders So Distrusted the Common Man

The Founders were proud to have created a government that made officials accountable, but kept the people's hand off the levers of power. The constitution they produced, in the words of a leading historian, "was intrinsically an aristocratic document designed to check the democratic tendencies of the period."[2] It separated the people not only from direct policy making but also from selection of almost all government officials.

From today's perspective, it is easy to overlook how undemocratic the original government was. The Constitution's primary accommodation to democratic sentiment was the House of Representatives, which was to be elected directly by the people. The Senate was to be chosen by state legislatures. The leader of the executive branch, the president, was to be chosen by a college of electors who themselves were expected to be chosen by state legislatures, and all other executive-branch officials were to be appointed by the president and the Senate. The judicial branch was to be appointed for life by the president and the Senate. Perhaps most surprising to a modern reader, nowhere in the Constitution was any person granted or guaranteed a right to vote, nor was it included in the Bill of Rights. In the eyes of James Madison, the leading architect of the Constitution, it was "the total exclusion of the people, in their collective capacity, from any share" of government that was the Constitution's "most advantageous superiority" over all other governments.[3]

While Madison did not speak for all of the Founders—his friend and political ally Thomas Jefferson was much more positive about the wisdom of the people—discourse during the founding era displayed a pervasive apprehension about participation by the common people. John Adams, the country's second president, believed that pure democracy would "soon degenerate into anarchy"; Benjamin Rush, a prominent signatory of the Declaration of Independence, thought a simple democracy was "the devil's own government"; and John Marshall, the first chief justice of the Supreme Court, declared that "between a balanced republic and a democracy, the difference is like that between order and chaos."[4]

The Founders came to these views in two ways. For one thing, they were shocked at the direction democracy had taken in the 1780s; after independence, the states had extended voting rights to a broader swath of the population and the newly enfranchised voters had replaced the wealthy gentlemen who had previously served as legislators with less-educated commoners from humble backgrounds. The new legislators, now subject to frequent elections, were more attentive to constituent interests ("parochial," in the words of critics) than their colonial predecessors, and in response to pressure from debtors, took action to suspend foreclosures, print paper money, and cut taxes. Elites (which the Founders were) viewed these developments with a mixture of distaste and horror, bordering on an abridgment of the sacred property rights of creditors. The new legislatures gave elites a sense of what might happen if ordinary people controlled the government.[5] Their fears of mob rule were exacerbated by armed uprisings by commoners in the 1780s, among which Shay's Rebellion in Western Massachusetts was the best known.

The Founders also drew "indispensable lessons" from their reading of the ancient Greek and Roman historians; their speeches and writing repeatedly referenced the Roman Republic and classical Greek city-states whose governments were anchored by popular assemblies. Elite education in the eighteenth century revolved around the classics, and a man was not considered educated without knowledge of classical authors such as Cicero, Livy, Sallust, Plutarch, and Thucydides. "The founders' classical conditioning was so successful that most learned to relish the classics as a form of entertainment, and to consider the ancients wise old friends."[6] James Madison prepared for the constitutional convention by spending the preceding summer reading through boxes of books on ancient history, compiling detailed notes on the strengths and weaknesses of ancient confederacies.

Based on their reading of the classical historians, the Founders concluded that popular assemblies—the most common form of democracy in the ancient world—were a threat to liberty and a source of political instability. According to the classical authors, popular assemblies inevitably were corrupted by demagogues who persuaded the people to strike down their traditional leaders and tyrannize property holders, leading to internal strife, chaos, and collapse of the state. In short, the classical texts reinforced the Founders' apprehensions formed by observing the "excessively" democratic new legislatures in the postcolonial 1780s.

Yet with the benefit of more than 200 years of subsequent research, modern historians have a better understanding of how the classical authors' aristocratic backgrounds colored their narratives. "The canon's ancient lineage inhibited the Founder's critical instincts," wrote historian Carl Richard, making them "largely oblivious to the literature's aristocratic and other biases."[7] These antidemocratic biases led to histories that celebrated elite rule while casting popular rule in a bad light. We now know that direct democracy was not to blame for the failures of ancient democracies, and may even have been a source of their success—as a closer look at ancient Rome and Athens shows.

Roman Republic

The Roman Republic was the ancient state the Founders most admired. It was "the utmost height of human greatness," according to Alexander Hamilton, and he and his colleagues Madison and John Jay honored the Roman Republic by publishing *The Federalist Papers* under the pseudonym "Publius," after Publius Valerius Publicola, credited as the leader of the group that overthrew the Roman monarchy and established the Republic in 509 BCE.[8]

The (unwritten) constitution of the Roman Republic evolved during its five centuries of existence, but the government was always a representative democracy with significant elements of direct popular decision making.[9] Its central premise was the sovereignty of the people, instantiated by a system that delegated administration and leadership to a small group of elites but gave the people the final right of approval.[10] Citizen assemblies gathered once a year to hold elections for tribunes, who had the power to propose and veto legislation, and for magistrates, who administered the government (advised by an elected senate, whose members had lifetime appointments).[11] While the magistrates together with the senate performed government functions (leading armies, collecting taxes, judging legal cases, etc.) and took the lead in formulating policy, the people retained ultimate sovereignty over important public decisions. In particular, all declarations of war, peace treaties, and laws required approval by an assembly of the people (what we would today call "mandatory referendums").[12]

The classical historians dated the onset of the Roman Republic's decline to 133 BCE, when the tribune Tiberius Gracchus promulgated a law distributing public lands to soldiers and limiting the holdings of elites.[13] This law prompted a violent reaction by the aristocratic senate, which incited a mob that beat Tiberius and 300 of his supporters to death. The century that followed was one of turmoil, civil war, dictatorship, and political purges, only stabilizing in 27 BCE when the Republic became the autocracy that we now call the Roman Empire. The classical historians blamed this civil strife on the rise of demagogues who manipulated the assemblies; according to "the unanimous voice of historians," explained a widely read pamphlet in 1788, the noble Republic fell because of "encroachments of the people upon the authority of the senate."[14]

Our understanding of the fall of the Roman Republic is quite different today. Few contemporary historians would attribute it to overly powerful popular assemblies; more likely they would point to a dysfunctional oligarchy, destructive competition for power between elites, and the growth of standing armies as the Republic came to dominate the Mediterranean. Moreover, as the Republic expanded to control territory thousands of miles distant from Rome, the assemblies ceased to represent the Roman people at large because only a few were able to physically gather in the city and cast their votes. By the final decades of the Republic, the assemblies appear to have lost most of their legitimacy and the locus of power had shifted to the senate, the consuls, and the generals.

The Founders, following the classical authors, tended to overlook the contributions of the popular assemblies while celebrating the aristocratic senate. They blamed the assemblies for the bad years at the end of the Republic, but gave them no credit for the five preceding centuries that they so much admired. In comparison with other ancient states, the Roman Republic performed commendably for much of its long history, providing stable government, a prosperous society, and a fair amount of individual liberty by the standards of the times. The constitutional system produced a state with enough capacity to absorb all of the peoples around the Mediterranean into a single political system, a system that with some modifications under the emperors was able to dominate the region for another five centuries (and even longer in the East, as the Byzantine Empire).

Classical Athens

The Founders' perspective on ancient Greece was similar. They admired much about classical Greece and its preeminent city-state Athens—especially its openness and love of liberty—but they traced its downfall to an excess of direct democracy.[15] Again, they saw its citizen assemblies as sources of turmoil and tyranny, vulnerable to demagogues who could manipulate the passions of the people.[16] "Had every Athenian citizen been a Socrates, every Athenian assembly would still have been a mob," wrote Madison in *Federalist* No. 55.

Athens, the quintessential democracy of antiquity, was the most successful of approximately 1,000 Greek city-states (*poleis*) that flourished during the classical period (fifth and fourth centuries BCE), operating as an independent democracy from 508 BCE until it was absorbed into the Roman Republic in 322 BCE. The foundation of Athenian government was its assembly (*ekklesia*), in which all free male citizens of age were allowed to vote. Typically, 6,000 to 8,000 citizens attended its 40-odd meetings per year. The assembly decided all important matters of state policy, including public finance, war, and peace. Working in tandem with the assembly was the Council of 500 (*boule*), whose members were chosen by lot for a (nonrepeating) one-year term according to a system that guaranteed a geographic dispersion of representation. The Council controlled the agenda for the assembly, determining which issues would come to a vote, and framing the questions to be decided. Assembly decisions were administered by a group of approximately 700 magistrates (including generals), about 100 of whom were elected by the assembly and the rest chosen by lot, again for one-year terms. Judicial matters were handled by citizen courts comprising 200 to 500 or more members chosen by lot.[17]

The evidence suggests that the system provided effective government.[18] Athens had the largest economy among the Greek city-states and was the trade center of the eastern Mediterranean. Its fiscal capacity was unmatched and it maintained by far the largest navy. Athens was attractive to immigrants, hosting the largest and most diverse foreign population, and was the cultural capital of the Greek world in terms of literature, art, and architecture. Its famous silver coinage, the "owl" tetradrachm, was for centuries the international currency of the region.

Even more to the point, recent scholarship suggests that Athens's democratic institutions and its strong performance were not a coincidence; it is likely that democracy *caused* the success of Athens. For its first two centuries, roughly 700 to 508 BCE, Athens was not a democracy—it was ruled by an oligarchy and then a dictatorship. During this period, it was an unremarkable Greek city-state. A revolt by the common people in 508 BCE sparked a series of innovations in government that resulted in the direct democracy institutions for which Athens is famous—and shortly thereafter, Athens began its ascent to regional dominance, which it maintained for about two centuries. Historian Josiah Ober describes this timeline in detail, rejecting the possibility of reverse causality (that

democracy was itself a product of Athens's prosperity) and spurious correlation (that an external factor caused the city-state's prosperity and its use of democracy), and concludes that much of Athens's success can be attributed to
its democratic institutions.[19]

Ober also presents a detailed analysis of how decisions were actually made
in the assemblies that flips on its head the Founders' conclusion that public
speakers were able to incite ordinary citizens into making harmful decisions.[20]
Rather than being manipulated by demagogues, assemblies were highly effective means to incorporate dispersed information into public decisions. Thanks
to the rotation in office due to one-year terms and selection by lottery, many
assembly members had experience in government, as well as extensive networks
with fellow citizens that they could tap for expert advice as needed.[21] Athens's
reliance on direct democracy allowed it to take advantage of the dispersed
knowledge of its citizens, and was an important source of the city-state's competitive advantage.

The Founders believed that direct democracy would be the cause of "innu-
merable evils," "frequent convulsions," and "capricious measures," as it had
been in ancient Rome and Athens, in the words of Noah Webster's influential
pamphlet at the time.[22] We now have better knowledge than the Founders had
about ancient democracies, and can see that they were misled by the classical
historians; in fact, direct democracy functioned well in the two ancient states
they most admired, the Roman Republic and classical Athens, and may even
have been part of the reason those states thrived.

Why Representative Democracy Was
Inevitable at the Founding

The Founders' aversion to direct democracy was not just theoretical—it was
also practical. The population was largely uneducated, information was costly
to acquire, and news traveled across the continent at a snail's pace. This made
it impractical to involve the general public in policy decisions, and almost inevitable that the Founders would place all policy decisions in the hands of
representatives when they drafted the Constitution in 1787.

To understand this, we have to appreciate how different the Founders' world
was from modern American society. In 1790, the country's 4 million people,
distributed among the original 13 colonies on the Atlantic seaboard, overwhelm-
ingly worked the land. According to the first census, 95 percent of the population lived in rural areas, and between 75 and 90 percent of those employed

were farmers. The largest "city" was Philadelphia, with 42,444 people, which today would be considered a modest town. Only four other cities (New York, Boston, Charleston, and Baltimore) had more than 8,000 people.

This largely rural population was largely uneducated. While over 90 percent of adult, white males could read (and most could write to some extent), few had any formal education. With the exception of some New England colonies, there were no public schools, and those that existed were grammar or petty schools (elementary schools) that students attended for about three years. Only about 10 percent of colonial children attended any school at all, as farmers and artisans needed children at home for labor. Some children of the wealthy had private tutors, but that was a tiny minority of the population. Higher education was likewise rare and reserved for the wealthy; there were only nine colleges in 1790, which graduated a combined total of about 200 students per year.[23]

Not only was education rudimentary, but access to information was extremely limited. In 1790, there were only 92 newspapers in the country, and only 8 of them were dailies (there are about 1,300 today). A typical newspaper might run four pages; eight pages was long. News dispersed slowly: in 1790, it took more than a month for news to travel the 257 miles from Pittsburgh to Philadelphia, and 40 days to receive a reply to a letter sent from Portland, Maine, to Savannah, Georgia. In 1790, the postal service delivered only half a million copies of newspapers, or about one per five people for the entire year. News also spread by personal mail, but the postal service carried only 300,000 letters in 1790, about one for every 10 people.[24]

In this environment, asking the people to make policy decisions would have been unworkable. Ordinary Americans lacked both the raw information and the education to do so. It was commonsensical to select a couple hundred of the country's most educated citizens, gather them in a single central location where they could receive and share information, and delegate decisions to them. Experts could travel to the capital in person to provide background on important issues as necessary, or could become legislators themselves.[25]

Relying exclusively on representatives has its risks, however, as the Founders understood well. Madison worried that "men of factious tempers, of local prejudices, or of sinister designs, may, by intrigue, by corruption, or by other means, first obtain the suffrages, and then betray the interests, of the people."[26] The Founders attempted to control the dangers of faction, but their solutions weren't always effective. Government corruption became a growing problem in the early nineteenth century and preoccupied reformers into the early twentieth century. The power of special interests, particularly large economic enterprises such as railroads, was a central public concern starting in the late nineteenth century, and remains an issue today.

While the drawbacks of entrusting representatives with exclusive control of public decisions have become increasingly apparent, the conditions that made it necessary to grant them this monopoly on power have faded. Today, the American public is highly educated by historical standards; there is not a significant educational gap between the people and their representatives. Media have become superabundant and information moves across the globe instantaneously, with 24-hour television and radio, the internet, and social media. Nothing prevents ordinary Americans from being as informed about current issues as their representatives are. The logic for giving representatives a monopoly on policy decisions, compelling in the eighteenth century, has lost its force in the twenty-first century.

———

It is hard to disagree with political scientist Ronald Dahl's view that the men at the constitutional convention were "perhaps as brilliant an assembly as has ever gathered" to found a nation.[27] But there is a danger is treating the documents they left—especially the Constitution and *The Federalist Papers*—as holy writ. As brilliant as the Founders were, they were operating with quite limited information about politics, economics, and law compared with what we know today, and they were designing for a preindustrial society that bears little relation to our modern world.[28] Reliance on the authority of the Founders can strangle innovation if taken too far.

In the case of direct democracy, we should not be swayed by the Founders' negative views.[29] Their instincts were based on what looks like a misreading of the history of ancient democracies, and their actual decisions were mainly pragmatic solutions to logistical challenges of the eighteenth century that are no longer relevant. The Founders' strong opposition has relegated direct democracy to the margins of political discourse, making it appear to be a radical idea that would dramatically reshape American government.[30]

Even recognizing the flaws in the underlying logic of the Founders' system of government, we might hesitate to modify the foundations out of an abundance of caution. Some would argue that overall the system has served us well and tampering with its basic structure is a needless risk. The problem with this line of argument is that the basic structure has already been tampered with over and over by successive generations of Americans, to such an extent that it would be almost unrecognizable to the Founders. The next chapter describes the evolution of American government since the founding era, laying out the far-reaching changes the structure has undergone. It shows that prodemocracy innovation, such as expanding use of referendums would be, is a recurrent feature of American democracy, and one that has built the country an even better democracy than the one it started with.

10

A Work in Progress

THERE IS AN ARGUMENT against direct democracy that goes like this: direct democracy would upset the traditional structure of American government, which, while not perfect, has seen the country through difficult times; therefore, it would better to stay within the parameters set down by the Founders.

What this traditionalist argument misses is that the country left the Founders' parameters long ago. The original structure no longer exists; it has been heavily revised over the years, both to correct its original deficiencies and to update it for changing times. American democracy is not a static system created by the Founders, but a work in progress, an evolving set of practices that each generation has updated, largely by extending the scope of popular participation.

This chapter tells the sometimes-overlooked story of the numerous modifications of American democracy since the founding. Many of the changes aimed to unravel the aristocratic biases of the Founders that we saw in the previous chapter. From a historical perspective, direct democracy would not be radical reform but a logical continuation of a long-term pattern of innovation in the country's democratic practices.

The chapter also fleshes out the story of populism, which turns out to be tightly interwoven with the story of democratic progress. Populism, in a sense, is the manifestation of an ongoing debate among Americans going back to the very beginning of the republic—a debate about the nature of self-government between those who want greater popular involvement in government decisions and those who want to leave decisions to elite experts. Understanding the deep roots of populism helps put the current surge in perspective and reveals how substantial political change—often beneficial—can follow in the wake of populist outbursts. As we will see, populism is not necessarily a destructive force; it can also be a catalyst for positive change.

The Populist Roots of American Democracy

Populism is in the nation's DNA. In 1776, the 13 British colonies that became the United States of America revolted against Great Britain, waging a war that resulted in their independence following the British surrender at Yorktown in 1781. The colonists justified their revolt on the grounds that they had no representation in the British Parliament, which they saw as violating their natural rights as free men not to be taxed and regulated without their consent. Independence was a means to throw off rule by a distant power and replace it with self-government. The very act of the nation's creation, then, was suffused with a populist impulse.

The rhetoric of the revolution emphasized Enlightenment concepts of natural rights and the social contract associated with English philosopher John Locke's *Two Treatises of Government*. Yet according to a notable historian of the revolution, the ideas of a radical eighteenth-century English opposition group called the "commonwealthmen" may have been even more important in fashioning the ideology of the revolution.[1] The commonwealthmen added to the mix something close to a populist view that states tend to be corrupted by the powerful and wealthy, who use government to advance their own interests at the expense of the people. The idea of a corrupted government resonated with the colonists, angered by British trade policies that favored economic interests on the distant home island over the colonies.

The Boston Tea Party, a key part of revolutionary lore, provides a vivid illustration. On the evening of December 16, 1773, a mob of masked Bostonians took over a ship in Boston harbor and dumped its valuable cargo of tea overboard—a critical turning point that sparked the British to pass a series of laws the Americans called the "Intolerable Acts" and ultimately led to the formation of the Continental Congress, the first colony-wide government.[2] Today the Tea Party is remembered as a protest against higher taxes, but the Tea Act that triggered it did not in fact increase taxes—it merely extended an existing tax that the colonists had been paying without objection for the previous three years. The novelty of the Tea Act was its grant of a monopoly to the East India Company on tea imports to the colonies, a provision made possible by the company's influence over the government in London.[3] The colonists' resistance to this twisting of government to benefit a private company anticipated populist reactions to the power of other economic interests that were to emerge later in American history.

Conflict and Change in the Early Republic

Once independence was secured in 1783, the colonists set about designing a government that provided self-rule. One by one, the individual states replaced their colonial charters with "republican" constitutions centered on a popularly elected legislature, and together they formed a national government, first under the Articles of Confederation and then under the Constitution. The debate over the Constitution brought out the enduring dispute about the role of the people. The "aristocratic" view was that government ought to be conducted by the country's "natural" leaders, those with the education, wealth, and status to govern wisely and impartially, with the people restricted to selecting those leaders. The "democratic" view was that ordinary people ought to participate in making laws and holding office.[4]

The aristocratic view, as we know from the previous chapter, prevailed—to the ire of those who carried the populist instincts forged in the revolution. A significant opposition, branded the "anti-Federalists," coalesced against adoption of the Constitution. Despite the name we now give them, most anti-Federalists were not opposed to creation of a stronger national government, but to the elitist tendencies of the Constitution and especially the House of Representatives, which they judged to have too few members to prevent its corruption by wealthy interests. "Every man of reflection must see, that the change now proposed is a transfer of power from the many to the few."[5] Although they lost the battle over adoption of the Constitution, their concerns remained latent in American politics and were to get more traction later as reformers chipped away at the government's aristocratic foundations.

The pushback started during the presidency of George Washington's successor, John Adams (1797–1801). Adams, like Washington, was a Federalist, and very much in the camp of those who favored leaving the actual business of government to the "natural aristocracy." Resistance grew during his presidency to the expanding federal government, leading to the emergence of grassroots organizations called Democratic-Republican Societies. The societies were anti-elite organizations composed of "middling people"—entrepreneurs, mechanics, small-time merchants, and yeomen farmers. They were united in their opposition to the financial plans of Treasury Secretary Alexander Hamilton, who had given a speech in favor of monarchy at the constitutional convention and who they saw as championing private financial interests in the Northeast, and in their agitation for social and political reforms that would undercut systems of deference to elites.[6] Resistance to the Federalists coalesced around the figure of Thomas Jefferson, eventually taking the form of the Democratic-Republican Party.

In the face of growing populist pressure, the Federalists chose to double down on their agenda. In 1798, using the pretext of an undeclared war against France, Federalist legislators passed and Adams signed a series of laws called the Alien and Sedition Acts, which made it a crime to "oppose any measure or measures of the government of the United States" or to write, print, utter, or publish "any false, scandalous and malicious writings" against the president or other elected officials. As the Federalists saw it, the government was run by impartial elites on behalf of the common good, and therefore criticism of the government was in effect a treasonous attack on the body politic. The Democratic-Republicans denounced the acts as an attempt to suppress free speech, another step in a Federalist conspiracy to create a monarchy. Their fears were confirmed when the government swiftly brought charges against publishers and editors of Democratic-Republican newspapers, in effect criminalizing the actions of the opposition party.

The conflict climaxed in the presidential election of 1800, in which Jefferson narrowly defeated Adams. This victory signaled the decisive rejection of the Federalist agenda, and the Democratic-Republicans went on to hold the presidency uninterrupted for the next 40 years. As the Democratic-Republicans chipped away at the aristocratic foundations of the founding government, those who argued—as Madison had in 1787—that the United States was not a democracy, but something entirely different called a "republic," were increasingly seen as antediluvian. To its citizens (and the international community), the United States became the exemplar par excellence of a democracy.

Jefferson was an odd choice to lead a populist movement. He was the scion of an elite planter family in Virginia, a slaveholder, highly cultured, highly educated, and a member of the elite by any definition. Yet he had a remarkable genius for expressing the aspirations of American democracy, and an instinctive affinity for the capacity of ordinary people to govern themselves. He was the primary author of the Declaration of Independence, and the person who "more than any other figure in the early republic, established (and was seen to have established) the terms of American democratic politics."[7]

Jefferson's instincts ran against the aristocratic tendencies of his peers. He demonstrated this on inauguration day, when in the morning he eschewed the grand processions of his predecessors and simply walked from his boarding house down the street to the Capitol to take the oath of office, and in the evening, when instead of hosting a series of inaugural balls, he walked back to his boarding house and stood in line for his turn at dinner.[8] Like others of his class, he believed government would function best if conducted by the natural aristocracy, but unlike them, he had faith in the common people: "I am not among those who fear the people. They, and not the rich, are our dependence for continued freedom."[9] He repeatedly emphasized that a free government could only be sustained by empowering the people, and showed a hostility to the corrupting influence of banks and corporations that would be echoed by the next generation of populists.[10]

In addition to capturing the presidency in 1800, the Democratic-Republicans gained control of the Congress, and triumphed at the state and local levels across the country. They embarked on a multipronged program to reshape American democracy by rolling back antidemocratic institutions of the Federalist Founders and by opening more doors for popular participation:[11]

Suffrage. The original colonies typically restricted voting to white males who held substantial property, usually in the form of land, so that as little as 10 percent of the adult population was eligible to vote.[12] Three states removed property requirements during the revolutionary period (Maryland, Pennsylvania, Vermont), but 77 percent retained such requirements in 1790. Their effect could be substantial: a study of New York found that two-thirds of adult males were unable to meet the pre-1820 property requirement to vote for state senator and one-third were unable to meet the requirement for the state assembly. During the Jeffersonian period, states rapidly dropped their property requirements and new states entered the union without them, so that by 1824 only 21 percent of states had substantial property requirements for voting.[13]

Qualifications to hold office. Postcolonial constitutions often imposed property requirements to hold public office. Of 24 pre-1800 constitutions, 13 required property to serve in the lower house of the legislature, 16 required property to serve in the upper house, and 11 required property to serve as governor. The amounts could be substantial, such as £10,000 to serve as governor in South Carolina, and not surprisingly the state legislatures were composed largely of wealthy men.[14] Most of these requirements were swept away in the Jeffersonian era. This, together with broadening suffrage, contributed to the rise of common men as political leaders.

Presidential electors. In the early republic, presidential electors were selected by state legislatures. Pennsylvania was the first state to switch to direct election of electors by the voters, which it did after the election of 1800. Other states quickly followed; the percentage of states providing direct election grew to 47 percent in 1804, 75 percent in 1824, and 92 percent by 1828.[15]

Direct democracy. As we saw in chapter 6, the practice of submitting new constitutions for popular approval began during the revolutionary period, and the use of referendums to amend constitutions had become the norm by midcentury.

Conflict and Change in the Age of Jackson

Populism reemerged in the 1820s, a time, according to Secretary of War John Calhoun, of a "general mass of disaffection to the government, not concentrated in any particular direction."[16] The resurgence had both economic and political roots. On the economic side, a major factor was the Panic of 1819. When increased agricultural production in Europe caused crop prices to fall, the Bank of the United States took the precautionary step of sharply reducing credit to state banks, which in turn called in their loans—pushing many farmers and small businessmen into bankruptcy and triggering a recession that lasted for several years. The Panic was "the first time that the American public had experienced collectively what would become a recurrent phenomenon, a sharp downward swing of the business cycle."[17]

The Panic called attention to the uncomfortable fact that banks had become central to the stability of the economy. This was as much a political issue as an economic issue. Unlike today when most banks are fully private entities (at least in the United States), in the nineteenth century most banks were quasi-monopolies created and capitalized by state governments and controlled by politically connected persons. It rankled democratic sensibilities that governments were creating banking monopolies for the financial benefit of the few (often the legislators themselves), and when banks gained the power to take down the country's economy and cause thousands of ordinary people to lose their livelihoods, it became a matter of public concern.

The Panic crystalized an unease about the spread of banks and growth of manufacturing that had been latent in democratic thinking for years. In retirement, former president Thomas Jefferson began to voice these concerns in his private correspondences, expressing hope that the country would "crush in its birth the aristocracy of our monied corporations which dare to challenge our government to a trial of strength, and to bid defiance to the laws of their country."[18] As similar views spread across the country, a new generation of politicians began to shape them into a political program.

Former general and war hero Andrew Jackson became the standard-bearer of the gathering populist forces. A self-made man, a wealthy planter and slave-holder, he was fiercely populist in outlook and described his political philosophy as "good old Jeffersonian democratic republican principles." His central tenet, repeated in his public statements, was simply, "the majority is to govern."[19] Known for his irascibility and explosive temper, he raged against the politicians in Congress and the monied interests that he believed had corruptly denied him the presidency in the controversial election of 1824.[20]

The surging populist sentiment carried Jackson to the White House in 1828, with 56 percent of the popular vote, the largest majority in American history to that time, and re-elected him in 1832. Jackson's victory was built on a coalition of small farmers, mechanics, and urban laborers in the North, and yeomen and planters in the South. It was thus made possible by the democratizing reforms of the Jeffersonian era that had opened up the franchise to men without wealth. In running his campaign, Jackson's supporters created the country's first mass political organization. His wing of the Democratic-Republican Party came to be called The Democracy by contemporaries and evolved into today's Democratic Party.

One of the major controversies of Jackson's presidency was whether to renew the charter of the second Bank of the United States (BUS).[21] Jackson and his followers fought, successfully in the end, to close down the bank, viewing it as a subversion of government by narrow financial interests. Unlike a modern central bank, the BUS was a privately owned business that held a tax-free monopoly on managing the US government's fiscal transactions and deposits. At the time, it was possibly the largest financial corporation in the world, with more capital than the annual spending of the federal government, and 25 branch offices scattered across the country. It issued 40 percent of all bank notes in circulation and could call for specie payments from state banks, forcing them to contract their credit. While the US government held 20 percent of the BUS's equity and chose 5 of the 25 directors, the bank's management was adamant that it did not answer to the government: "no officer of the government, from the president downwards, has the least right, the least authority, the least pretense, for interference in the concerns of the bank," in the words of the BUS president.[22]

In short, the BUS was a government-created private monopoly with immense power to affect the economy and deliver benefits to private individuals

who operated outside democratic control. Just as troubling, the BUS had become active in partisan politics, using its resources to elect friendly politicians,
loan money to friendly newspaper publishers, and organize national lobbying
campaigns.[23]

Jackson's veto message killing the BUS was one of the most populist mes-
sages ever issued by a US president:

> Many of our rich men have not been content with equal protection and equal
> benefits, but have besought us to make them richer by act of Congress. . . .
> If we can not at once . . . make our Government what it ought to be, we can
> at least take a stand against all new grants of monopolies and exclusive privi-
> leges, [and] against any prostitution of our Government to the advance-
> ment of the few at the expense of the many.[24]

Of course, there is an element of caricature in Jackson's rhetoric. Many of those
who supported the BUS were not trying to line their own pockets; rather, they
hoped that a national bank would promote economic development by expanding credit and add stability to the banking system. What they failed to
recognize—and what Jacksonian rhetoric so skillfully exploited—was the
incompatibility of a privately owned, government-created monopoly with the
country's evolving democratic mores.

Populist impulses were also behind another prominent Jacksonian policy,
"rotation in office," or the "spoils system" of patronage. The new administration
fired a large fraction of government workers, replacing them with persons loyal
to the administration. While some Jacksonians supported rotation for purely
partisan reasons, and patronage later came to be associated with corruption,
Jackson's motivation appears to have been to make government more democratic by preventing the formation of a permanent class of government insiders
disconnected from the people (what we call technocrats, today). For the same
reason, he also favored term limits for appointed executive-branch officials,
elected officials, federal judges, and the president.

The "surging demand for expanding democracy" that carried Jackson to
power and animated his agenda increased the pressure to make government
more responsive to the people.[25] Out of this pressure cooker emerged several
important reforms to American democracy:

> *Suffrage.* Property requirements to vote continued to fall away. From 1824
> to 1855, four states dropped their property requirements, and six new
> states entered the union without property requirements. As a result,

the percentage of states with property requirements dropped from 24 to 7 percent. Moving in the same direction, between 1830 and 1855 six states removed taxpaying requirements to vote.[26]

Election of governors. Prior to 1800, only 12 of the 23 postcolonial constitutions allowed the people to elect their states' governor; the 11 others gave that power to the state legislature.[27] During the Jeffersonian era states began to drift away from appointed governors, and during the Jacksonian era election by the people became the norm. States also began to elect executive-branch officials other than the governor.[28]

Nomination of presidential candidates. After Washington, presidential nominees were chosen according to what came to be called the congressional caucus system: each party's congressmen and senators met and selected the nominees who were to be considered by the voters. There were no primary elections, conventions, or other ways for anyone other than elites in the capital to influence which candidates were nominated. Criticized as a system of "aristocratic intrigue, cabal and management," the caucus system was swept away after 1824, to be replaced by party conventions.[29]

Direct democracy. Referendums as a check on legislatures became more common, as discussed in chapter 6. Rhode Island was the first state to require popular approval of debt, in 1842, and over the next six years mandatory referendums of a similar nature were adopted in Michigan, New Jersey, Iowa, New York, and Illinois. Iowa was the first state, in 1846, to require popular approval before the state could charter a bank. Similar requirements were imposed in Illinois and Wisconsin in 1848, Michigan in 1850, and Ohio in 1851.

The reforms in the first half of the nineteenth century left the country much more democratic than it had been at the founding. A largely unintended consequence of the move to universal white male suffrage was that the United States granted voting rights to industrial workers well before they became a large part of the electorate, unlike in Europe where laborers had to fight long and hard for their political rights. As a result, the labor movement was incorporated into the political system from the beginning and could bring attention to its issues through existing political channels, contributing to less acrimonious resolution of disputes than in Europe, where anarchists and revolutionary movements flourished.[30]

The populist wave that carried Jackson to power began to dissipate with the Panic of 1837 and a series of crises involving admission of new states to the Union that were intertwined with the issue of slavery. By midcentury slavery had become the focal point of contention in American politics, a situation that was only resolved by a bloody civil war (1861–65) in which Northern armies suppressed an attempt by 11 Southern states to secede from the Union. Populism did not reappear as a central issue until sometime after the end of the Civil War and Reconstruction, in the wake of the Industrial Revolution.

Conflict and Change in the Industrial Age

Populism reemerged in a new muscular form, to meet a new challenge, in the late nineteenth century. Its leaders saw their fight as the latest installment in a long-running struggle at the heart of American democracy: "We are engaged in one of the great battles of the age-long contest waged against privilege on behalf of the common welfare. We hold it a prime duty of the people to free our government from the control of money in politics," declared President Theodore Roosevelt.[31] Their opponents this time were the giant industrial corporations—railroads, mining, and manufacturing companies—that had arisen during the Industrial Revolution.

Two movements that grew independently of each other after the Civil War converged in the 1880s to produce the populist surge.[32] The first centered on farmers in the West and South, who started farmers' alliances, in the late 1870s, originally to spread knowledge about modern agricultural practices. Realizing they faced other common challenges—boom and bust cycles linked to fluctuations in global prices and dependency on an increasingly concentrated railroad industry to move their crops to market—they initially explored the idea of creating large business organizations to counterbalance the power of the concentrated interests they faced. With a membership in the millions by the 1880s, they launched a variety of cooperative enterprises: grain elevators, cotton gins, supply stores, warehouses, cotton sellers, and insurance programs. They even began to plan for a cooperative railroad that would run from the Gulf of Mexico to Canada. However, these cooperative enterprises were unsuccessful and few survived for long.

When their attempts at creating economic counterweights to what they saw as oppressive market forces failed, farmers turned to the government for protection—but found there, too, that railroads and industrial interests exerted undue influence. Railroads, for example, put government officials on their payrolls (legally) and distributed free passes to politicians, officeholders, prominent lawyers, and newspaper editors.[33] Buffeted by economic downturns in 1873, 1884, 1890, and an especially severe recession in 1893, the frustration of farmers took the form of a populist program to rid the government of special-interest influence and restore popular control.

The other key movement involved industrial workers. In the East, a nascent labor movement arose following the emergence of large industrial companies. Faced with the concentrated strength of their employers, workers attempted to create counterbalancing power by forming labor unions. The first national union was the Knights of Labor, founded in 1869. Originally a secret organization because the legality of unions was in doubt, by 1886 membership had grown to over 700,000 members scattered over 15,000 local assemblies.[34] Labor unions pressed for higher wages and improved working conditions. Early union efforts focused on helping workers through market channels, such as strikes and boycotts, not through the political process.

However, as industrialization advanced, governments revealed an inclination to intervene on behalf of companies, and against workers. In 1877, in response to wage cuts announced by the four largest railroads, workers in West Virginia walked off the job, followed by workers across the East and Midwest. The Great Railroad Strike, as it was called, shut down rail traffic across the country for several weeks in the summer. The strike came to an end when President Rutherford B. Hayes declared the strike an "insurrection" and sent in federal troops to get the trains running, in the process transforming a peaceful dispute into a bloody fight that left 45 people dead. This set an example of deploying armed force against strikers that was followed by subsequent presidents and governors.

Workers also found themselves confronting a hostile judiciary, particularly federal courts. In 1890, reformers had managed to secure the nation's first antimonopoly law, the Sherman Antitrust Act, that prohibited "every contract, combination in the form of trust or otherwise, or conspiracy, in restraint of trade." In a bitter irony, the Supreme Court refused to apply the law against the American Sugar Refining Company that monopolized the sugar industry, but used it instead to declare strikes by labor unions unlawful restraints of trade.[35] Recognizing "the ability of corporations and large employers to gain more and more influence over the courts and the ability of those courts to deploy force in support of private companies," industrial workers, like farmers, concluded they would have to fight for their rights in the political arena.[36]

The paths of the farmers in the South and Midwest and laborers in the East thus converged on a belief that political action was necessary. If the forces of monopoly were going to use the government to gain an unfair advantage, the only solution was to take back the government. This led in the late 1880s to establishment of an explicitly populist political party, the People's Party, or Populist Party. The party's 1892 platform declared:

> The fruits of the toil of millions are boldly stolen to build up colossal fortunes for a few, unprecedented in the history of mankind; and the possessors of these, in turn, despise the republic and endanger liberty. From the same prolific womb of governmental injustice we breed the two great classes—tramps and millionaires. . . . [W]e seek to restore the government of the Republic to the hands of "the plain people," with whose class it originated.[37]

The Populist Party focused on three broad issues: government action against monopolistic businesses, government action on behalf of farmers and workers, and greater democratization. On the latter, specific proposals included direct election of US senators; the initiative, referendum, and recall; term limits for the president; and secret ballots.

In 1887, a populist candidate took the Oregon governorship, and by 1897 populists occupied the governor's offices in six states. In the 1890 election, the populists sent 11 members to the US House of Representatives and one to the Senate. Populist representation rose to 22 congressmen and 5 senators following the election of 1896. Even when populist candidates lost, their presence disrupted the normal competition between Democrats and Republicans, siphoning votes away from the majority party.

The Populist Party ran its own presidential candidate in 1892, but in 1896 it fused with the Democratic Party behind the candidacy of William Jennings Bryan. The campaign, which revolved around the issue of whether or not to issue silver currency, ended in a decisive defeat for Jennings, and turned out to be the high-water mark for the Populist Party. By 1900, there were no Populist Party officeholders at the national level, and the party's last governor left office in 1901.

Even as the party faded, the populist impulses remained, and the issues of government corruption and capture by special interests began to attract the attention of middle-class citizens. Their concerns melded with existing populist concerns to produce a broader and stronger reform movement, called the progressive movement, that ran from about 1900 to 1920. The progressives managed to achieve most of the populists' goals and then went well beyond them.

The surge in populist sentiment and action resuscitated the old Federalist arguments against popular rule. In the words of President William Howard Taft while vetoing a populist reform (the recall):

No honest, clear-headed man, however great a lover of popular government, can deny that the unbridled expression of the majority of a community converted hastily into law or action would sometimes make a government tyrannical and cruel. Constitutions are a check upon the hasty action of the majority.[38]

But Taft was out of touch with the spirit of the times. A better thermometer of public opinion was Theodore Roosevelt, president from 1901 to 1909 and perhaps the most popular politician of the era. His speeches are run through with concerns over the power of special interests, and the need for the people to retake control. His response to Taft was:

No sane man who has been familiar with the government of this country for the last twenty years will complain that we have had too much of the rule of the majority. The trouble has been a far different one that, at many times and in many localities, there have held public office in the States and in the nation men who have, in fact, served not the whole people, but some special class or special interest.[39]

The populist and progressive movements produced perhaps the highest volume of democratizing reforms in the country's history, moving the country even farther from the Founders' framework. A list of the most important reforms would include:

Secret ballots. Traditionally, voting was a public act, done in front of crowds that gathered around the polling site on election day. Initially, citizens verbally stated their vote to an election clerk who entered it into a poll book; later they submitted a decorated or color-coded ballot provided by the party of their choice. The populists agitated for the "Australian ballot," in which votes were cast confidentially, and by the turn of the century every state had moved to secret ballots.

Primary elections. Since the Jacksonian era, each party's presidential nominee was selected at national conventions attended by delegates selected at state-level party conventions. Ordinary voters were left out of the process entirely. In 1901, Florida became the first state to choose party delegates in a primary election. By 1920, 20 other states had moved to primary elections. During the Progressive Era, states also began to hold primary elections for other federal and state offices.

Direct election of US senators. One of the antidemocratic artifacts of the US Constitution was the provision assigning selection of US senators to state legislatures. This method of selection gave political bosses significant influence and completely shut out the voters. In the face of populist pressure, more and more states allowed voters to make the choice themselves. By 1912, 30 states had switched to direct election, in some cases using the newly adopted initiative process to bring about the change. In 1914, the 17th Amendment was ratified, making direct election of US senators universal.[40]

Women's suffrage. The movement for women's suffrage began before the Civil War but showed little progress until the late nineteenth century. Perhaps the most common objection was that allowing women into the political arena would cause destruction of the family. The earliest successes were at the state level; between 1878 and 1898, 24 states adopted laws allowing women to vote on school matters and 5 states adopted laws allowing women to vote on municipal or tax matters. Wyoming provided full suffrage for women when it entered the union in 1889; Colorado, Utah, and Idaho did the same in the mid-1890s. While women's suffrage was not a core issue for most populists, some suffrage activists became populists, and the cause benefited from the populist surge. The Populist Party's success in Colorado, including capturing the governor's office, was crucial for the state's passage of a suffrage law in 1893. The major gains for women's suffrage came after 1910, during the progressive movement, when the suffrage movement converged with broader progressive concerns. Between 1910 and 1919, 17 states adopted laws permitting women to vote in presidential elections, and 16 states fully enfranchised women. In 1920, the 19th Amendment to the US Constitution banned discrimination in voting rights based on sex.[41]

Direct democracy. As we saw in chapter 6, South Dakota was the first state to adopt the initiative and popular referendum—as part of a constitutional amendment drafted while the Populist Party held the governor's office. For the first time, state voters had the power to propose laws themselves and to reject laws passed by the legislature. During the following two decades, 21 other states adopted either the initiative or the popular referendum. Many cities provided initiative and referendum rights in their charters during this time as well.[42]

Ban on corporate contributions. The Progressive Era witnessed the first national legislation seeking to sever the connection between corporate money and politics. This effort was a logical outgrowth of the populist belief that money gave corporations undue influence with the government. The Tillman Act of 1907 made it unlawful for any bank or corporation "to make a money contribution in connection with any election to any political office."[43] While the law lacked teeth and ultimately proved ineffective, it was the first step toward construction of today's extensive regulatory apparatus for campaign finance.

Behind this efflorescence of democracy was a dark side: disfranchisement of blacks in the South. Populism created a difficult challenge for its Southern supporters: the underlying impulse to empower the common people so they could fight back against powerful interests could give African Americans more power as well—an idea that clashed with the white majority's prejudices. The "solution" to this conflict, for the populists, was to support the efforts of white conservatives to remove black voters from the body politic by disenfranchising them, clearing away an issue that might have produced resistance to the rest of their agenda.

Between 1890 and 1905, all Southern states adopted new constitutions or laws that disenfranchised African Americans by imposing registration requirements that on their face were racially neutral, to avoid conflict with the 15th Amendment, but were discriminatory in effect or applied in a discriminatory manner. The new registration rules included lengthy residency requirements, poll taxes, and literacy tests. The effects were profound: in Louisiana the number of black registered voters dropped from 130,000 in 1896 to 1,342 in 1904. The percentage of black citizens who voted in the region fell into the single digits. As this troubling example highlights, although the country has generally progressed in the direction of more democracy, sometimes it has gone backward instead.[44]

The populist surge that began in the 1880s lost energy once the United States entered World War I (1917–18), and for the most part was spent by 1921, when President Woodrow Wilson left office. The onset of the Great Depression in 1929 and then World War II (1939–45) brought other challenges to the front for the next several decades.

Democratic Changes Up to the Present

Populism was largely dormant in the second half of the twentieth century, perhaps sated by the spate of reforms at the beginning of the century.[45] But American democracy did not stand still. Americans continued to revise and reform the structure of their democracy, opening it up to ever more popular participation.[46]

Powerful democratizing movements emerged at the end of the 1950s and ran through the 1970s. The central issue at first was the civil rights of black

Americans, but the movements blossomed into a broader rethinking of the civil rights of all groups across the country. A key accomplishment was the destruction of the Jim Crow system of segregation in the South that had been erected at the turn of the nineteenth century.

The civil rights movement spurred several important democratizing changes. The first was the restoration of voting rights to African Americans, rights that had been denied for decades because of discriminatory registration laws. A key step in this reform was the federal Voting Rights Act of 1965. Almost a century after the Constitution had been amended to give black Americans a de jure right to vote, they finally gained a de facto right. A second change was the Supreme Court's adoption of the one-person-one-vote principle in a series of rulings in the 1960s. The effect of this principle was to force states to redraw their district boundaries to equalize their populations. By upending the long-standing practice of apportioning seats based on historical geographic areas, the ruling removed power from rural constituencies and transferred it to dense urban areas.

The civil rights movement overlapped with the Vietnam War. By the late 1960s, significant opposition to the war had emerged, merging with the civil rights movement. A voting age of 21 years had been a "remarkable constant" in American democracy, dating back to colonial charters, but to many it seemed undemocratic that young men could be drafted into the army and forced to fight without giving them the right to vote: How could they be old enough to fight but not old enough to vote?[47] After unanimous approval in the House and Senate, the states ratified the 26th Amendment to the US Constitution in 1971, lowering the voting age to 18 years across the country.

———

Looking back over two centuries of American history, we can see that American democracy has always been a work in progress, never a finished product. Each generation of Americans has modified the template established by the Founders. And by and large, they have done so in ways that made the country more democratic, giving the people more power to govern themselves (table 10.1). The current structure of government looks nothing like the quasi-aristocracy that the Founders created—and we are better off because of it. Expanding the scope of democracy by holding more referendums would not be undermining the venerable structure established by the Founders, as some fear; it would be following a time-honored path of updating and improving it. The next part of the book lays out a menu of possible updates, and systematically evaluates their benefits and risks.

TABLE 10.1 Expansion of American Democracy from the Early Republic to Today

	Then	Now
Eligible to vote	Only white men over the age of 21 with substantial property Ineligible to vote: those without property, women, blacks, Asians, American Indians	Men and women over the age of 18, without regard to race or property
Voting process	Public act	Secret ballots
Presidential candidates	Chosen by sitting congressmen and senators	Chosen by voters in state primary elections or caucuses
Presidential election	Winner chosen by electors selected by state legislatures	Winner chosen by electors selected by voters
US senators	Chosen by state legislatures	Chosen by voters in direct election
Officeholder qualifications	Substantial property required	No property requirement
Governors and other state-level executive officials	Chosen by legislature	Chosen by voters in direct elections
Party nominees	Chosen by party leaders	Chosen by voters in primary elections
Referendums	None	Required for state constitutional amendments, state borrowing, tax increases, and other issues
Initiatives	None	Available in many states, allowing citizens to propose new laws and constitutional amendments
Recall	None	Available in many states, allowing citizens to remove elected officials and judges from office
Apportionment	Voters in some areas given more legislative seats, usually to disadvantage of urban voters	One person one vote: all voters given the same representation

PART III

The Benefits and Risks of Direct Democracy

11

Six Reforms

WE HAVE SEEN how the long-run evolution of government caused policy to drift out of the hands of the people, and we have reviewed how direct democracy is being used across the world to contain democratic drift. With a rich collection of examples in hand, we are now in a position to consider how referendums might be used in the United States to enhance popular control.

I begin this task by outlining six concrete potential reforms. Since drift is most profound in the United States at the federal level, the focus is on introducing direct democracy into national decisions. Ultimately, we want to understand how each reform would work, how difficult it would be to implement, and its potential advantages and drawbacks—and we want to ground these conclusions in careful review of historical evidence and social-science research.

Covering all this ground takes several chapters. This chapter focuses on describing the reforms, illustrating their existing analogs if any, and considering their feasibility. The next chapter takes an in-depth look at two well-known referendums, and the chapters that follow carefully consider the benefits from expanding direct democracy, as well as some important concerns (the competence of voters, the distorting power of interest groups, and the vulnerability of minorities to majority decisions).

For ease of reference, table 11.1 lists the six proposals discussed in this chapter, in approximate order from most to least feasible. The US Constitution makes no provision for direct democracy and gives Congress the exclusive power to legislate—which means that any reform that transferred legislative authority to the people would require an amendment to the Constitution and face a steep uphill climb. The most feasible reforms are those that do not require a constitutional amendment, and, fortunately, there are several promising possibilities. I explore them all to give a sense of the range of options that are

TABLE 11.1 Direct Democracy Reforms at the National Level

#1	Advisory referendums—called by Congress
#2	Advisory referendums—called by petition
#3	Advisory referendums—required on specific issues
#4	Binding referendums—required on specific issues
#5	Binding referendums—called by petition (national initiative and referendum)
#6	Constitutional amendments—proposed by petition

conceptually available and to illustrate strengths and weaknesses of different approaches—even though some are quite hypothetical at this point.[1]

Proposal #1: Advisory Referendums—Called by Congress

The easiest way to introduce direct democracy at the national level would be through advisory referendums on issues selected by Congress and the president. Holding such votes would be allowable under the Constitution—Congress could simply pass an act calling for a national referendum election. This is not a new idea: Congress member Dick Gephardt, a Democrat from Missouri (later House majority leader), introduced legislation in 1980 calling for three advisory referendums every two years. Under his proposal, Congress would hold hearings to determine issues of importance and then select three issues on which to solicit public feedback. Congress would also provide for publication of a nonpartisan information pamphlet discussing the issues. He was unable to get any traction on his proposal.

The advantages of occasional advisory referendums are easy to see. They give the people a chance to express their views, they help elected officials understand what the people really think, and they could help end gridlock on issues if they reveal a national consensus toward a particular path. Holding advisory referendums would bring the United States up to speed with practices in other democracies throughout the world that were discussed in previous chapters. The risks are minimal. In the event that an election outcome was flawed in some way, Congress would not be obligated to follow a purely advisory vote.

Consider the DREAM Act, a proposed law that would provide a path to naturalization for those who entered the United States illegally when they were younger than 18 years old.[2] Opinion surveys indicate that roughly three-quarters of the public, including majorities of both Democrats and Republicans, support creating a path for so-called "DREAMers" to become US citizens, and the past three presidents (George W. Bush, Barack Obama, Donald Trump) expressed support for legislation to this end.[3]

Yet two decades after the initial introduction of the DREAM Act in 2001, it remains stalled in Congress. In part the logjam is due to disagreements over the precise path to citizenship that would be opened up. If a national vote were held on a particular proposal, both sides could take their argument directly to the American people and let the public decide. If the vote revealed clear support for a course of action, Congress might be prompted to act—and if it revealed a preponderance of opposition to the idea, the issue could be put to rest. This would be a step toward alleviating the public's deep frustration with government's failure to "get things done," the feeling that partisan posturing is overriding the common good, and the unwillingness of elected officials to compromise.[4]

Many issues might be profitably submitted to a national advisory referendum. International agreements come to mind, since many countries now consult the people on such matters. To take two recent examples, the country could have held national referendums on the Paris Agreement on climate change, which committed countries to reduce greenhouse gas emissions, and the Trans-Pacific Partnership (TPP) free-trade agreement. The current American approach to international agreements is unstable, involving no direct consultation with the people and almost no consultation with the people's representatives in the Senate, as discussed in chapter 2. Taking a decades-long trend almost to the limit, President Obama completed 98 percent of his international agreements without seeking the advice or consent of the US Senate by framing international agreements as executive agreements rather than as treaties (including the Paris Agreement and TPP).[5] Because such agreements are unilateral actions of the president, they can be rescinded unilaterally by a later president, as when President Trump swiftly canceled President Obama's most prominent international agreements. Holding a national vote would provide more stability to American commitments: presidents would be deterred from concluding agreements that lacked popular support in the first place, and would hesitate to rescind their predecessor's agreements if the public had endorsed the agreements in a referendum.

Proposal #2: Advisory Referendums—Called by Petition

A variant on the preceding proposal would be to hold national advisory referendums, but allow *citizens* to propose the questions instead of Congress. This would be similar to the European Citizens' Initiative (ECI), discussed in chapter 7, that allows citizens to propose questions for consideration by the European Commission. Congress could create this procedure through an ordinary law; as long as the outcome was advisory, a constitutional amendment would not be required (although Congress would probably be more hesitant about this idea than the first proposal because it would surrender some control over which issues go to a vote). The law would have to set the rules for collecting signatures and could be structured so that a referendum automatically occurs after enough signatures are collected, or—as with the ECI—the decision to call the referendum could be left to Congress's discretion.

This process has the advantage of allowing issues to percolate up from the people. If Congress has a monopoly on deciding which issues go to a vote, the same forces leading to gridlock in legislation, such as partisanship and special-interest influence, might prevent important questions from coming to a referendum. Under a petition system, groups that struggle to get the attention of legislators would have the opportunity to place their issues before the public and demonstrate support. Based on recent examples from the states, we might expect to see animal rights activists seek a vote on treatment of farm animals, drug reformers seek a vote on legalizing marijuana, progressives seek a vote on increasing the minimum wage, taxpayer groups seek a vote limiting taxes, civil rights activists seek a vote ending affirmative action, and so on. Term-limits activists would be chomping at the bit to restrict the terms of members of the House and Senate.

The basic concept could be extended in a couple of ways. One would be to allow citizens to call for a vote on an *existing* law (an advisory petition referendum). The referendum would ask voters if they support the law or wish to repeal it. Again, the outcome of the vote would have to be advisory to avoid constitutional issues. This would be similar to Italy's *abrogativo* referendum process, discussed in chapter 7, except that the referendum outcome in Italy has the force of law.

Another way to extend the concept would be to allow citizens to call a vote on administrative rules and regulations. With the growth of the administrative state, the preponderance of lawmaking today occurs in the form of rules formulated by administrative agencies, and these decisions are far removed from popular control. If the referendum outcome indicated popular disapproval, Congress would have the option of vacating the rule through its normal powers. In some cases, it might not be necessary to hold a vote; the petitions themselves might alert Congress to a problem, and Congress could investigate and act on its own. In addition to providing a safety valve for citizens to challenge undesirable regulations, the very existence of such a possibility could alter the nature of the rules that are promulgated—regulators would consult with key individuals and groups in order to find rules that do not attract a challenge.

Proposal #3: Advisory Referendums— Required on Specific Issues

The first two proposals leave it to politicians or petitioners to determine whether a referendum is held. There may be issues for which a referendum should occur automatically. Ronald Reagan proposed such a mechanism before he became president during an appearance on the *Tonight Show* in 1975: "I still say the answer to our problems in this country . . . is to have a law that says there is a percentage limit of the people's earnings that government cannot go beyond without the consent of the people."[6]

The proposed referendum process would trigger an election whenever Congress took a specified action, such as increasing taxes. Congress could create this process through ordinary legislation, without necessitating a constitutional amendment, as long as the outcome of the referendum is advisory. As with the previous proposal, Congress would cede control over what goes to a vote, which would likely create some resistance among sitting officials.

There is a direct analog to this process in the governance of corporations: a company is required to hold a shareholder vote on executive compensation every three years. The vote is advisory—the directors can ignore a negative recommendation from the shareholders—but as a practical matter, directors do not like to disregard clear instructions from shareholders. Directors who ignore shareholder recommendations often find themselves voted out of office at the next election.[7] One could imagine a similar dynamic for government policies— if legislators explicitly ignored clear instructions from the voters, their re-election prospects might be endangered.

Mandatory referendums seem natural for issues where representatives have a conflict of interest, such as laws pertaining to their compensation and benefits, terms of office, and redistricting. Requiring a canvass of voter opinion might inhibit naked self-interest when they make these decisions. Taxes and debt are also natural issues for mandatory referendums, as shown by the prevalence of tax and debt referendum laws in the states. Tax laws can be distorted from the public good by pressure from special interests, and debt decisions can be distorted by the short-run perspective of politicians who do not expect to hold office indefinitely. An advisory vote would create pressure to align tax and debt policies with public preferences, counteracting special-interest influence and legislator myopia.

————

Next we move to proposals in which the referendum outcome has the force of law. Because the Constitution gives Congress the power to make laws, these reforms would likely require a constitutional amendment, making them much more difficult to bring about.

Proposal #4: Binding Referendums— Required on Specific Issues

A bold reform would be to require referendums on certain government actions and give the outcome the force of law, essentially requiring voter approval of those policies. Instituting this would likely require amending the Constitution. Such referendums could be considered for matters of high national importance, where the consent of the people is especially important.

The so-called Ludlow Amendment, sponsored by Indiana's Democratic congressman Louis Ludlow, was an example of just such a reform. Ultimately unsuccessful, the amendment would have required a national referendum before the country could declare war. Ludlow introduced the amendment several times in the 1930s, arguing that the common people who would serve and die in a war ought to be able to vote on whether to enter a conflict. Opinion surveys showed that over 70 percent of Americans supported the amendment, reflecting the isolationist temperament of the time. The amendment failed due to determined opposition from President Franklin Roosevelt, who saw it as impracticable and incompatible with representative democracy.

Referendums of this nature are already in place in some countries, as mentioned in previous chapters. Switzerland requires a national vote before the country enters into an international security agreement, and Ireland requires one before it signs international treaties. Mandatory referendums are common among the American states; all but one of them require a vote on constitutional amendments and many require votes on taxes, debt, relocation of the state capital, liquor prohibition, and other matters.

Proposal #5: Binding Referendums—Called by Petition

A variant of the preceding proposal would be to allow citizens to repeal existing laws through petition referendums, which also would require a constitutional amendment. This would be like Italy's *abrogativo* process, which has triggered 72 referendums in the seven decades it has been available. Switzerland, as one might expect, has a national referendum law of this form as well, which has been available and frequently used since 1874. The processes appear to be popular in both countries.

An even more far-reaching reform would be to allow citizens to propose new laws by petition and approve them by popular vote, a full-bore national initiative process. This too would require a constitutional amendment. Clearly, giving citizens control of the agenda as well as the power to make final decisions would be a fundamental change to American government. It would put the US government in uncharted waters, although other governments have been navigating those seas for some time. Several countries permit initiatives at the national level, including Switzerland, Taiwan, and Uruguay, and 24 American states and a majority of American cities provide initiative rights as well.

Proposal #6: Constitutional Amendments— Proposed by Petition

The constitutional amendment process is broken. It has become almost impossible to amend the US Constitution, and as a result the nation's fundamental law has become ossified and outdated. To the extent it is updated, it happens at the hands of unelected judges—as we saw in chapter 2—rather than through a democratic process, which contributes to democratic drift. Direct democracy could be deployed in several ways to unblock the constitutional amendment process.

One reform that has the virtue of not requiring a constitutional amendment would be to allow citizens to propose constitutional amendments to Congress by petition. Congress would consider the proposals but would not be required to approve them; if Congress chose to move forward, it would follow the Constitution's article V process. While conceptually easy to implement, this process could amount to nothing in the end because it does not require Congress to act; in this regard it is similar to the EU's ECI process, discussed earlier. It is possible, however, that the process of collecting signatures, by demonstrating popular support for an idea, could prompt Congress to look at the issue seriously.

A more substantial reform would be to allow citizen proposals to go straight to the states for approval, bypassing Congress. This is not an option under article V, so it would require a constitutional amendment of its own. Creating an amendment path of this sort would break Congress's monopoly over which amendments are considered. For instance, opinion surveys suggest that most Americans would support term limits on members of Congress, but Congress is unlikely to impose such a limit on itself.[8]

Perhaps the most "extreme" proposal of all would be to allow citizens to propose constitutional amendments by initiative, and then approve them by referendum. Several states allow initiatives of this form and, predictably, so does Switzerland.

———

At the most basic level, populist sentiment originates from a belief that government has slipped out of control of the people and into the hands of elites, special interests, and other influential groups. Putting decisions directly into the hands of the people targets remediation at the root of the problem. If the people have more control over decisions, they will not feel that policy is controlled by elites. This chapter lays out several concrete proposals to give the people more control by using referendums.

Discussions of direct democracy usually start with the idea of a national initiative process; this is the form of direct democracy pushed by activists, often to the exclusion of all other forms. In my list, a national initiative comes at the end of the discussion, after a series of less risky proposals have been adopted. My sense is that while the idea of a national initiative process has some merit, it is too unrealistic to consider as a first step. Adopting it would require a constitutional amendment, meaning approval by two-thirds of House and Senate members and three-quarters of state legislatures. On top of this significant legislative hurdle, there is the question of public opinion: Would Americans be comfortable with such a profound change right out of the gate?

I believe it makes more sense to go in steps, starting with reforms that are easy to implement and have been "road tested" by other democracies. Advisory referendums called by Congress are the natural starting point. If this proved to work well, as I believe it would, confidence would build for more far-reaching reforms over time.

Most people have an instinctive reaction to direct democracy. For some people, the idea of giving the people a voice is immediately appealing; it fills others with a sense of dread. What is important to realize, in either case, is that those instinctive reactions are just that—instinctive—and therefore not entirely trustworthy. Democratic government, especially in a vast, mature democracy like the United States, is a complicated interconnected system, involving elected officials, technocrats, judges, interest groups, and ordinary voters. The effect of referendums on such a system is bound to be complicated as well. This means that many of our initial instincts and intuitions about direct democracy might be incomplete or even wrong. The purpose of the next several chapters is to sharpen our intuitions by laying out the various ways in which referendums shape and are shaped by the larger political system, relying heavily on historical evidence. By comparing our intuitions to the actual facts, we can understand how the pieces fit together and arrive at a reasoned opinion on direct democracy.

12

A Tale of Two Referendums

PROPOSITION 13 AND BREXIT

SOMETIMES REFERENDUMS WORK WELL; sometimes they don't. Sometimes they allow the people to wrest control of policy from special interests; sometimes they provide another channel for rich groups to exert influence. Sometimes they settle long-running disputes and stabilize policy; sometimes they amplify existing controversies. In short, like all forms of democracy, they can make things better if done properly, and create problems if done wrong.

One goal of this book is to understand how to do direct democracy properly. As a guide, this chapter tells the tale of two famous referendums, California's Proposition 13 in 1978 and the United Kingdom's Brexit referendum in 2016, one that worked well and one that did not. Both are well known, and both were controversial. To understand them requires cutting through the rhetoric and getting into the details. I start with a narrative history of both referendums, sorting out the facts from the myths, and use that as a springboard to the more systematic discussion of referendums that follows.

Proposition 13

California gives us a preview of how referendums might work at the national level. For one thing, the state is immense—in wealth (GDP greater than the UK's), people (40 million), land area (a little bigger than Japan), and cultural influence—and it offers a good testing ground for how citizen lawmaking works in an advanced, complex, diverse society. Second, the state's extensive experience with initiatives and referendums illustrates many of the important issues. Third, the state is often viewed as a bellwether, and its history hints at what might be in store for the rest of the country and world going forward.

Because California is so often mentioned in discussions of direct democracy (often in a misleading way, in my experience), it is good to have an accurate description of the facts available.

Proposition 13, approved in 1978, is the most famous ballot proposition in American history. While memory of the proposition's origins may be fading, it remains a foundational element of the state's government. Jerry Brown, who opposed the proposition in 1978 while governor, in his more recent 2014 gubernatorial campaign called it "a sacred doctrine that should never be questioned."[1] Proposition 13 has become a lodestar for direct democracy proponents, and an example of everything that is wrong with citizen lawmaking for opponents. Any assessment of direct democracy has to grapple with the causes and consequences of Proposition 13 and penetrate the fog of its mythology.

The seeds of Proposition 13 were sown decades before the proposal appeared on the ballot. In the years after World War II, California's population surged, its economy boomed, and the state spent heavily on infrastructure, education, and social programs. The swelling of government mirrored the rest of the country, which also pursued expansive economic policies after the war. Figure 12.1 shows the growth in revenue collected by the state, in real per capita terms, from 1955 to 1990.[2]

By the late 1960s, cracks were appearing in the postwar consensus for big government. Property taxes became a particular flash point as housing prices seemed to rise without end. Proposition 9, in 1968, was the first in a series of

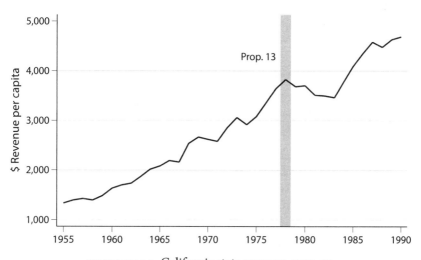

FIGURE 12.1. California state revenue, 1955–90

initiatives that sought to cut property taxes. The proposition capped property taxes at 1 percent of value, increased exemptions, and limited how revenue could be used. In what would become a recurring pattern, the legislature countered with modest tax cuts and its own proposal, Proposition 1A, that simply offered to increase the property tax exemption. Proposition 9 was opposed by public- and private-sector labor unions, major corporations, and leaders of both the Democratic and Republican parties, as well as by GOP governor Ronald Reagan—and on election day was soundly rejected, 32 to 68 percent. Voters instead adopted Proposition 1A.

Proposition 14, another tax-cutting initiative, made it on to the ballot in 1972. It proposed a more modest tax rate cap of 1.75 percent. The legislature once again countered with a modest increase in the property tax exemption. With many of the same opponents, Proposition 14 was also rejected, 34 to 66 percent.

In 1973, Governor Reagan placed his own tax-cutting initiative on the ballot. Reagan had misgivings about the legislature's failure to consider serious tax relief and was frustrated by its approval of a one-cent *increase* in the sales tax— even though the state anticipated a surplus of $700 to $850 million on a budget of just over $7 billion. "If you are looking for a good investment, invest in taxes, they always go up," Reagan quipped.[3] Proposition 1 was a fiscal conservative's dream: it froze property tax rates and required voter approval for future increases; it cut and limited income taxes; it restricted future spending growth; it required two-thirds approval in the legislature for future tax increases; and it required an immediate 20 percent income tax rebate to be funded from the surplus. After Reagan called a special election to decide Proposition 1, the legislature approved an immediate 20 to 35 percent income tax rebate, meaning a vote for Proposition 1 would actually *increase* income taxes in the short run. On election day, voters rejected the initiative 46 to 54 percent.

In 1974, Reagan declined to run for re-election and was replaced by 36-year-old Democrat Jerry Brown, the youngest person to be elected California governor in the modern era. Brown, a former Jesuit seminarian, was the son of former governor Pat Brown, remembered for his ambitious infrastructure spending, who had been defeated by Reagan in 1966. The Democrats also took control of both chambers of the legislature, giving them unified control of the government for the first time since 1966. Under the new political leadership, state spending exploded, growing an average of 12.5 percent per year from 1974 to 1977. As high as the spending growth was, state revenue grew even faster. Fueled by rising housing prices and income, revenue growth averaged 18.4 percent per year during that period.

While the state's treasury amassed record revenue, its residents struggled with a stagnating economy and spiraling property tax burdens. Housing prices rose at a dizzying pace of 22 percent on average per year from 1974 to 1977, increasing property taxes in their wake. Homeowners watched with anxiety when a neighboring home sold for a record price, knowing that it portended a steep rise in their tax bills. When the clamor for tax relief became too loud for the legislature and governor to ignore, they began to consider relief plans; but none of their plans were able to navigate through the thicket of pro-spending interest groups in the legislature. The failure of the government to take action was especially galling to homeowners because, by the start of 1978, the state was sitting on a $5.8 billion surplus, an "obscene" amount, according to the Democratic state treasurer, considering that general fund expenditure at that time was $16 billion.[4] In a pure representative democracy, the only option for ordinary citizens would have been to gnash their teeth and try to elect new legislators and a new governor. Because the initiative was available, history took a different path.

Howard Jarvis, a "burly and profane spud of man," was a retired 75-year-old former newspaper publisher and manufacturing businessman who had been active in Republican circles for decades, running for office unsuccessfully several times. His United Organizations of Taxpayers had failed to qualify initiatives in several earlier petition campaigns, so in 1978 he joined forces with Paul Gann, who ran an organization called the People's Advocate. Relying only on volunteers, in short order they collected 1.2 million signatures for a new tax-cutting proposal, more than twice the required 500,000, and the most ever for an initiative at that time. Jarvis's proposal, Proposition 13, limited property taxes to 1 percent of assessed value, rolled back assessments to their 1976 values, capped future assessment increases at 2 percent per year, required a two-thirds vote of the legislature to increase taxes, and imposed a mandatory referendum on local-government tax increases. California's Legislative Analyst estimated that the proposal would reduce local property tax revenue by 57 percent.[5]

Following the familiar pattern, the legislature responded by placing a watered-down tax-cut proposal of its own on the ballot, Proposition 8, which would have taxed residential property at a lower rate than commercial property, limited property tax revenue increases to the rate of inflation, and cut property taxes overall by 30 percent.

Proposition 13 was opposed by Governor Brown, the leaders of the Democratic Party, and many prominent Republicans. The opposition also counted a long list of business, civic, and labor organizations: public employee unions; the AFL-CIO;[6] the Los Angeles and San Diego chambers of commerce; the

Sierra Club; numerous newspapers; the California Manufacturer's Association; and major corporations based in the state, including Bank of America (then the nation's largest commercial bank). No one campaigned more often and more adamantly against Proposition 13 than Governor Brown, who predicted it would be "a disaster for California" and called it "the biggest can of worms that has ever been presented to government anywhere."[7]

Jarvis was not worried: "The more large corporations that come out against us, the better I like it. That will make a lie out of the opposition claim that was made for the first few months of the campaign that this measure will enrich big business."[8] The primary spokesman for Proposition 13 was Jarvis himself, but former governor Reagan and Nobel Prize–winning economist Milton Friedman appeared in television commercials in support. The initiative almost sold itself, however. When Los Angeles County announced the biggest assessment increases in 30 years one month before the election, the *LA Times* recounted:

> No campaign worker ever made a pitch to the salesman who walked into the office of Californians for Proposition 13 one morning. He had read the day before that new assessments were available at the assessor's branch office on Van Nuys Blvd. He said he had just learned his had gone up 105%. His next stop was at Californians for Proposition 13, where he gave Ms. Nerpel a contribution. "Never in my life have I been involved in politics," he said. "I got drafted, went over to 'Nam, fought their war for them. I wasn't even too upset about Nixon." But the property tax increase, he said, "is like the movie *Network* where everyone shouted they were mad as hell and didn't have to take it anymore."[9]

On June 6, 1978, a remarkable 70 percent of registered voters turned out to approve Proposition 13 in a landslide, 65 to 35 percent. At the same time, voters turned down the legislature's counterinitiative, Proposition 8. A postelection survey found that 56 percent of nonvoters who had an opinion on the issue were in support. Proposition 13 was favored by 45 percent of self-described liberals and 65 percent of moderates as well as 82 percent of conservatives, and by a majority of both Democrats and Republicans.[10] The decade-long road from the failed Proposition 9 in 1968 had ended in decisive passage of one of the most far-reaching tax-limitation laws in American history.

––––––

The "tax revolt" ignited by Proposition 13 instantly became a national talking point, dominating news in the following weeks, and commanding the covers of leading news magazines and the op-ed pages of leading newspapers. In November 1978, only five months after the California landslide, 16 states voted on their own tax-limitation measures, approving 12 of them. Within five years, nearly half of the states in the country had adopted a law that restricted future taxes and spending, and almost every state had provided some form of tax relief. At the federal level, Proposition 13 breathed new life into the Kemp-Roth tax-cut plan that Congress eventually passed in 1981 after Ronald Reagan became president, which in its final form (Economic Recovery Tax Act of 1981) cut personal income tax rates 25 percent across the board, trimmed corporate income taxes, and increased estate tax exemptions.

In California, the response by political leaders was swift. Governor Brown, facing re-election in November, declared himself a "born-again tax cutter" and pivoted on a dime to a more fiscally conservative position. Seeking "to carry out the will of the people," he instituted a hiring freeze on state workers, froze cost-of-living adjustments for public employees and welfare recipients, took a tough bargaining position with public-sector unions, and proposed a constitutional amendment to permanently limit the growth of state and local spending.[11]

The legislature also got the message, responding with a $1 billion cut in income taxes, as well as a cut in taxes on home sales, and other tax breaks for senior citizens, welfare renters, and the disabled. It also made $5 billion of the state surplus available to local governments to offset revenue losses from Proposition 13. Liberal Democrat Leroy Greene, chair of the Assembly Education Committee, described the new environment: "I doubt there's anyone here who is going to want to vote for a tax increase. Whenever we put more money on the table, there's somebody there to grab it every time. We've got to put less money on the table and slap hands when they grab."[12] Spending and revenue plunged in 1979, and stayed flat for five years.

Although the state's politicians seemed willing to accept the will of the voters, some powerful interest groups were not—particularly the education establishment, which, as the largest recipient of public spending, had a vested interest in preserving the flow of revenue to the state's coffers. Just days after the election, they filed two lawsuits asking the state supreme court to block implementation of Proposition 13; one from the California Teachers Association, the state's biggest teachers' group, and the other by the California Federation of Teachers and the state service employees' union. Two more lawsuits followed shortly thereafter, one by school superintendents and community colleges, and another by eight counties. The court rejected all of the challenges.[13]

The anti-tax tide continued to surge over the next decade. In 1979, voters approved Proposition 4, which limited government spending growth to the inflation rate plus the growth rate of population, by an even larger margin than Proposition 13: 74 to 26 percent. Called the "Gann Limits" after the initiative's author Paul Gann, the spending restrictions also required the government to refund taxpayers any revenue it collected in excess of the spending limit. In 1987, Republican Governor George Deukmejian announced his intention to rebate surplus revenue to taxpayers as required by Proposition 4, declaring, "California has gone from government deficits to taxpayer dividends." Democratic leaders and public employee unions objected, urging diversion of the revenue to education instead, but Deukmejian prevailed and taxpayers pocketed $1.1 billion in refunds.[14]

Local governments soon discovered a loophole in the language of Proposition 13. While the initiative had required voter approval for "tax" increases, it did not explicitly require voter approval for increases in property-related "fees" and "special assessments." After the state supreme court allowed governments to raise fees under this interpretation, taxpayer groups lobbied the legislature to close the loophole, but without success. It took yet another initiative, Proposition 218, approved in 1996, to close down these backdoor tax increases.

Pro-spending interests persisted, however, led by public employee unions and their Democratic allies in the legislature. Gradually, they managed to chip away at the Gann Limits. After failing to persuade voters to repeal Proposition 13 and weaken the Gann Limits, in 1988 they proposed Proposition 98—which carved out a fraction of revenue in excess of the Gann Limits for public schools (and also required 40 percent of the state budget to be spent on education)—and persuaded a narrow majority of voters, 51 percent, to approve it.

They had even better luck in 1990. The legislature and governor placed Proposition 111 on the ballot, with the deceptive title "The Traffic Congestion Relief and Spending Limitation Act of 1990." The ballot summary described it as enacting a statewide traffic-congestion relief program, but buried beneath the traffic-congestion language it also "update[d] the state appropriations limit to allow for new funding for congestion relief, mass transit, health care, services for the elderly, and other priority state programs." In fact, the proposition implemented the unions' long-sought goal of tying the Gann Limits to the growth of income as well as inflation and population, allowing much faster spending growth. With defenders of the limits poorly organized and underfunded, the election received limited attention and voters approved the proposition 52 to 48 percent.[15]

As a result of Proposition 111, the state was able to embark on nearly two decades of explosive spending—from 1991 to 2007 total expenditure grew 284 percent, while inflation rose only 52 percent, until it was hit hard by the 2007 financial crisis, and went through a series of budget crises as it struggled with the consequences of its addiction to overspending.

The story of Proposition 13 has several themes that are explored in more detail in the coming chapters: the failure of politicians to adopt common-sense reforms until voters take matters into their own hands with an initiative, the responsiveness of politicians to a clear demonstration of voter preferences, the dependence on politicians to implement initiative laws, and the ability of special interests to fight back with their own initiatives. The tale of Brexit that is up next illustrates another set of opportunities and risks.

Brexit

On June 23, 2016, the United Kingdom held a national election on whether to take the country out of the European Union, widely known as the "Brexit" referendum. An unusually high 72 percent of the electorate went to the polls, amid heavy rain storms, and voted to exit by a narrow margin of 51.9 to 48.1 percent. The outcome was a shock to pundits and politicians; it threatened to upset the decades-long project toward European integration, and plunged UK politics into turmoil from which it has yet to emerge as of this writing. To supporters, Brexit was a much-needed antidote to the antidemocratic, centralizing drift of European politics, but for critics it was an example of why referendums should not be used to resolve important public issues. A closer look at exactly what Brexit did and did not do can help us clear away misconceptions and draw lessons for future referendums.[16]

Brexit had its origins in the late 1990s and early 2000s when opponents of the EU—dubbed "Eurosceptics"—organized and began to gather strength. The EU is part of a broader project to build an integrated Europe, something along the lines of a United States of Europe in the minds of its most ambitious supporters. The EU began as a free-trade zone, gradually expanding from economic into political issues and establishing its own parliament and administrative structure, headquartered in Brussels. In 1973, the UK joined the European Economic

Community (EEC), which was transformed into the EU in 1993 by the Maastricht Treaty.

The EU could claim some credit for economic prosperity and for helping to maintain peace in a region that had been the center of two destructive world wars in the twentieth century. Still, citizens were troubled by some aspects of the EU enterprise. The free flow of labor across the region allowed large movements of immigrants into a country, without the country's approval. Some labor unions considered the free-trade zone to be tilted in favor of corporate interests, and some businesses felt overregulated by bureaucrats in the center. Moreover, the accumulation of power in Brussels upset citizens who valued the preservation of their nation's distinct culture, values, and way of life.

The emergence of the UK Independence Party (UKIP) signaled the arrival of anti-EU sentiment as a political force. UKIP was founded in 1991, essentially as a single-issue Eurosceptic party, but languished on the fringes until Nigel Farage, provocateur and former commodity trader, became leader in 2006. The party broke through in 2013, capturing 22 percent of the national vote in local elections, and ran first nationally, with 27 percent of the vote, in the European Parliament elections the following year. It drew its support by siphoning off voters from both of the two mainstream parties, the Conservative Party and Labour Party.

Attempting to contain the growing appeal of the anti-EU message, in 2013 Conservative prime minister David Cameron announced that the government would hold an advisory referendum on EU membership before the end of 2017. The promise was then explicitly included in the party's election manifesto for the May 2015 parliamentary elections in order to quell a revolt by Eurosceptics within the party. When the Conservatives unexpectedly captured a parliamentary majority, the government set in motion plans for the referendum.

European nations have been holding referendums on integration matters for more than 40 years; of the 16 countries that have joined the EU over its past three rounds of expansion, 13 held national referendums on the decision.[17] While the UK did not hold a referendum when it originally joined the EEC, it did hold one on whether to remain a member in 1975. A majority of 67 percent voted to remain, and despite some initial controversy, the validity of the referendum was widely accepted in the end.[18]

Cameron, a lifetime politico with moderate globalist views, had reservations about the EU, but favored the UK remaining as a member, both for economic reasons and as a way to enhance the country's political clout. A referendum held two attractions for him: he could use the threat of an exit vote as leverage in upcoming negotiations with the EU, in which he hoped to carve out a more independent position for the UK; and if the electorate backed his revised terms of membership, which was widely expected, he could put the issue to rest for a generation, as the 1975 referendum had done.

In February 2016, with the referendum looming, Cameron flew to Brussels for negotiations with the key EU leaders on reforms in the UK's relation to the EU. After two days of almost nonstop discussions, a bleary-eyed Cameron emerged with an agreement that he touted as providing a "special status" in the EU that allowed the UK to "be in the parts of Europe that work for us" and "out of the parts of Europe that don't work for us." But the revised terms were panned by the media and pundits, who said that Cameron got almost nothing from the EU. Upon returning to London, Cameron triggered the EU Referendum Act, setting an election date four months out, and declaring, "the British people must now decide whether to stay in this reformed European Union or to leave."[19]

The campaign was fiercely contested, with media saturation before and during the official 10-week campaign. The members of Parliament from the major parties were split, with some on the "Leave" side and others with "Remain." The official campaign organizations, Vote Leave and Britain Stronger in Europe, each received £600,000 of public money, free mailing to each household, free television time, and were allowed to spend up to £7 million of their own funds. The Leave campaign emphasized loss of sovereignty and immigration; its official slogan was "Take back control." The Remain campaign focused on the economic cost of leaving. Both sides had articulate champions, and television provided time for each side to make its case to the public. It is doubtful that many voters went to the polls without having heard the main arguments.

Through election day, Brexit took a course that was familiar from many previous European referendums: an energetically contested campaign with an engaged citizenry turning out to express its views. However, after the voters spoke, rejecting EU membership, things began to fall apart. The morning after the election, having been repudiated by the voters, Cameron resigned as prime minister. The Conservative Party selected Theresa May to replace him.

Initially, it seemed like the UK would move toward a smooth exit from the EU. May, a banker and longtime Conservative politician, was an unlikely choice since she had been a supporter, albeit lukewarm, of remaining in the EU, but she took a firm position that there was no turning back: "Brexit means Brexit. The campaign was fought, the vote was held, turnout was high, and the public gave their verdict. . . . I am very clear that I will deliver Brexit."[20] The leaders of the major parties also expressed their intent to implement the will of the voters, even though many of them had also favored remaining. The general public appeared ready to accept the outcome as well (including about half of those on the losing side; see next chapter): one year after the election, 68 percent of voters believed that the country should abide by the referendum and exit; to do otherwise would be undemocratic.[21]

In March 2017, May won the support of Parliament to start the exit process by invoking article 50 of the Treaty of Lisbon, committing the UK to be out by March 2019. It was then up to May and the EU to negotiate the terms of separation.

In November 2018, May completed negotiations with the EU on a withdrawal agreement. The agreement mapped out the post-exit structure of the UK's relation to the EU and the rights of EU citizens, provided a transition period, and required the UK to pay the EU about £40 billion, its estimated share of the EU's budget over the remainder of the current budget cycle.

Hardcore Brexiters saw the deal as a cave-in that kept the UK enmeshed in a web of EU regulations, particularly when it came to trade policy. A particularly thorny issue in the settlement was a "backstop" to ensure that Northern Ireland's border with the Republic of Ireland remained open after the exit. The agreement kept the UK in the EU's customs union, and hence subject to the EU's economic regulation, until a follow-up agreement on the border was devised—meaning potentially indefinitely.

During the first few months of 2019, May tried in vain to gain parliamentary approval for the agreement, losing three parliamentary votes. One of them was the largest parliamentary defeat of any British prime minister in the democratic era. In desperation, she even tried cutting a deal with the opposition Labour Party when she could not attract enough support from her own party. Although the country was set to exit with or without a plan, Parliament refused to accept any of the exit plans, and also voted not to exit without a plan—apparently rejecting all available options. The EU extended the UK's official exit date to April 2019 and then October 2019. In the spring of 2019, after several cabinet members quit in protest of the arrangement, May was forced to resign. More than three years after the British electorate had voted to leave the EU, the UK was still a member, and the country's politics remained in turmoil.

———

Why did things become so dysfunctional after the election? The turmoil in British politics after Brexit is surprising and unusual. In the case of Proposition

13 in California, we saw that once the votes were counted, the political leadership accepted the people's verdict and moved to implement their will, cutting taxes and slowing government growth. This was despite the fact that most politicians had opposed Proposition 13. Similarly, Brexit initially looked no different than dozens of other referendums held across Europe related to European integration. After the voters chose to leave the EU, there appeared to be a clear path forward that would have implemented the will of the voters and been perceived as legitimate by most citizens.

Part of the responsibility lay with the politicians who failed to find the path out. They may have lacked the necessary skills, or dragged their feet on purpose because they privately preferred the UK to remain in the EU. But the politicians charged to implement Brexit were also dealt a bad hand by the referendum's architects; the design of the referendum put them in an extremely difficult position. Two critical flaws were baked into the Brexit referendum from the beginning—and the strife that ensued shows how poor design can nullify the benefits that might otherwise accrue (more on these benefits in the next chapter, and on best practices for referendum design in chapter 18).

The first was not presenting voters with a concrete proposal. The government did not negotiate an exit plan with the EU, and then ask voters to approve or reject it, nor did it ask voters to choose between concrete exit options. Instead, voters were posed a general question: "Should the United Kingdom remain a member of the European Union or leave the European Union?" The problem is that the UK could leave the EU in many ways, ranging from various "soft exits" in which the country remained part of the EU's customs union or single market to a "hard exit" involving complete separation. No one can be sure what the Leavers wanted when they voted to exit, and the Leavers themselves could not be sure what options they were choosing between. This put the government in an awkward position when it came to formulating an actual exit plan.

After Prime Minister May negotiated her exit plan with the EU, it became clear that there were sharply different opinions within Parliament on the details. The members splintered into several factions, each of which had a specific plan it favored. Unfortunately, none of the individual plans enjoyed majority support. Even though a majority agreed to exit, the country was forced to remain because no plan could garner a majority. The ambiguity of the referendum question made it impossible to cut the knot by appealing to the will of the people since each group could claim that its position best reflected what the voters had in mind.

It would have been better for the referendum to ask voters their opinion on a specific exit plan. In the 1975 referendum on EU membership, voters were asked if they wanted to continue under specific terms that had been recently negotiated. Most referendums on EU integration are of the same nature—the government first negotiates a treaty, and then voters are asked to approve it. The Brexit referendum did it backward, asking voters to approve a treaty first, then charging the government to negotiate it afterward. The lack of a concrete proposal made much of the pre-election discussion about the effects of Brexit entirely hypothetical. Attempts to quantify the economic costs of leaving, for example, were pure conjecture, given uncertainty about the exact form exit would take.

Asking voters a general question rather than presenting a concrete proposal also encouraged the campaigns to tap into voter emotions about sovereignty, economic growth, and immigration, rather than to consider the actual consequences of a particular exit scenario. Without knowing the details of what exit would involve, some people on both sides may have voted based on general feelings about globalization and sovereignty. Some voters even said they were casting their votes in order to protest against the government. All of which immensely complicated the task of inferring which specific exit proposal the voters would prefer.

Yet another problem with posing a general question is that it leaves little room for policy makers to return to voters if they have second thoughts, or believe voters would prefer a new, third option. Irish voters twice rejected EU referendums, once in 2001 on the Treaty of Nice and once in 2008 on the Lisbon Treaty. In each case, the government corrected the perceived deficiencies in the original proposal—by excluding language calling for participation in a common defense policy in the first case and by issuance of "Irish Guarantees" in the second case—and voters approved the revised proposals. Similarly, after Danish voters rejected the Maastricht Treaty in 1991, the government negotiated four exclusions with the EU, and voters approved the revised treaty. By not placing a specific proposal on the table for Brexit, there were no specific defects that the government could try to correct. Seeking a second vote, without offering a substantially different proposal, would look like an attempt to force the people to vote until they chose the government's favored outcome.[22]

The other problem with Brexit was requiring only a simple majority for approval. In principle, if 50 percent plus one person voted to exit, that would have counted as the winning outcome. Thomas Jefferson warned long ago that "great innovations should not be forced on a slender majority."[23] The 51.9 percent majority on Brexit is a slender majority.

Slender majorities create several problems. One of them is doubt about whether the election outcome represents the true majority view of the population. Given that 28 percent of registered voters chose not to participate, one might wonder if the overall majority—taking into account nonvoters—might actually have been in favor of remaining. Opinion polls suggest that abstainers would not have changed the outcome, but the margin was small enough to make it debatable. A related problem with slender majorities is that a small shift in public opinion can cause the majority position to flip after the election. It only required 2 percent of Leave voters to change their minds to create a majority for remaining in the EU. This placed politicians in an awkward position, having to work toward implementing an outcome that they were not sure the majority still wanted. It also led to pressure for a re-vote by those who wanted to stay in the EU, hoping that they would fare better with a second bite at the apple.

There are ways to avoid the risk of making a fundamental change based on a slender majority. One is to require a supermajority of votes for approval. The state of Florida requires a 60 percent majority in order to amend its constitution. With such a rule, if a proposal passes, there is little doubt that the majority supports it.[24] Another approach is to require a proposal to be approved twice. The state of Nevada requires constitutional amendments to be approved in two consecutive elections, two years apart. This mitigates the risk of making a change based on a momentary passion. If a dramatic event triggers an emotional response in the public that leads to passage of a proposal, the heat of that event will have faded two years later. The Brexit referendum could have avoided some of its problems by requiring a supermajority or by requiring approval in two separate elections.[25]

———

In light of these flaws, why did the decision makers structure the referendum in the way they did? This is not easy to answer conclusively. The question itself was drafted by the government, and was revised from the initial wording upon recommendation of the Electoral Commission, which felt it might be slanted.

It does not appear that requiring a supermajority to exit was ever contemplated, perhaps because supermajorities run against British tradition. A special report on referendums in the UK issued by the House of Lords in 2010, following testimony by dozens of experts, explicitly recommended that "there should be a general presumption against the use of turnout thresholds and supermajorities."[26] Experts testified that supermajorities were undemocratic, a violation of the one-person-one-vote principle, and essentially alien to British democracy, which does not use supermajorities in Parliament or in other elections. To hold a referendum with a supermajority requirement would have broken with tradition, and probably would have been viewed as manipulative by those opposed to the EU. Such a referendum might not have put the issue to rest for a generation, as the prime minister hoped.

The issue of holding two referendums—the first on the basic idea of exit and the second on a specific plan—was actually on the table.[27] In June 2015, Dominic Cummings (the mastermind of the Vote Leave campaign) posted a long entry on his blog speculating about the possibility of a "double referendum," focusing on what he saw as the pros and cons from each side's perspective (Leavers might benefit because it would be easier for voters to cast a "protest" vote in the first round, knowing they could say no in the second round; Remainers might benefit from having two chances to stop the exit).[28] The issue was taken up by prominent Tories, including London mayor Boris Johnson, but in October 2015, an aide speaking for the prime minister shot down the idea:

> Some of those advocating "leave" are suggesting that the referendum is just the first half and that if the majority of the UK public voted to leave, then the UK government would have a stronger hand to embark on a second negotiation with the rest of the EU and hold a second referendum. The prime minister is clear that is simply not going to happen.[29]

It is hard not to conclude that Cameron expected to put the issue to rest with a single vote, and did not want to jeopardize the prospects of victory in the first round by holding out the possibility of a do-over. The main reason for a single referendum on a broad question, then, appears to be the government's wish to maximize its prospect of winning on June 2016; the possibility of what would happen if the government lost does not seem to have been a factor.

In this sense, then, the problems with Brexit can be attributed more to elected officials than to the voters. The politicians structured the vote in a way that created downstream problems, not because the structure was democratically desirable but because it served their short-term political aims.

———

Any analysis of direct democracy requires some sort of reckoning with Proposition 13 and Brexit, as two landmarks in the history of referendums. This chapter tells their story in some detail, in a way that I hope is largely free of the rhetorical gloss that usually accompanies them and creates obstacles for an objective assessment. However, because these are such exceptional cases, we should be careful about generalizing from them. Indeed, one message of the book is that we need to look at direct democracy from a broad perspective, and not draw general conclusions from a handful of specific cases.

The next chapter begins the process of making some general statements about direct democracy. While I use these two prominent referendums to motivate some tentative principles about what works and why, I also "test" those notions by examining the broader historical experience using data from the United States and the sizable published research literature.

13

Potential Benefits of Referendums

DIRECT DEMOCRACY SOUNDS GOOD; it appeals to our basic human aspirations for autonomy and self-determination. But an assessment needs to go beyond that—well beyond. We need to understand not only how direct democracy empowers the people, but also how its effects propagate across the political system and alter the behavior of elected officials, bureaucrats, judges, voters, and interest groups. This chapter walks through the potential benefits of direct democracy; subsequent chapters explore potential drawbacks.

#1: Allows the People to Choose the Policy They Want

The most obvious benefit of direct democracy, of course, is that it allows the people to choose the policy they want. Without direct democracy, government officials choose the policy *they* want. Government officials might make different choices than the people would make because they misunderstand citizen preferences, what I would call "honest mistakes"; because they prefer a different policy; or because they are unduly influenced by special interests. By eliminating the middlemen, a referendum avoids the risk of a policy that the people dislike.[1]

California's tax revolt in the late 1970s is a good illustration. It is unlikely that the governor or legislature would have cut taxes as much as Proposition 13 did, or would have agreed to limit their future spending authority as Proposition 9 did. They may have gotten around to approving some sort of tax relief eventually, but their actions over the preceding 10 years suggest it would have been modest. Brexit illustrates the point as well; the outcome was not what a majority of members of Parliament would have preferred. That the two referendums produced what most consider right-wing outcomes is coincidental; as discussed earlier, referendums just as often lead to left-wing policies, such as minimum-wage increases and marijuana legalization (as well as tax *increases* in California—more on that below).

The potential impact of letting the people choose is larger for initiatives and mandatory referendums than advisory referendums. In advisory referendums, sitting officials choose the menu of options, and they may or may not give voters meaningful choices. Mandatory referendums, which force the government to seek approval for certain actions, allow the people to impose their preferences on issues raised by the government. Initiatives allow citizens not only to choose between alternatives on the ballot, but also to select the alternatives to be decided; the people's choices are no longer tied to the agenda of sitting government officials.

The option to overrule the choices of government officials is most valuable when the government otherwise would pursue policies not favored by the public. Government can be pulled away from the public interest by pressure from powerful interest groups, such as business organizations and public employee unions. This appeared to be a factor in the California tax revolt, where the legislature's failure to deliver commonsense tax reform was due in part to the political power of public employee unions, state and local government workers, and major corporations.

Government can also be sidetracked from the public interest when elected officials have personal interests at stake in a policy decision. A prime example is legislator term limits, which a large majority of the public supports, but most legislators oppose—not surprisingly, because it limits their career options. Of the 24 states that allow initiatives, 21 have adopted legislator term limits, while only 2 of the 26 noninitiative states have done the same—a stark example of the power of the initiative in cases where public and government interests diverge. Legislator compensation, ethics rules, and matters related to elections fall into the same category.

Allowing the people to choose the policy they want may be particularly valuable when political parties are highly polarized, as in the United States over the past decade. With the extinction of moderate legislators, policy outcomes are driven to one of the polar extremes. Policies move to the left when the left-wing party is in control, and jump to the right when the right-wing party is in control, as happened when the Democratic Obama administration gave way to the Republican Trump administration in 2017. To the extent that citizens are more centrist than the parties (as opinion surveys suggest they are), polarization is likely to create a disconnection between policies and the public's preferences. Letting citizens choose can exert a moderating effect on policy choices.

#2: Allows the People to Communicate Their Preferences to Government Officials

Recall that in the decade before Proposition 13, voters had rejected three previous tax-cutting measures that were, if anything, more moderate, and they elected candidates from both parties who were opposed to tax cuts. Politicians at the time would have been justified in drawing the conclusion that voters did not have an appetite for large tax cuts. Proposition 13, however, revealed that public opinion had undergone a swift and sharp transformation. Based on this new information, the governor and legislature quickly adopted a more fiscally conservative posture. It might have taken the political class much longer to detect and act on the shift in public opinion without Proposition 13. A second benefit of direct democracy, then, is allowing the people to communicate their preferences to their representatives.

Of course, the people have other ways to communicate their preferences. Referendums turn out to have some advantages over those alternatives.

One way voters can signal their policy preferences is through candidate elections, by voting in politicians who support policies they like, and voting out opponents of those policies. The problem is that since candidates take positions on multiple issues, a vote for a candidate might indicate support for some but not necessarily all of the candidate's positions; it isn't clear what a voter thinks about any particular issue based on his or her candidate choice. Moreover, sometimes candidate elections do not even present voters with an option that expresses their position. The day Proposition 13 was on the ballot, Californians were also voting in the gubernatorial primary. The Democratic primary had one candidate (incumbent Governor Brown) who opposed the initiative, leaving Democrats no way to express support for tax cuts. Similarly, in the UK parliamentary election immediately before Brexit, neither major party supported leaving the EU. In order to signal a desire to leave, a voter had to support the UKIP, implicitly endorsing the rest of its right-wing agenda. There was no appealing option for a person who wanted to communicate a preference for left-wing policies *and* for exiting the EU.

Another way to gauge voter preferences is through opinion surveys. Opinion surveys are invaluable tools for capturing public opinion, and their practice has been honed by decades of scientific research, but they have their limitations. For one thing, polling accuracy depends on having a representative sample, and determining which subpopulations will turn out to vote and need to be included is never clear-cut. Brexit is an illustration. While pre-election polls indicated a tight race, most showed a majority in favor of remaining in the EU. The polling was so one-sided in this respect that betting markets the day before the election gave exit only a 20 percent chance of winning.[2]

Another, more fundamental challenge with opinion polls is that respondents may be uninformed about an issue and lack incentives to spend time figuring out their true views when responding to a pollster. "Voters may say one thing to pollsters when they know what they say will not have any real-life consequences, but they may well say another at the end of a serious referendum campaign, when they know that the outcome will control what the government does or refrains from doing," observed one study comparing referendum voting to opinion polls.[3]

In contrast, referendum elections are more likely to reflect the informed sense of the electorate. A referendum election is preceded by a campaign in which competing interests make their case to the voters through advertising and other forms of outreach; and citizens have the opportunity to talk with family, friends, and coworkers; learn from online discussions, social media, talk radio, and television; and hear the opinions of experts. This leads to a more informed population than the one that responds to an (off-election) opinion poll.

It is well established that election campaigns produce information that changes opinions. Figure 13.1 provides an illustration, showing public opinion on nine California propositions in September (poll), October (poll), and November (election outcome) 2016.[4] Voter opinion did not change much for some propositions, typically issues that were already familiar, such as Proposition 55 that extended a temporary income tax increase, and Proposition 62 that proposed to repeal the death penalty. For other propositions, involving issues that were unfamiliar to voters before the campaign, opinion shifted significantly during the campaign.

A dramatic example was Proposition 61, which required the state to pay no more for prescription drugs than the price paid by the federal government. The September poll, before the campaign had begun in earnest, showed 76 percent in favor, presumably based on the appeal of the simple idea of controlling costs. But during the expensive campaign ($20 million by the "yes" side and $111 million by the opposition), voters learned that the initiative's effects were uncertain—it could conceivably even increase prices for many people—and that almost all major groups in the state were opposed to the proposition, including both Democratic and Republican groups, labor unions, the chamber of commerce, and most of the newspapers. Support melted away to 47 percent on election day. Two of the nine propositions (61 and 62) swung from overall approval to failure on election

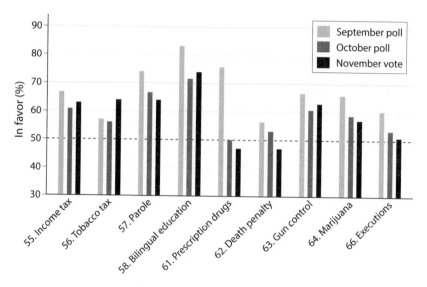

FIGURE 13.1. Evolution of support for California propositions during 2016 campaign

day, and the average swing from September to November was 10 percent.[5] In short, the responses people give to a pollster on an issue they haven't thought about is an unreliable measure of what they think once they have become informed.

All of this helps explain why a referendum can communicate information about voter preferences better than an opinion poll. It also suggests that the effect of referendums goes beyond the laws they approve or reject—the information they produce can influence the behavior of political actors long after the election is over. Recent political science research demonstrates exactly this behavior, showing that members of Congress and state legislators change their roll-call votes to better conform with constituent preferences once they are revealed in referendum elections.[6]

#3: Allows the People to Change Policy without Changing Their Representatives

We don't need referendums—goes a common argument—because if the people don't like the policies chosen by the incumbents, they can just vote them out of office. While there is something to this argument, it actually points to another benefit of direct democracy: it allows voters to change policy *without having to change their representatives.*

Elected officials perform a variety of duties. In addition to creating laws and regulations, they oversee government bureaucracies; provide constituent services (such as intervening with bureaucrats); and serve as ambassadors for their cities, states, and nations; among other things. Some representatives might do an excellent job performing these duties, and voters might not want to remove them over disagreement on a single issue. Without direct democracy, the only way to change policy is to replace the representatives. With direct democracy, voters can adopt policies they prefer without having to cut loose a public official they otherwise admire—what might be called "unbundling" the issue.[7]

Proposition 13 provides an example. California voters liked Governor Jerry Brown. He wasn't a "typical politician," scored high on imagination and "bringing new ideas to government," and the glamor of his romance with pop singer Linda Ronstadt didn't hurt.[8] He was considered a shoo-in for re-election in 1978, and expected to run for president in 1980. But in staking out a firm position against the tax cuts in Proposition 13, he was completely out of step with voters. Once Proposition 13 passed, giving voters the tax relief they desperately wanted, they were spared the tough decision of whether to remove Brown and he was re-elected in a landslide, capturing 56 percent of the vote. If the initiative process had not been available, Californians would have faced the unpalatable choice of either removing Brown from office or continuing to endure high taxes. Proposition 13 allowed them to sail around this Scylla and Charybdis.

In parliamentary systems, when facing a question of national importance, the parliament can dissolve itself and call a "snap election" to seek a vote of confidence from the people. This is similar to a referendum, except that instead of voting directly on the question, voters are asked to vote for parties based on their positions on the question. This has the drawback that voters may end up replacing a government they like in most respects in order to bring about change on a single issue. Countries with parliamentary systems can avoid going down this path by calling a national referendum on the question instead, in effect unbundling the issue from parliamentary elections.

#4: Reduces Side Deals and Corruption in Policy Making

The next benefit is not widely recognized, and requires a bit more explanation. Two more tax-related episodes from California help bring out the main ideas.

Like the rest of the country, California struggled to stabilize its public finances after the financial crisis of 2007–8. After general fund revenue plunged from $100 billion in 2007 to $85 billion in 2008, GOP governor and former action-movie star Arnold Schwarzenegger and the Democratic-controlled legislature faced a $20 billion shortfall in the upcoming budget. The state's balanced-budget rule prohibited deficit financing, and the constitution required a two-thirds majority to pass a budget, giving the minority Republican legislators a veto on any plan. Predictably, Democrats and their allies (teachers and government workers) called for income tax increases to plug the hole, while Republicans and their allies (business interests and taxpayer groups) wanted spending cuts. Before they finally struck a deal, 85 days after the constitutionally mandated budget deadline, the state had furloughed workers, paid its bills with IOUs, and watched its debt rating fall from A− to BBB. The deal split the difference between the parties by cutting spending and increasing sales and income taxes and vehicle license fees.

To secure the necessary two-thirds votes, Schwarzenegger cut side deals with wavering legislators. Democratic senator Lou Correa got an additional $70 million per year distributed to local governments in Orange County that he represented. Moderate Republican senator Abel Maldonado got a constitutional amendment on the ballot to create on open primary, which he hoped would help him attract independent voters when he ran for statewide office. Republican senator Roy Ashburn got a $10,000 tax credit for new home buyers. Some said other legislators were promised appointment to cushy state boards.[9]

There was an immediate outcry against the deal. Democratic groups objected to the spending cuts, Republican groups objected to the tax increases, and everyone seemed to find the process itself distasteful. One assembly member called it "blackmail, extortion, skullduggery. If any integrity is left in this house we should send it back."[10] Republicans in both the assembly and senate sacked their leaders who had signed onto the deal. Los Angeles talk-radio personalities John Kobylt and Ken Chiampou, whose show reached one million listeners every afternoon, hammered the deal day after day and launched a "heads on a stick" campaign to recall three legislators who had "caved" on taxes. Former assembly leader Mike Villines was defeated in a run for state office, becoming a lobbyist; former senate leader Dave Cogdill ended up in a minor local government position; and Maldonado lost his campaigns in 2006, 2010, 2012, and 2014.[11]

The story was different in 2011, when the state once again faced a projected deficit, this time of $27 billion. Again, Democrats and their allies argued for tax increases while Republicans and their allies argued for spending cuts. The governor this time was Jerry Brown, who had been re-elected in 2010, 22 years after the end of his previous term. Democrats still had majorities in both chambers, but the two-thirds requirement to pass a budget had been repealed by voters in 2010, so Republicans had little leverage.[12]

While Democratic control of the government made a tax increase seem likely, events transpired in a different and surprising way. During his campaign in 2010, candidate Brown had promised "no new taxes without voter approval."[13] Brown made it clear that he personally favored a tax increase to plug the budget hole, but stuck to his promise that the people would have to sign on it. Instead of trying to work a tax increase through the legislature, he qualified an initiative for the ballot, Proposition 30, that proposed temporary income and sales tax increases. Brown declared that without these tax increases, the deficit would have to be closed entirely with spending cuts—and it was up to the voters to make the choice. The campaign over Proposition 30 was fiercely contested, and intensified by the introduction of a competing measure that proposed even larger tax increases. More than $100 million was spent by the contending sides. In November 2012, voters approved the governor's initiative by a comfortable margin of 55 to 45 percent.

A proverbial deafening silence followed. While the losers were unhappy, there were no recall campaigns, organized protests, or "heads on sticks." The referendum election appeared to settle the matter, and everyone went about their business.

What explains the different public reaction to higher taxes? The tax increase imposed by Governor Schwarzenegger and the legislature in 2008 had the whiff of corruption from its side deals to buy legislator votes. In contrast, there were no side deals involved in the tax increase that the voters imposed on themselves with Proposition 30. Referendums have the benefit of avoiding the side deals, and sometimes outright corruption, that are part of the legislative process. There is no practical way to deliver personalized favors to an electorate of 10 million people.

Side deals are part of the routine business of every legislature, and they can help the public if legislators hold out for public-minded reasons and the accommodations make the law better.[14] The problem is when side deals distort policy decisions away from what is in the public interest. If a legislator gains a pork-barrel project just to curry favor with his or her constituents, the public loses because it has to pay for a project that wasn't needed.[15] If a legislator gains appointment to a public office personally or for a family member, the public loses because the position is not filled by the most qualified candidate. Moreover, when policy making takes place in an environment of side deals, it undermines public confidence in government and fuels suspicion that government works for special interests rather than the people. Referendums skirt these complications entirely by replacing the legislative process with a simple vote of the people.

#5: Helps to "Settle" Policy Disputes

Some amount of conflict is inevitable in any society; people have different interests, values, and information about alternative courses of action. Direct democracy allows issues to be settled in an orderly way, after a free exchange of information, bringing closure to disputes. The idea of bringing closure to an issue is closely connected to the concept of *legitimacy*, something that is important but challenging to define and measure, and not well understood by social scientists. Keeping in mind the speculative nature of this concept, there is some reason to believe that direct democracy may enhance the perceived legitimacy of policy decisions.

Consider Brexit. Obviously, the referendum did not settle or bring closure to the issue—the previous chapter discusses why this was the case—but it provides an illustration of how the public views referendum outcomes in terms of legitimacy. Figure 13.2 shows public opinion on leaving the EU at the time of the referendum and one year later.[16] The interesting point is that half of the people who had voted to remain believed, one year later, that the country should exit. Counting these so-called "re-leavers" brought the postelection exit majority to 68 percent. Re-leavers still preferred to remain in the EU, but felt an obligation to abide by the majority view: "As deeply sad as it makes me, I feel they [the government] have a duty to take us out of the EU to address public anger at perceived inequality. We do not want to end up with a Trump. We ignore the people who voted to leave at our peril." Another said that overturning the referendum would "be seen as undemocratic."[17]

The re-leavers seemed to believe in abiding by democratic outcomes, even one they didn't agree with. This behavior is consonant with more rigorous social science research indicating that people consider decisions reached by referendum to be more legitimate than decisions by elected representatives.[18] To be sure, some citizens on the losing side may have *lost* confidence in democracy after the election, but it seems likely that if Parliament had swiftly implemented Brexit and taken the country out of the EU, a large majority of the population would have considered it a legitimate policy outcome.

Public opinion on California's Proposition 13 followed a similar path. The initiative passed with a large majority; one month later an opinion survey found

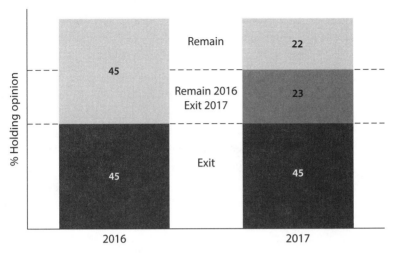

FIGURE 13.2. Changing public opinion on leaving EU

that among those who voted against the initiative, 14 percent had changed their minds and were now in favor.[19] The history of California tax increases after the Great Recession points in the same direction. The first tax increase, in 2008, was pushed through the legislature with a package of special deals for wavering legislators and set off a storm of protests for about a year. The second tax increase, in 2010, was achieved through an initiative, and was accepted by the public with little controversy once the votes were counted.

A comparison of abortion law in the United States and Italy, discussed in the introduction, offers another example. Both countries legalized abortion in the 1970s under similar formulas: always permitted in the first trimester, sometimes in the second trimester, and rarely in the third trimester. The United States did it through a Supreme Court ruling, while Italy did it through a referendum. In the United States, the issue has been fiercely contested for half a century and remains at the center of politics; in Italy the issue appears to have been settled, and has moved to the periphery of politics.

Some Americans see their country's ceaseless turmoil over abortion as unavoidable, an inevitable by-product of the emotional nature of the issue. But to observers outside the United States, with the examples of other countries in mind, it was a self-inflicted wound caused by the way the policy was decided. The *Economist* summarized it this way:

Why does abortion remain so much more controversial in America than in the other countries that have legalized it? The fundamental reason is the way

Americans went about legalization. European countries did so through legislation and, occasionally, referenda. This allowed abortion opponents to vent their objections and legislators to adjust the rules to local tastes. Above all, it gave legalization the legitimacy of majority support. . . . America went down the alternative route of declaring abortion a constitutional right.[20]

Direct democracy's ability to legitimize a public decision, at least as suggested by these examples, has the potential to make policy more stable over time. Referendums might increase stability by building a sizable public consensus around the chosen course of action. When a legislature determines policy, especially if the vote is close, the losers might see a path to reversing the outcome if they can switch control of a few seats, giving them an incentive to stir up their partisans to tip control in a few key races. In contrast, if a law is approved by referendum, reversing the outcome requires changing the minds of millions of voters, a much bigger hill to climb.

On the other hand, referendums could make policy less stable because they avoid the multiple procedural gates through which ordinary legislation must pass to become law: in the United States, approval by two legislative bodies and concurrence by the executive. Collectively, these hurdles make change difficult and create "gridlock" that immobilizes policy. In the United States, policies at the federal level can be sustained long after they have lost their popular support if a faction gains control of a key gatekeeper; a notorious example was the ability of white supremacists in the South to block civil rights measures for decades because they had enough votes in the Senate to filibuster reform measures.[21]

In any case, it is debatable how much policy stability would be "optimal." Too much policy change impedes businesses and individuals from making plans and investment decisions. Too little policy change strangles innovation and prolongs anachronistic laws. Casual observation suggests that policy stability is not all that different under direct compared to representative democracy, so this might be a secondary consideration in the end. The legitimacy benefit of direct democracy, then, is not so much in stabilizing policy as in reducing dissension and conflict regarding policy decisions that have been made.

———

Three other potential benefits of direct democracy are worth mentioning. I have left them for last because I view them as less central for the argument.

#6: Utilizes a Wide Pool of Information

When a legislature makes a policy decision, it draws on the information and knowledge of its members, their aides, expert witnesses, and lobbyists, a group that typically numbers in the hundreds at most. When an agency makes a decision, the number of people may be even smaller, and when a court decides, smaller still. A referendum election, in contrast, can involve millions of people, drawing on a much wider pool of knowledge and information. The ability to utilize a wider pool of information constitutes another advantage of direct democracy.

There are two ways a dispersed pool of information can improve public decisions. One is through information aggregation: to the extent that each person makes errors when forming an opinion on an issue, these errors tend to cancel out in the aggregate through what statisticians call the "law of large numbers." This property of elections was first noted by a French political scientist in the eighteenth century, and in his honor is named the Condorcet jury theorem; more colloquially, we call it the "wisdom of crowds."[22] The second advantage of a wide pool of information is that it increases the chance that important pieces of information will be recognized and taken into consideration, and reduces the risk of groupthink by technical experts. Josiah Ober, a leading classical historian, attributes the flourishing of ancient Athens to the ability of its direct democracy "to make effective use of knowledge dispersed across a large and diverse population," calling its "superior organization of knowledge" the "key differentiator that allowed the community to compete effectively against its rivals."[23]

#7: Leads to More Citizen Trust and Engagement

By bringing policies into alignment with citizen preferences, direct democracy should increase trust in government.[24] We can assess this potential benefit by comparing trust in initiative and noninitiative states, using data from a 2014 Gallup poll that asked citizens, "How much trust and confidence do you have in the government of the state where you live when it comes to handling state problems—a great deal, a fair amount, not very much, or none at all?"[25]

For the sample as a whole, 58 percent of citizens had a great deal or fair amount of trust and 42 percent had not very much or no trust in their state government—but trust (great deal or fair amount) was higher in initiative states, 61 percent, compared with noninitiative states, 56 percent.[26] While this comparison does not control for a host of other factors that might influence trust in state government, it is nonetheless interesting as a descriptive fact that citizens living in initiative states were about 5 percent more trusting than citizens living in noninitiative states.

A related potential benefit of direct democracy is what has been called "educative effects": by participating directly in policy decisions, citizens become more educated and knowledgeable about government and society, and more inclined to participate. This idea goes back to the Progressive Era:

> Where the initiative and referendum do not exist, the people have little encouragement to devote time and effort to the study of public questions, for, even if they desired, they have no power to change laws or conditions. Therefore, chief among the advantages of the initiative and referendum is the unlimited field afforded for individual and community development.[27]

While the mechanism by which democracy influences voter information and engagement is straightforward, measuring the size of the effect is not. A fair amount of evidence indicates that ballot propositions increase turnout by a few percentage points. The scholarly literature on voter information is less conclusive; most evidence points to modest increases but some finds no effects.[28]

#8: Increases Policy Competition, Innovation, and Responsiveness

This final benefit applies only to the initiative process. In a purely representative democracy, only policies proposed by legislators and other government officials come to a vote. The initiative allows ordinary citizens to make proposals as well. In this sense, direct democracy introduces competition into politics, breaking the legislature's monopoly over the policy agenda. Political competition, broadly defined, has long been seen as important for making policy responsive and innovative, but most attention has been focused on the competitiveness of candidate elections. The initiative process allows ordinary citizens who might not want to hold elective office to develop new policies and bring them to a vote of the electorate.

The city of Seattle's decision to provide "democracy vouchers" is a good example. In a 2011 *New York Times* op-ed piece, Harvard professor Larry Lessig, frustrated with the dominance of corporate money in campaign finance, proposed giving each American a $50 voucher that could be contributed to a political campaign, resuscitating an idea that had been around for decades.[29] Lessig's column caught the eye of Alan Durning, founder of a sustainability think tank in Seattle. Durning helped draft and qualify an initiative that proposed to mail each resident four $25 vouchers before each election, which residents could then distribute to candidates of their choice, as long as the candidates agreed not to accept cash donations above $250, with the program funded by a property tax increase. In November 2015, voters approved his initiative I-122 with 63 percent in favor, and the program received national attention when it was rolled out in 2017.[30]

The ordinary citizens like Durning who formulate and advance policy proposals are in effect "policy entrepreneurs." They create new policy ideas and offer them to the political marketplace, where voters can "buy" them or take a pass. Other prominent examples are Howard Jarvis, the sponsor and leading proponent of Proposition 13; Douglas Bruce, a property manager and real estate investor who wrote Colorado's tax-limiting Taxpayer Bill of Rights (TABOR); Ward Connerly, a businessman and University of California regent who promoted a series of successful initiatives banning racial preferences in the 1990s and early 2000s; Tim Eyman, a conservative activist in Washington, who has placed more than 20 initiatives on the ballot; and Tom Steyer, a progressive hedge-fund manager in San Francisco, who supported an initiative closing a tax loophole exploited by corporations. Policy entrepreneurship also comes from organized interest groups, like labor unions, environmental organizations, and taxpayer groups, and animal rights groups have been quite successful in the twenty-first century in promoting initiatives that improve living conditions for farm animals.[31]

———

Table 13.1 summarizes the potential benefits from direct democracy. It is important to underscore that the potential benefits have not been justified because they would bring about specific policy outcomes; I am not arguing that direct democracy is beneficial because it leads to (say) lower taxes or more liberal social policies. One reason for taking this position is that direct democracy does not have an ideological policy bias; it is simply a tool that brings policy into alignment with majority opinion. The other reason is a normative belief that institutions ought to be chosen in order to advance democratic principles, in this case the principle of rule by the people, rather than to deliver short-run policy outcomes (more on this later).

TABLE 13.1 Benefits of Direct Democracy

Benefit	Shorthand	Description
1	Deciding	Allows the people to choose the policy they want
2	Communication	Allows the people to communicate their preferences to government officials
3	Unbundling	Allows the people to change policy without changing their representatives
4	No deals	Reduces side deals and corruption in policy making
5	Closure	Helps to settle policy disputes
6	Information	Utilizes a wide pool of information
7	Trust	Enhances citizen trust and engagement
8	Competition	Allows policy entrepreneurship

This chapter focuses on the benefits of direct democracy, but as Brexit suggests, things can also go wrong. There are three important issues that might give us pause about using direct democracy more widely. The first issue is at the very heart of direct democracy: How confident are we that ordinary people will make informed and reasonable decisions? The second relates to interest groups: What is the risk that wealthy and organized groups will use referendums to bias policies in their favor? And the third concerns minority rights: How much of a threat does majority rule pose to the fundamental rights of minority groups? The next three chapters address these issues, one by one. Because of the centrality of these questions for any assessment of direct democracy, they have received a great deal of attention in the scholarly literature, and we can ground the assessment in a healthy body of empirical research.

14

Are Voters Up to the Task?

VOTING IS surprisingly complicated. A typical ballot asks voters to weigh in on headline races like president, governor, and US senator, but also umpteen other issues. They must choose a long list of representatives—state officials such as lieutenant governor, attorney general, secretary of state, treasurer, controller, and legislators, and local officials such as mayor, county commissioner, city council member, sheriff, and school board members. They also vote on judges—Supreme Court, court of appeals, superior courts. Finally, there are ballot measures, also at the state, county, and city levels. Clearly, no one is going to have deep knowledge about each and every one of these elections. In a democratic society, it seems only right for the people to take part in these decisions, but the complexity of the task does create nagging doubts about the quality of government that is going to result. This is especially true for direct democracy, where voters are not delegating to representatives but making the final decisions themselves. Are voters willing to invest the time and energy to become sufficiently knowledgeable and informed? Are they capable of putting aside selfish and emotional concerns and looking to the common good? In short, are voters up to the task of making important public decisions?

At first glance, there is reason for pessimism. Political scientists have amassed copious evidence that ordinary people have fragmentary information about the details of government, politics, and policy. Survey research consistently reveals that citizens struggle to answer factual questions such as the name of their member of Congress or Supreme Court justices, and they cannot identify issue positions of prominent public figures.[1] Voters often complain about the complexity of ballot propositions and describe them as confusing. To direct democracy skeptics, the conclusion is obvious: "Voters possess neither the knowledge nor the expertise to understand and evaluate the measures on which they are voting."[2]

Similar negative assessments flourished after the UK's Brexit vote in 2016. News stories proliferated about "leavers" not understanding what their vote meant, claiming they didn't really want to leave and were just blowing off steam, or had only voted Leave because they assumed that Remain would win. That Google searches for "What is the EU?" spiked immediately after the vote is evidence in the eyes of skeptics that voters did not understand what they were voting for.

Yet, despite what appear to be unpromising ingredients, scholars of voting behavior have generally found that voting displays a much higher degree of rationality than one might expect, and voting outcomes in aggregate look more coherent than a focus on individuals suggests. Indeed, the historical experience with democratic self-government in the United States seems to confirm that voters are somehow able to overcome their limitations and make good choices in the voting booth. Concerns over voter competence should not be dismissed, but they are not as self-evident or as severe as they might first appear.

This chapter shows how this surprisingly positive conclusion about the possibility of enlightened self-government can emerge from unpromising raw materials. Information shortcuts, the power of aggregation, and the structure of ballot measures allow a mass electorate with limited information on an individual basis to make coherent and informed public decisions.

When Is a Vote "Competent"?

To evaluate voter competence, we must first specify what we mean by a "competent" vote.[3] We need a definition that allows for the possibility that competent people can disagree: it would be pointless to adopt a definition that, in effect, classified those votes that agree with us as competent and the rest as incompetent.[4] Democracy is predicated on the assumption that reasonable people can disagree over policy. At the same time, our definition must allow for the possibility that decisions can be misguided; we might disagree because some of us are mistaken.

To arrive at a definition, it is useful to draw a distinction between a person's *values and interests* and the person's *information*. Values are ethical and philosophical beliefs and interests are personal stakes in a situation. Information is data—facts about the world that pertain to the effects of a proposed policy. A person uses information to evaluate the consequences of alternative policies, favoring the policy that best advances his or her values and interests. In this framework, individuals can disagree about the merits of a policy because they have different information or because they have different values (or both). For example, a person's view on whether to use capital punishment may depend on *information* such as whether it has a deterrent effect on crime and how much it costs to execute a convicted criminal, and also on *values* such as his or her views on the sanctity of life and whether retribution is a just reason for punishment. People can disagree about a policy even if they have the same information, if they have different values.

With this in mind, we can now define: *a vote is competent if it advances a person's values and interests, based on the best information that is available.* A person's vote would not be competent if it was in support of policy X when the person would have supported policy Y if aware of information that was known to others at the time. This definition does not judge a person's values and interests, as those are matters of individual discretion; it only judges whether a person's vote is effective in advancing those values and interests. If campaign advertising routinely misled citizens to vote against their own values and interests, then we would say that voting is not competent. Similarly, voting would not be competent by this definition if citizens were driven by passing emotions to cast votes that they later regret. With a working definition of competence, we can now look more closely at when elections will and will not produce competent outcomes.

How Elections Can Be Informative Even if Voters Are Not Informed

A natural strategy for overcoming voter ignorance is to provide voters with more information. This is the motivation for civic campaigns that reach out to voters through candidate forums, town meetings, informative websites, public service advertising, and so on. While not without value, such efforts are unlikely to make much of a dent in the prevalence of uninformed voters. This is because most voters *choose* to be uninformed about political matters, and it is "rational" for them to do so in a benefit/cost sense. The benefit of becoming informed— that the information might lead to a better election outcome—is vanishingly small because of the remote chance that one vote will swing an election, while the cost of acquiring information is substantial, especially for obscure down-ballot races. The resulting state is called "rational ignorance" following the pioneering work of economist Anthony Downs.[5]

Fortunately, there are some surprising ways that elections can be informative without having to sweep away voters' rational ignorance.

Information Shortcuts

While civics textbooks envision people studying the issues in depth before voting, most people base their decisions on advice from informed persons or organizations that they trust, and on signals that reveal underlying tendencies such as a candidate's party affiliation. Such information is widely available—from media outlets, interest groups, community leaders, bloggers, politicians, coworkers, family, and friends. Political scientists refer to these as information "shortcuts," "cues," or "heuristics." As opposed to what might be called "substantive information" pertaining to the details of specific policies and their consequences, information shortcuts are small pieces of information that signal the consequences of a vote without conveying much of the underlying content.[6]

Consider an environmentalist deciding how to vote on the "Preserve Our Forests" initiative. The title is enticing, but the environmentalist is unsure what the proposal would actually do: would it limit timber harvesting, which she would like, or is it actually a deceptively titled proposal that would roll back regulations and untether timber companies?

Now, the environmentalist could try to become substantively informed by reading the hundreds of words of legalese that comprise the law—challenging for anyone without a law degree, expertise in statutory interpretation, and knowledge of forest regulation terminology and practices. Alternatively, the environmentalist can seek an information shortcut, such as the recommendation of the Sierra Club, a major environmental organization. If the Sierra Club shares her values, she can accurately register her pro-environment preferences by following the Sierra Club's recommendation. Similarly, a pro-timber-industry voter can follow the recommendation of the timber industry. (The timber industry's recommendation also provides a shortcut for the environmentalist; she knows to vote *against* that recommendation.)

When the environmentalist follows the Sierra Club's recommendation, she is voting competently (as defined above): her vote is the one she would have chosen if fully informed. However, she is not substantively informed about the proposal; she would not be able to answer detailed questions about it or provide a substantive rationale for her vote.[7]

This way of making decisions—relying on expert advice rather than firsthand knowledge of the underlying trade-offs—is one we use extensively for nonpolitical as well as political matters. With limited time, we cannot afford to become substantive experts whenever we have to make a choice. We buy consumer products or services, for example, after consulting family and friends, Yelp reviews, and evaluations in consumer reports. When we are sick, we do not study published medical research to determine which drug will be most effective; we rely on the advice of our doctor. We would not be able to function in society without information shortcuts—the advice and recommendations of others. The ability to draw on a wealth of informed opinion to help us make decisions allows us to harness vastly more knowledge than if left to our own devices.

Our reliance on information shortcuts is self-evident on reflection. Yet the fact that voters behave this way is vaguely disquieting to some and makes direct democracy an unnecessary evil to others. Why suffer this crude manner of decision making when we could simply leave policy making in the hands of our elected representatives, who could base their decisions on substantive information?

The flaw in this argument is the assumption that our representatives themselves vote based on substantive knowledge, when in fact they also rely on information shortcuts for most of their decisions. This claim might seem exaggerated, but consider that the 114th Congress (2015–16) enacted 329 laws, passed 708 resolutions, and voted on 683 other bills or resolutions that did not end up passing. Some of the votes were ceremonial matters, such as naming a federal building, but others were regulations of considerable complexity such as fixing Medicare reimbursement rates, updating the PATRIOT Act, fast-tracking approval of free-trade agreements, and overhauling the No Child Left Behind law. The DRIVE Act alone, a six-year funding plan for highways, ran almost 500 printed pages.

Obviously, the senators and congress members did not personally read the text of each proposed law or conduct extensive background research before each vote. Nor did the president personally read the text of every law he signed or vetoed. Instead, they all relied on information shortcuts, advice from trusted advisors such as party leaders, key supporters, legal advisors, and interest groups with shared values. The business of lawmaking is too complicated for it to be any other way.

In short, we cannot purge information shortcuts from the policy process simply by delegating to representatives. The difference between lawmaking by citizens and lawmaking by legislators is not a matter of shortcuts versus substantive information, but a matter of which shortcuts are going to be used and who chooses them. Voters can register their preferences effectively using information shortcuts even if they lack detailed substantive knowledge about politics and policy. This is part of the explanation of how elections can be informative even if voters are uninformed.

The Wisdom of Crowds

Another way that elections can accurately register voter preferences, despite those preferences being based on limited information, is through the "law of large numbers" or "wisdom of crowds," discussed in the previous chapter. The idea, to recap, is that if each voter has only a piece of the full set of information, each voter might make a mistake in his or her voting decision, but when all of the votes are added up in an election, the errors in their individual votes tend to cancel out, so the final outcome accurately represents the underlying information.

A large theoretical literature has been developed to identify when aggregation does and does not help overcome information problems. One important limit is that aggregation is effective only when policy differences arise from differences in information.[8] If disagreements are due to differences in values, then eliminating information errors does not get to the root of the problem. Whether to allow driverless cars is an issue about which people might disagree because they have different information about their safety, while disagreements over abortion and capital punishment are probably more dependent on underlying value differences than information differences. For decisions in which disagreement is fundamental and not due to information differences, aggregation can still be useful in clarifying the underlying state of opinion—it accurately reveals the proportion of the population with various values—but it does not help adjudicate the underlying difference in values.

The wisdom of crowds is thus not a panacea for the limited information of voters, but it does provide another tool to chip away at the problem. Vote aggregation and information shortcuts together provide a powerful combo for making elections informative.

Deliberation

A line of scholarly work argues that deliberation is important for making good decisions, and comes down on the side of lawmaking by legislators instead of citizens in order to bring more deliberation into policy decisions. Deliberation here means making decisions based on consideration of alternative views and expert opinion, followed by thoughtful reflection on the available information. Some experimental research suggests that deliberation and discussion can lead to better decisions, but there is also evidence that deliberation can polarize opinions and impede achievement of consensus.[9] Either way, common sense suggests that public decisions can benefit from discussion, and public debate may have collateral value for a democracy in terms of educating the citizenry.

What is less obvious are the twin assumptions that legislatures are rich in deliberation, while referendum elections are not. When it comes to legislatures, the notion of deep and probing floor debate is more the stuff of cinematic imagination than reality today: most legislation is written by party leaders and lobbyists behind closed doors; legislators give floor speeches for the TV cameras, before an empty chamber; and committee hearings are opportunities for advocates to place into the record their predetermined policy views. Legislators may be able to devote more time and attention to consider policies than referendum voters, but instances of a bill emerging from the leadership at the last minute, giving members no time to read it before voting, are not usual. The idea that the legislative process—floor debates, committee hearings, and the like—is a dispassionate and thorough search for truth is more of an aspiration than reality.

Moreover, the notion that referendum elections involve no deliberation or discussion is also questionable. Most ballot measure campaigns extend over months, during which citizens are exposed to contending arguments from the campaigns, mass media, and interest groups. For particularly contentious issues, civic organizations, universities, and media outlets host events in which experts debate and discuss, and the blogosphere provides a rich forum for the exchange of views. Many voters discuss and deliberate with coworkers, family members, and friends. The United Kingdom's Brexit referendum is a good example, where the options were widely discussed, and every voter had a chance to hear the contending arguments. Based on a review of the research, two leading experts on public opinion, Benjamin Page and Robert Shapiro, concluded that the process of "public or collective deliberation" results in the public forming opinions "that are generally stable, coherent, internally consistent, responsive to the available information, and sensible."[10]

———

The bottom line: although voters appear to operate with limited substantive information about government, politics, and policy, this does not necessarily prevent them from voting in a way that reflects their values and interests. In theory, voters can use information shortcuts to manage their information limitations; aggregation through elections can wash out individual-level errors; and exposure to a variety of information sources can serve a deliberative function, allowing citizens to form coherent opinions on public issues. The next question is how well these theoretical possibilities work in practice.

How Accurately Do Voters Express Their Interests?

How do we go about determining whether people do in fact vote their interests in elections? One approach, which sounds almost too simple, is to identify what seem to be a voter's interests, and then examine whether his or her votes in fact advance those interests. A long line of research, much of it in economics, studies candidate elections from this perspective. Economist Sam Peltzman conducted a series of studies estimating to what extent voters reward incumbent politicians for good economic performance and punish them for bad performance. He found that voters punished incumbents for poor economic performance, discriminated between outcomes that were and were not under the politician's control (e.g., governors were punished for bad state performance, but not for nationwide downturns), distinguished between transitory and permanent changes to their welfare, and responded differently to types of spending growth they liked and disliked. Not only did citizens cast votes that appear to process information correctly, according to Peltzman, but "one would be hard put to find nonpolitical markets that process information better than the voting market."[11] Not all researchers would go quite so far, but plenty of other studies report findings with a similar flavor.[12]

While promising, this evidence from candidate elections does not immediately translate to direct democracy elections. Candidate elections offer an excellent information shortcut that is not available in referendum elections—party membership. It could be that citizens vote competently in candidate elections because the party cue is available, but do worse on ballot measures where party cues are not available.

Fortunately, we can also draw on several studies that examine ballot measure voting. By and large, these studies find a strong connection between citizens' interests and their votes on ballot measures. In a study I conducted with economist Matthew Kahn, we looked at county voting patterns on 16 environmental initiatives in California. We found that counties that faced an economic cost from environmental regulation were significantly more likely to vote against pro-environment propositions, and conversely.[13] Other studies have found that citizen votes register their economic interests on growth control, city-county consolidation, and public transit measures, among other issues.[14]

While conceptually simple, studies in this vein share a potentially important limitation: they have to assume that the researcher knows what the voter's interest is. In my study with Kahn, for example, we had to assume that in counties with high employment in forestry and construction, which would have suffered from logging restrictions, it was in voters' interests to oppose forest protection measures. While plausible, we don't have any proof that interests align as we assume. It would be nice to have evidence that does not require the researcher to make assumptions about the voters' interests.

Political scientist Arthur Lupia came up with a clever study that cleverly addressed this limitation. The "laboratory" for Lupia's study was five complicated California insurance propositions in 1988. Frustrated California drivers at the time were paying among the highest auto insurance rates in the country, but the state legislature had failed to provide relief because no plan could run the gauntlet between the insurance industry and the trial lawyers, two special-interest titans of the state capital. The insurance industry wanted to bring down rates by limiting attorney fees and pain-and-suffering awards, which the trial lawyers naturally opposed. Fed up, consumer advocates qualified an initiative (Proposition 103) that mandated across-the-board rate reductions of 20 percent, limited future rate increases, and removed the industry's antitrust exemption. With this industry-unfriendly proposal looming, the insurance industry leapt to action, qualifying three initiatives of its own (Propositions 101, 104, 106) that targeted trial lawyers, and nullified key provisions of Proposition 103. Trial lawyers responded with their own proposal (Proposition 100), a watered-down version of Proposition 103 that contained language nullifying the insurance-industry initiatives.[15]

Voters were left to sort out these five complex and confusing proposals.[16] The text that appeared on the ballot—not particularly helpful—is reported in table 14.1.[17] If ever there was a situation that challenged the ability of voters to understand what they were voting on, this was it. A saving grace is that voters had ample opportunity to hear from the contending groups and receive information shortcuts. Spending on the five initiatives reached $82 million in total, the lion's share by insurers. To put this in perspective, that year's presidential candidates, Republican George H. W. Bush and Democrat Michael Dukakis, spent $80 million and $77 million, respectively, on their campaigns.

Lupia surveyed voters as they left the polls on election day, asking how they voted and what they knew about the insurance measures. Based on their

TABLE 14.1 California Insurance Initiatives, November 1988

100	INSURANCE RATES, REGULATION. INITIATIVE. Reduces good driver rates. Requires automobile, other property/casualty, health insurance rate approval. Adopts anti-price-fixing, anti-discrimination laws. Fiscal Impact: Additional state administrative costs of $10 million in 1988–1989, paid by fees on insurance industry. Possible state revenue loss of $20 million.
101	AUTOMOBILE ACCIDENT CLAIMS AND INSURANCE RATES. INITIATIVE. Reduces automobile insurance rates, limits compensation for non-economic losses for four years. Fiscal Impact: Additional state administrative costs of $2 million in 1988–1989, paid by fees on insurance industry. Possible state revenue loss of $50 million annually for four years.
103	INSURANCE RATES, REGULATION, COMMISSIONER. INITIATIVE. Reduces auto, other property/casualty rates. Requires elected Insurance Commissioner's approval of rates. Prohibits price-fixing, discrimination. Fiscal Impact: Additional state administrative costs of $10 to $15 million in 1988–1989, to be paid by fees on insurance industry. Unknown savings to state and local governments from reduced insurance rates. Gross premium tax reduction of approximately $125 million for first three years offset by required premium tax rate adjustment. Thereafter, possible state revenue loss if rate reductions and discounts continue but gross premium tax if not adjusted.
104	AUTOMOBILE AND OTHER INSURANCE. INITIATIVE. Establishes no-fault insurance for automobile accidents. Reduces rates for two years. Restricts future regulation. Fiscal Impact: Additional state administrative costs of $2.5 million in 1988–1989, paid by fees on insurance industry. Possible state revenue loss of $25 million annually for two years.
106	ATTORNEY FEES LIMIT FOR TORT CLAIMS. INITIATIVE. Limits amount of contingency fees which an attorney may collect in tort cases. Fiscal Impact: Net fiscal effect on state and local governments is unknown.

answers to a series of detailed substantive questions, he classified each voter as substantively "informed" or "uninformed." Based on whether they knew the recommendations of consumer advocate Ralph Nader, the insurance industry, and the trial lawyers, he classified each voter as having a "shortcut" or "no shortcut." Following the definition that a person's vote is competent if "it is the same choice that she would make given the most accurate available information about its consequences," Lupia wanted to see how close the votes of people with shortcuts came to the votes of the substantively informed comparison group.[18]

Figure 14.1 shows the distribution of votes across the five measures according to what voters knew. The baseline group, informed voters (*leftmost bars*), had a clear preference for the two propositions that were most consumer

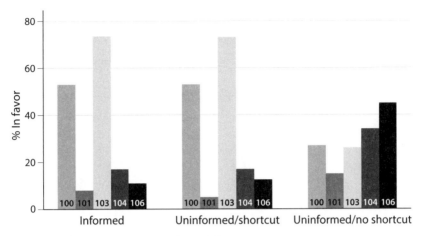

FIGURE 14.1. Votes for California insurance initiatives

friendly, topping out with 74 percent support for Proposition 103. For those who were uninformed and had no shortcut (*rightmost bars*), the pattern was very different. What is striking is the voting pattern of those who were substantively uninformed but had a shortcut (*middle bars*): they were able to mimic the behavior of informed voters.

Information shortcuts were extremely effective for the elections that Lupia studied, and subsequent research has found them effective in other elections, but they do not always work so well.[19] For direct democracy to register preferences accurately, ample and effective shortcuts must be available (or the issue has to be so simple that it doesn't require more information). Lupia and Mathew D. McCubbins attempted to sort out the conditions under which shortcuts allow competent voting, and identified a healthy supply of shortcut providers whose interests are known by voters and competition among shortcut providers as two important factors.[20] These conditions do not always hold, but when they do, information shortcuts can allow for competent voting even in the absence of substantive understanding.

Do Voters Make Irresponsible Fiscal Decisions?

A different criticism leveled at ordinary people is that they lack the judgment and temperament to make important public decisions. Alexander Hamilton opined during the Constitutional Convention that "the people are turbulent and changing: they seldom judge or determine right."[21] This criticism is

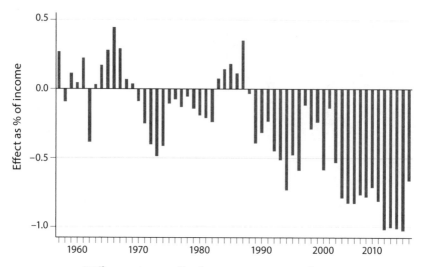

FIGURE 14.2. Difference in spending between initiative and noninitiative states

especially common when it comes to taxes and spending, issues for which voters are accused of being self-centered and short-sighted: given the power to make decisions themselves, it is said, ordinary people will lavish spending on themselves while simultaneously cutting their taxes, failing to appreciate that budgets must balance.

There is a lot of evidence on this question, too, and the message is reassuring. For the most part, when voters have the power to make tax and spending decisions, their policy choices look similar to those made by elected representatives. If anything, voters appear to be a bit more fiscally conservative. To frame the discussion, figure 14.2 shows the year-by-year average difference in spending over the past six decades between American states that allow initiatives and states that do not allow initiatives. Spending is expressed as a percentage of income, so the last bar means that in 2016 initiative states spent on average 0.66 percent less as a fraction of income than noninitiative states. The estimates control for other factors that determine spending, such as population and region.[22]

As this figure shows, in the late 1950s and 1960s initiative states tended to spend more than noninitiative states. The patterned reversed in the 1970s and early 1980s during the tax revolt, when initiative states spent less on average, and reversed again (briefly) in the mid-1980s. But remarkably, starting in 1988, a spending gap opened up that has persisted for 30 years and has widened as the twenty-first century progressed, hovering at about 1 percent of income over the last five years. Considering that state and local spending was about 19 percent of income on average, the gap represents about a 5 percent difference in spending between initiative and noninitiative states. The basic picture, then, is that initiative states generally spent less than noninitiative states over the past half century. The same pattern appears for tax policy: total tax revenue is lower in initiative than noninitiative states. Research on Switzerland going back more than a century also finds a negative relation between initiatives and state (canton) spending.[23]

Far from engaging in reckless spending, initiative states tend to spend slightly less than states run only by legislators. A natural question in regard to this evidence is whether the spending differences are due to direct democracy or whether citizens in initiative states just happen to be more fiscally conservative to begin with. Contrary to the conjecture, several studies of public opinion data have shown that citizen ideology on average is no different in initiative than noninitiative states.[24] The most natural explanation for figure 14.2 is that ordinary citizens are (somewhat) more fiscally conservative than legislators, and when they are allowed a direct say on taxes and spending, they implement more conservative tax and spending policies.[25] Regardless of the explanation, the facts suggest that voters are at least as responsible fiscally as legislators.[26]

Although this discussion has focused on the initiative process, mandatory referendums may be just as important in practice, and their story is similar. Recall that many states and cities require voter approval for tax increases and bond issues. The evidence, almost without exception, shows that mandatory referendums lead to more fiscally conservative outcomes. Economist Lars Feld and I conducted a study in this vein: we compared the spending of Swiss cantons (similar to US states) that required voter approval on new spending programs with cantons in which the legislature could approve new programs on its own and found that cantons requiring referendums spent an eye-popping 19 percent less on average than their nonreferendum peers.[27] Researchers have conducted similar studies in a variety of other contexts—New York school districts, Swiss cities, American states, cross-national samples—invariably reaching a similar conclusion: mandatory referendums on spending reduce spending (by 2 to 19 percent, depending on the context), and mandatory referendums on debt reduce borrowing (by 10 to 25 percent, depending on the context).[28]

A final criticism of giving voters power over fiscal decisions is that they will choose incompatible spending and tax policies. They will approve spending programs without considering costs, and cut taxes without considering how public services will be funded. Nowhere has this claim been made more often than in California, the epicenter of ballot-box budgeting, where pundits routinely accuse the voters of irresponsibly approving initiatives that taken together make the state ungovernable. Voters have misused the initiative process, so the argument goes, by committing the state to fund numerous spending programs while at the same time limiting tax increases, to such an extent that the legislature does not have enough levers to balance the budget. "By 1990, only eight percent of the budget was controlled by the legislature; voters controlled the remainder through the voter initiative process," claimed a leading casebook on the law of democracy in 2007.[29]

This claim, if true, would constitute a powerful indictment of direct democracy, but is it true? A few years ago I spent considerable time trying to track down the source of the "fact" that 92 percent (or 70 percent or 80 percent, the numbers vary depending on the author) of the California budget was earmarked by initiatives. I followed citations back to their sources until the trail went cold—which it always did, usually ending with a journalist attributing the fact to another journalist in a kind of echo chamber.[30] Eventually, I concluded that the only way to get to the bottom of it was to do the calculation myself.

The task is straightforward, although it takes a little work. I reviewed all initiatives ever approved in California (111 when I did the study in 2010), flagged those that had committed the state to spend at least $1 million (there were 20, listed in table 14.2), and then calculated the amount of money committed by each for the 2009–10 fiscal year.[31]

The initiative with by far the largest fiscal impact was Proposition 98 (1988), which locked in $34.66 billion of state spending for education. The next most expensive measure was Proposition 63 (2004) that dedicated $1.752 billion to mental health services. In total, these 20 initiatives locked in $39.4 billion. To put the amount in perspective, total state spending for that year was $119.2 billion, so initiatives locked in about 33 percent of the budget—not very close to 92 percent. And even this 33 percent figure gives an exaggerated sense of the actual constraints placed on the budget because the state would have appropriated most of the money committed to education by Proposition 98 even without the initiative. Without Proposition 98, only 4 percent of the budget was locked in by initiatives.[32]

To round out the picture, I also investigated whether initiatives constrained the revenue side of the budget. I found that they created no barriers to raising the personal income tax and only modestly constrained the state sales tax, by far the two most important revenue sources for state governments (providing 66 percent of state revenue nationwide).[33] Initiatives imposed almost no limits on the five most important revenue sources, and actually increased three of

TABLE 14.2 California Initiatives Committing the State to Spend, 2009–10

Year	Proposition	Description	$ Billion
1988	98	Education	34.660
2004	63	Millionaire surtax for mental-health services	1.752
2002	49	After-school programs	0.550
1998	10	Early childhood development	0.528
2000	21	Juvenile crime (for prisons)	0.449
1994	184	Three strikes and you're out (for prisons)	0.434
1988	99	Tobacco tax (funds for antismoking, wildlife, research)	0.286
2002	50	Water-projects bonds (authorized $3.44 billion)	0.228
2006	84	Water bonds (authorized $5.388 billion)	0.132
1990	116	Rail bonds (authorized $1.99 billion)	0.101
2004	71	Stem-cell-research bonds (authorized $3 billion)	0.092
2004	61	Children's-hospitals bonds (authorized $750 million)	0.070
1990	117	Wildlife protection	0.030
2008	3	Children's-hospitals bonds (authorized $980 million)	0.029
1988	103	Automobile insurance (administrative spending)	0.027
1988	70	Natural-resource-preservation bonds (authorized $776 million)	0.021
1988	97	Cal/OSHA	0.010
1974	9	Political reform (California FPPC administration)	0.004
1990	132	Gill net ban (enforcement spending)	0.002
1986	65	Toxic discharge (enforcement spending)	0.002
Total appropriation by initiatives			**39.407**
Total state expenditures (excluding federal funds)			**119,244.9**

FPPC, Fair Political Practices Commission

them.[34] Initiatives only restricted property taxes (Proposition 13, of course) and death and gift taxes, which together account for only 2.7 percent of state revenue nationwide.

Clearly, the "fact" that only 8 percent of the budget is in the hands of the legislature is incorrect. Voters have used initiatives to constrain the budget in various ways, but overall, they did not make the budget unmanageable.

This review of the evidence on fiscal policy gives little reason to fear that voters are too irresponsible to make tax and spending decisions. If anything, they tend to be slightly more fiscally conservative than their representatives. And if we are worried about myopic fiscal decisions, theory suggests we should be more concerned about elected officials. Legislators have inherently short horizons—their eyes always on the next election—giving them an incentive to fund programs that deliver benefits today and push the costs into the future. A legislator might be tempted to borrow to fund a public project, anticipating that he or she will have moved on to another office by the time the debt comes due and taxes have to be raised to pay for it. It was this sort of behavior, in addition to outright corruption, that contributed to government defaults in the nineteenth century, and led to the introduction of mandatory referendums for borrowing decisions in the states. Ordinary citizens have fewer reasons than legislators to mortgage the future to pay for the present.

Other Reasons for Informed Decision Making in Referendum Elections

Three other features of referendum elections make them amenable to decision making by the general public. First, the choices on a ballot proposition are binary, the voter chooses either *yes* or *no*. This simplifies things considerably because voters do not need to make a comprehensive assessment of the consequences of each proposal—they only need enough information to compare the two options and determine which is relatively better. Making a relative comparison is much less informationally demanding than making absolute assessments, especially since one of the options—voting *no*—is the status quo, which the voter already understands since he or she has been living with it.[35]

Second, while we might hesitate before asking voters to resolve complicated and technical issues, many ballot propositions present fairly simple choices. This is not to say that the underlying issues are trivial or that the implications are minor, but rather that the core issues are not difficult to understand. This is the case for many social issues that have come before the voters in recent years, such as whether to permit same-sex marriage, capital punishment, physician-assisted suicide, or recreational use of marijuana. Many fiscal issues are also easy to understand, such as whether to issue bonds for school buildings and water projects, grant a property tax exemption to veterans who were disabled during military service, exempt food from the sales tax, abolish inheritance taxes, or impose a temporary income tax surcharge on high-income taxpayers. Moreover, direct democracy can be structured precisely to present voters with the sort of issues that hinge on matters of principle more than technical details, something I discuss at length in chapter 18.

And third, voters have a safety valve if they find a ballot measure too confusing: they can just vote *no*. If a proposition fails, policy remains at the status quo; nothing has changed and no harm has been done. Research finds that many voters in fact behave in precisely this way, rejecting proposals that they find too confusing or too technical.[36]

The collection of evidence I have discussed here runs against a recent strand of research, widely reported by the media, claiming that voters are irrationally affected by "irrelevant" events. The most colorful claim is that shark attacks along the coast of New Jersey in 1916 caused people to vote against the incumbent president. Other studies in this vein claim that voters are more likely to support incumbents when the local college football team wins, and turn against incumbents after a tornado, flood, or other natural disaster. Based on this evidence, some argue that voters are fundamentally irrational, and therefore democracy (any form, not just direct) is problematic. This is not the place to engage in depth with that lively literature, but for the reader who is not a political scientist, I would note that the core empirical claims are highly contested (the endnote provides references for the reader who wants to dig deeper). Several papers published in reputable journals by reputable scholars challenge the empirical findings, claiming that they are statistical artifacts, and to my reading, there is something to their argument. Moreover, even if voters can be influenced by irrelevant events, the estimates suggest that the effects are small; the majority of voters appear to behave reasonably on the whole.[37]

———

With so much evidence available that voters are uninformed about basic political and governmental facts—such as the names of their elected representatives and how much money the government spends—anyone proposing that voters make *more* public decisions ought to explain how this could possibly work out well. That is what I have tried to do in this chapter. I explained theoretically how use of information shortcuts and the wisdom of crowds allow voters to accurately register their preferences in elections, and I presented evidence showing that voters generally make sensible and, when it comes to taxes and spending, moderately conservative decisions (relative to elected officials).

Finally, it seems important to keep our concerns about the capabilities of ordinary voters in the proper perspective. We are beyond the point of arguing whether ordinary people can govern themselves. The American people have governed themselves for 250 years with admirable results; and California, the state in which ordinary citizens play the largest direct role in making policy, is a role model in many respects for the sort of prosperous and open society that many around the world aspire to. The competence of voters to make the most fundamental decisions directly was settled more than a century ago by the near-universal practice of requiring popular approval of constitutions. At some point, questions about the competence of voters become questions about self-government itself. The issue, it seems to me, is not so much whether voters are qualified to make important policy decisions, but how to present voters with the questions they are most fit to decide (those concerning core principles and values) while leaving technical matters to the experts—and how to structure referendum elections to best reflect the public's views. I have more to say about this in the chapters that follow.

15

The Challenge of Interest Groups

INTEREST GROUPS ARE a blessing and a curse for democracy. All of us have interests—as consumers, workers, investors, taxpayers, and so on—and banding together to protect those interests is right and proper. Interest groups are the glue that holds democracy together; without them the political system could not incorporate the diverse views of all its members.[1] Yet interest groups can also undermine democracy if they advance their members' interests to the detriment of the general public. The Founders hoped that interest groups would check one another's ambitions, but this only works with evenly balanced competitors; the system breaks down if one group is vastly more powerful than the others. That concern is precisely what animates populism: that concentrations of wealth have created an unfair playing field allowing those with the most resources to bend government decisions for their private benefit.

Interest groups can influence legislators and regulators in several ways. They might "buy" favorable policies with campaign contributions or promises of future employment. They might work to put business executives into government positions regulating their own industries through the "revolving doors" between government and industry. And by lobbying, they might provide information and expertise that steer policies in directions they favor.[2] All of these channels of influence, it should be noted, have something in common: they run through the *representative* parts of democracy—legislators and regulators. This raises the possibility that special-interest influence can be reduced by taking the decisions away from representatives and giving them to the people instead.

That idea has been the driving force behind direct democracy ever since industrialization created great concentrations of wealth and organized interest

groups came to the forefront. In the words of progressive Democratic president
Woodrow Wilson:

> Let us ask ourselves very frankly what it is that needs to be corrected. To sum
> it all up in one sentence, it is the control of politics and of our life by great
> combinations of wealth. . . . [The initiative and referendum] are being pro-
> posed now as a means of bringing our representatives back to the conscious-
> ness that what they are bound in duty and in mere policy to do is to repre-
> sent the sovereign people whom they profess to serve and not the private
> interests which creep into their counsels by way of machine orders and com-
> mittee conferences.[3]

The hope of reformers then and today is that by giving the people a tool to counteract the organizational and resource advantages of interest groups, direct
democracy can restore popular control over policy, reducing democratic drift.

At the same time, there is a contrary argument that direct democracy actually *enhances* the power of interest groups. According to award-winning journalist David Broder:

> The experience with the initiative process at the state level in the last two de-
> cades is that wealthy individuals and special interests—the targets of the
> Populists and Progressives who brought us the initiative a century ago—have
> learned all too well how to subvert the process to their own purposes.[4]

This more pessimistic view stems from a belief that voters can be manipulated
by campaign advertising into supporting the agendas of wealthy interest groups,
to the detriment of their own interests.[5]

What is one to make of these diametrically opposing arguments? Does direct democracy reduce the power of concentrated economic interests or make
them even more influential? This chapter examines data from American history,
both distant and recent, in search of an answer—and finds very little evidence
that business interests thrive when the people make the laws. To the contrary,
business interests seem to fare much better when policy decisions are made
by elected officials.

A Century of Business-Related Propositions

The question to be answered is: Historically, have business groups been able
to use the initiative process to secure laws that help them, or have initiatives been
used to curtail the power of business groups? (I focus on business regulation

because corporations and business groups are the most important interest groups by conventional metrics, such as total spending.)

To answer this question, I assembled a complete list of the 2,609 statewide initiatives that went to a vote from 1904, when the first initiative was decided in Oregon, through 2018. (I use this list repeatedly in this and the next chapter, focusing on initiatives because they are the most high-powered form of direct democracy.) Starting from the complete list, I extracted every initiative that proposed a law targeted at an identifiable industry. I then classified each initiative as likely to have helped or harmed the industry based on examination of the text of the measure, explanations and arguments in voter guides, and media accounts.[6] Three industries attracted the most attention: energy, with 113 initiatives; finance, with 44 initiatives; and tobacco, with 44 initiatives. Common initiative subjects for energy were regulation of nuclear power plants and radioactive waste, regulation of electricity rates, gas taxes, and severance taxes on oil; for finance, usury laws and automobile insurance rates; and for tobacco, cigarette taxes and smoking bans. I start by focusing on these three industries because that is where the preponderance of business-related initiatives are targeted.

Figure 15.1 shows the content of initiatives related to these three industry clusters. The top panel shows the number proposed each year, distinguishing pro-business from anti-business initiatives by symbol. We see, for example, that one pro-business initiative was proposed in 1912, and two anti-business initiatives were proposed in 1914. What immediately jumps out from this figure is the prevalence of anti-business over pro-business initiatives. This pattern is persistent over time, becoming especially pronounced after 1970. The rise in anti-business initiatives in the 1970s is somewhat unexpected because the Supreme Court's *Bellotti* decision in 1978, which removed all limits on initiative campaign spending by corporations, gave corporations complete freedom to fund pro-business proposals. Overall, 82 percent of initiatives related to these three industries were anti-business.

The picture would be less bleak for business interests if it were the case that they managed to defeat the anti-business initiatives while securing passage of the pro-business initiatives. But the lower panel, which shows the number of initiatives that voters approved, reveals that business interests did not fare well on election day: an astounding 96 percent of those initiatives that passed were anti-business. Taking into account election outcomes, we can say that business was better off as a result of an initiative if (1) the proposal was pro-business and (2) it passed. This happened for 1 percent of the initiatives overall, and for literally zero percent of finance and tobacco initiatives. On the other hand,

Proposed

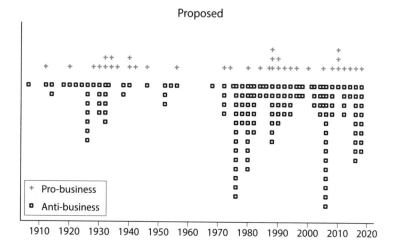

Approved

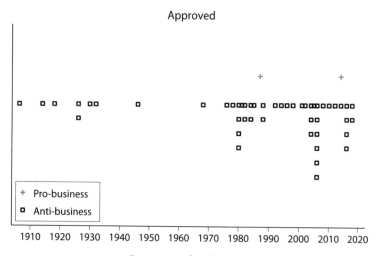

FIGURE 15.1. Business-related initiatives, 1904–2018

anti-business initiatives were approved 24 percent of the time.[7] The idea that the deep pockets of businesses allow them to dominate the initiative agenda, and win passage of favorable laws, is not supported in the historical record. To the contrary, businesses were usually playing defense on initiatives, and almost never managed to secure favorable legislation through the initiative process.[8]

The figure also provides a vivid illustration of the dangers of making inferences from just a few select cases. The bottom panel shows that there were

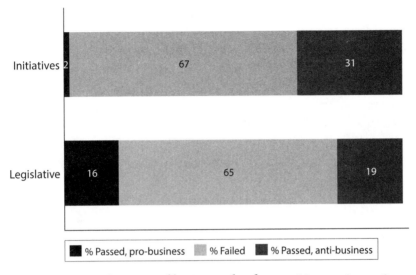

FIGURE 15.2. Outcome of business-related propositions, 1980–2018

indeed two initiatives that resulted in passage of pro-business laws. If one were to focus on those two cases, it might seem that the initiative process is business friendly. But with the entire universe of initiatives laid out before us, we can see that those two cases are not representative; in fact they are exceptions to the general rule of anti-business initiatives.

We can put this evidence in perspective by comparing how business interests fared under proposals that originated from the legislature. Recall that many states require legislators to secure popular approval for their policies, especially when they require amending the state constitution or issuing bonds. To the extent that legislatures are susceptible to interest group pressure, we would expect their proposals to be less threatening to business interests.[9]

To examine this possibility, I collected information on all legislative proposals since 1980 that were on the ballot in states that allow initiatives. I identified legislative proposals related to the energy, finance, and tobacco industries and, as before, classified each proposal as beneficial or harmful to the industry.

Relatively few business-related proposals came from the legislature—only 31 out of 2,018 propositions—in contrast to the 123 business-related initiatives out of a total of 1,293 over the same time period. While the small set of legislative proposals cautions against drawing strong conclusions, the data available show that legislative proposals were pro-business more often than initiatives (29 versus 17 percent). And, as figure 15.2 shows, businesses were also much more successful with legislative proposals: 16 percent of pro-business legislative pro-posals passed, compared with 2 percent of pro-business initiatives, while 19 percent of anti-business legislative proposals passed, compared with 31 percent of anti-business initiatives.

None of this evidence supports the idea that corporations have been able to use the initiative process to advance their interests. To the contrary, business interests were usually on the defensive in initiative campaigns, and more often than not, initiatives produced laws that hamstrung rather than helped businesses. Businesses appeared to fare much better when dealing with the legislature.

Winners and Losers in California 2000–2016

The preceding evidence looked at referendums directly targeted at the energy, finance, and tobacco industries. This leaves out propositions that were targeted at businesses in general, such as a change in the corporate income tax; have in-direct effects, such as a bond issue for public-school facilities that would create business for the construction industry; or pit business groups against one an-other, such as a requirement that electric utilities switch from coal and oil to clean energy sources. It would be difficult to identify all of these consequences simply by reading the text of propositions, but there is an alternative, simpler way to do it: by looking at campaign contributions.

If a business group makes a sizable contribution in support of a proposition, we can infer that the proposed law would help the group, and conversely for a contribution against it. This classification scheme gives us another way to assess whether business generally wins or loses from direct democracy (and although I speak of business interests here, the same approach works for other interest groups such as public employee unions).

The focus here is on California—specifically, the 166 propositions that went to the voters from 2000 to 2016. California law places no limits on contributions to ballot measure campaigns, nor does it limit spending, so contributions in excess of $100,000 are common. Ballot measure committees (essentially all enti-ties that spend money on campaigns) are required to file quarterly reports disclosing all contributions of $100 or more. From these disclosure statements, I collected information on 373,440 distinct contributions—amounting to $3.0 billion in total. (To put this number in perspective, during the same period contributions to candidates for the state assembly and senate totaled $1.3 billion.)[10] The disclosure statements give the name of each contributor,

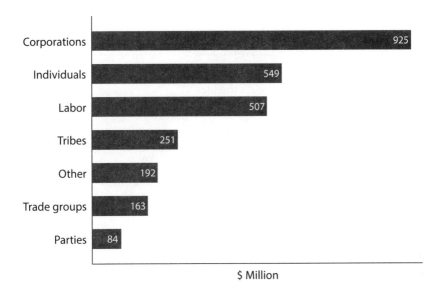

FIGURE 15.3. Large contributions in California, 2000–2016

which I used to assign it to a broad group, such as corporations or labor unions. I focused on persons and organizations that contributed $100,000 or more to a campaign (accounting for 87 percent of the $3 billion total). The question I seek to answer is: Which groups were able to advance their agendas using the initiative process, and which groups were playing defense?

To give a sense of which groups felt their interests were at stake in proposition campaigns, figure 15.3 shows aggregate contributions by type of contributor. The preponderance of large contributions, $925 million in total, came from business corporations. Trade groups, which often represent big business, contributed another $163 million, bringing total business contributions to almost $1.2 billion. Labor (mainly public employees, but also private-sector unions) contributed $507 million—still a sizable amount, but only half of what businesses gave—while Indian tribes contributed $251 million, almost all on a handful of gambling-related propositions. Wealthy individuals were important players as well, contributing $549 million; they crossed the ideological spectrum, with libertarians such as Charles Munger and progressives such as Thomas Steyer. Parties and politicians were minor players, contributing only $84 million.[11]

Before attempting to draw general conclusions, table 15.1 gives more detail on the 20 campaigns that attracted the most contributions. Topping the list was

TABLE 15.1 California Ballot Measures with Largest Total Contributions, 2000–2016

| Proposition | Contributions ($ millions) | | Election |
	Total (% support)	Contributors >$10 million	
Prop 87 (2006) $4 billion for alternative energy, new taxes on gas and oil	154 (39)	Stephen Bing 50*, Chevron 38, Aera Energy 33, Occidental Petroleum 10	F 45–55
Prop 61 (2016) Required state to pay same drug prices as federal government	128 (15)	AIDS Healthcare Foundation 19*	F 47–53
Prop 32 (2012) Prohibited political use of payroll-deducted union dues	107 (33)	CTA 21, Charles Munger 18*	F 43–57
Prop 56 (2016) Increased tobacco tax	103 (31)	Philip Morris 44, R. J. Reynolds 25, Thomas Steyer 12*, CAHHS 10*	A 36–64
Prop 30 (2012) Temporarily increased income and sales taxes	89 (68)	Philip Morris 35, CTA 12*	A 55–45
Prop 8 (2008) Defined marriage as solely between one man and one woman	89 (46)	. . .	A 52–48
Prop 86 (2006) Increased tobacco tax, revenue dedicated to hospitals	83 (20)	R. J. Reynolds 25, CAHHS 11*	F 48–52
Prop 68 (2004) Required tribal gambling to pay a state tax	72 (39)	. . .	F 16–84
Prop 75 (2005) Prohibited political use of payroll-deducted union dues	72 (24)	CTA 12, Alliance for Better California 10*, Council of Service Employees 10	F 47–53
Prop 46 (2014) Increased pain-and-suffering awards	71 (16)	NORCAL Insurance 11, The Doctors Company 11, Coop. American Physicians 10	F 33–67
Prop 79 (2005) Provided prescription-drug discounts for low-income residents	65 (36)	CTA 12*	F 39–61

Proposition	Total (% support)		Contributors >$10 million	Election
	Contributions ($ millions)			
Prop 38 (2000) Authorized-school voucher program	63	(49)	CTA 38, Timothy Draper 23*	F 29–71
Prop 45 (2014) Regulated health insurance rates	61	(7)	Kaiser Permanente 19, Blue Shield 12	F 41–59
Prop 29 (2012) Increased tobacco tax, increased cancer-research funding	60	(20)	Philip Morris 33, R. J. Reynolds 14	F 49.8–50.2
Prop 55 (2016) Extended temporary income and sales tax increases	57	(99)	CAHHS 25*, CTA 21*	A 63–37
Prop 37 (2012) Required GMO labels on food	57	(19)	. . .	F 49–51
Prop 38 (2012) Increased income tax	48	(99)	Molly Munger 44*	F 29–71
Prop 16 (2010) Limited public agencies from retail power business	47	(99)	PG&E 46*	F 47–53
Prop 76 (2005) Limited state spending	46	(36)	CTA 14, Alliance for Better California 10*	F 38–62
Prop 23 (2010) Suspended greenhouse gas law	42	(26)	. . .	F 38–62

Note: The table lists the 20 propositions that attracted the most contributions during 2000–2016. All 20 propositions were initiatives. CTA = California Teachers Association; CAHHS = California Association of Hospitals and Health Systems; GMO = genetically modified organism. An asterisk indicates that a contribution was in support; otherwise a contribution was in opposition. The election result was approved (A) or failed (F); the percentage in favor and against is reported below the outcome.

Proposition 87 in 2006, which proposed to spend $4 billion on alternative energy, financed with a tax on gas and oil. Big chunks of the $154 million in large contributions came from Stephen Bing ($50 million in support), heir to a real estate fortune, and three oil companies—Chevron, Aera Energy, and Occidental Petroleum ($81 million combined in opposition). Voters sided with the oil companies, rejecting the measure 45 to 55 percent; in this case, business interests won the battle, but it was a purely defensive victory; they would have preferred not to have had to fight at all. This turns out to be a common pattern, although the dollar amounts here were exceptional.

Proposition 61, requiring the state to pay no more for prescription drugs than the US Department of Veterans Affairs, came in second with $128 million in large contributions, mostly from large drug companies in opposition. It likewise failed, again a defensive win for business interests in a battle they would rather not have had to fight. Two other propositions were in the $100 million club: Proposition 32 in 2012, which sought to limit political use of union funds, pitting Republicans and business interests against Democrats and labor unions, and Proposition 56 in 2016, which increased taxes on tobacco products.

The table also lists individual or group contributions of $10 million or more to give a feel for who made particularly large contributions. The largest single contribution, $50 million, came from an individual, Stephen Bing, in support of Proposition 87. Most of the large contributions came from corporations, especially tobacco companies opposing tobacco tax increases, but two came from public employee unions. Overall, big contributions were roughly evenly divided between support and opposition campaigns.

Turning to the main question of which interest groups win or lose under direct democracy, figure 15.4 reports how often each group was on the "defensive," defined as having made a contribution to the opposition campaign.

For initiatives, the most "defensive" groups were corporations, with 54 percent of their contributions in opposition; and labor unions, with 52 percent in opposition. Wealthy individuals were the least likely to make defensive contributions; 72 percent of their contributions were in support of a proposition. Clearly, then, we should not think of initiatives as primarily a tool used by corporations and labor unions to secure favorable legislation; rather it seems that individual activists—particularly wealthy individuals such as Tom Steyer, discussed earlier—drive the agenda, often with proposals that are unfriendly to corporations and unions.

We can use contribution data to shed light on whether powerful interests fare better with the legislature than with initiatives by again comparing initiatives with legislative proposals that require voter approval. This is an imperfect comparison because it excludes laws passed by the legislature that did not require voter approval, but once more it appears that powerful interests fare better with legislators than with initiatives. While 54 percent of corporate contributions to initiative campaigns were in opposition, only 2 percent of their contributions on legislative proposals were in opposition. The same pattern

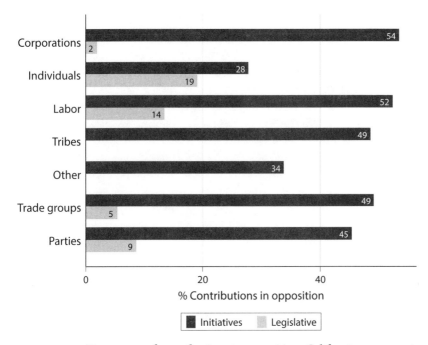

FIGURE 15.4. Percentage of contributions in opposition, California 2000–2016

holds (albeit to a lesser degree) for labor unions and the other organized groups. A natural explanation of these findings is that the legislature takes care with its proposals not to threaten the interests of organized groups, or, put differently, the legislature may be "captured" by these groups.

A key question is whether corporations and other economic interest groups win or lose from initiatives after all the dust has settled from campaigning. Figure 15.5 characterizes the overall impact of propositions on the different groups. A contributor "benefited" if it supported a proposition that passed, by gaining a favorable law. A contributor "lost" if it opposed a proposition that passed, because an unfavorable law came into effect. If the proposition failed, I classify the contributor as neither benefiting nor losing because the law did not change. Let me clarify that the issue here is not whether a group won or lost *on election day*, but whether it was better or worse off *as a result of direct democracy being used*. The oil companies won on election day by defeating Stephen Bing's Proposition 87, but this does not mean they benefited *from the initiative*—to the contrary, they would have been better off had the initiative never been proposed.[12]

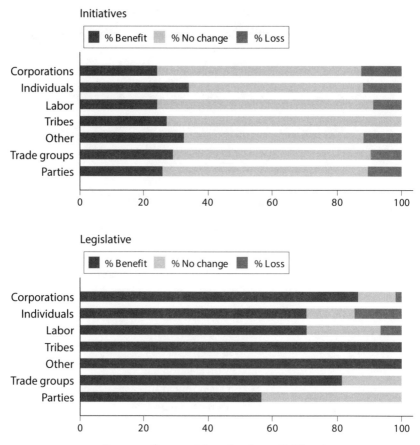

FIGURE 15.5. Impact of proposition elections, California 2000–2016

The top panel focuses on initiatives. Corporations were the least likely (24 percent) among all groups to benefit from initiatives and the most likely (12 percent) to lose. Labor's results were almost identical to those for corporations. Wealthy individuals (34 percent) were the most likely to benefit; tribes were the least likely to lose. Looking at the lower panel, every type of large contributor benefited from legislative measures more than half of the time, and none were hurt by legislative proposals with regularity. Corporations benefited 86 percent of the time and lost 2 percent of the time, and trade groups benefited 81 percent of the time and were not on the losing side for any legislative proposal. Labor won 70 percent of the time and lost 7 percent of the time.

Clearly, legislative proposals were much better for business and labor groups than initiatives.[13]

The Limited Effect of Money

The main conclusion—based on a century of experience across the states and a closer look at California—is straightforward: business interests generally do not prosper under direct democracy; they seem to fare better when the legislature makes the laws. At first glance, this conclusion may seem puzzling because we have seen that business groups far outspend the other interest groups. Why do they have so little to show for all that money?

Part of the reason, obviously, is that the preponderance of business spending is defensive. Corporations are getting a return on their investment by fighting off the many hostile proposals that they face, but these are only tactical victories that maintain the status quo; they do not change the legal landscape to their advantage. Even if every defensive dollar led to defeat of an anti-business proposal, at most it would produce a holding pattern for business interests.

Another reason business interests do not thrive under direct democracy is that campaign spending, where their deep pockets give them a competitive advantage, does not guarantee victory on election day. Figure 15.6 illustrates this by plotting the difference between spending in support and in opposition to a measure, and then showing the outcome with light and dark gray coding. There was no mechanical connection between the side that spent more and the election outcome, and even when spending was one-sided it was not conclusive. In fact, three of the four propositions with the most one-sided spending in support (the four rightmost bars) failed.

Saying that election outcomes depend on more than money is not really controversial. Political observers will recall that Hillary Clinton outspent Donald Trump about two to one in the 2016 presidential election and still lost. Money matters at the margin, as confirmed by several field studies on the effect of advertising on votes, but likely has diminishing returns.[14] The pool of persuadable people is finite; once they have been reached it is harder to move the rest of the electorate. And people may be persuadable only on certain issues; on other issues they are not going to change their minds no matter how many times they hear a TV commercial.

Political folk wisdom has long held that spending in opposition to a proposition is more effective than spending in support. The figure fits this story in the

Bar height = total spending in support − total spending against

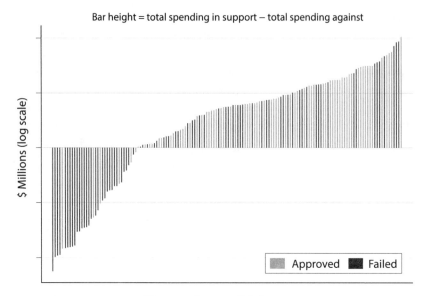

FIGURE 15.6. Net spending on California propositions

sense that most of the unsuccessful propositions lost the spending battle (the preponderance of dark bars on the left). Negative spending may be effective because voters are risk averse and can be persuaded to vote *no* by raising reasonable doubt in their minds; with enough money, opponents can throw enough mud at the wall for something to stick.[15]

Having said this, we still might wonder why business interests spend so much money in support of proposals. Political scientist Elisabeth Gerber suggested one possible explanation: in a survey of economic, professional, and business groups, the top reason they gave for advancing initiatives was to "signal support to the legislature" and "pressure the legislature to pass laws" (ranking well above to "pass initiatives").[16] Corporations may know they are likely to lose but hope that by demonstrating greater-than-expected support, they can convince the legislature at least to consider the issue. Another possibility is that corporations are attempting to deter hostile legislation in the future by signaling their willingness to fight over an issue. This is a common explanation for the immense spending by tobacco companies against smoking bans and tobacco taxes.

In short, corporations and business groups have a lot of money and are willing to spend it. Most of their spending is defensive, however; it enables them to fight off hostile propositions. For the most part they are not effective in using direct democracy to bring about new laws in their favor.

While the focus has been on business interests, the dominant spender, we should not ignore other powerful interest groups, especially labor unions. Public employee unions—teachers, police, fire fighters, and other government workers—are especially important at the state and local levels, as suggested by their campaign contributions and their numbers: as of 2005, 21.7 million people worked in the public sector, 15 percent of the labor force, and over 64 percent of them were employed by local governments.

Government workers are unique among interest groups in that they have a hand in choosing (through elections) the people who sit on the other side of the bargaining table from them during contract negotiations. This is likely to give public employee unions a hand up in negotiations and allow them to negotiate higher salaries. Direct democracy, which we have seen appears to counteract the power of interest groups, should allow voters to prevent excessive union contracts and keep wages closer to market values. This is what I found in a study of 650+ American cities. Comparing cities that allowed initiatives with those that did not, city workers were paid 18 percent less in the direct democracy cities, controlling for other determinants of compensation.[17] This evidence reinforces that idea that direct democracy weakens the power of concentrated economic interest groups in general, not just corporations and business groups.

Yes, Direct Democracy Does Reduce
Interest Group Influence

Given how one-sided the evidence is that interest groups lose under direct democracy, it is curious that the contrary argument—that direct democracy *enhances* the power of special interests—continues to surface. Do those advancing the contrary argument know something that we are missing? Or do they know perfectly well that direct democracy is bad for wealthy interest groups and are simply shilling for interests that stand to gain from limiting it?

Consider the task force convened by the National Conference of State Legislatures (NCSL) that issued a report in 2002 titled *Initiative and Referendum in the 21st Century*.[18] The task force's gloomy conclusion was that the "initiative has evolved from its early days as a grassroots tool to enhance representative democracy into a tool that too often is exploited by special interests." The report recommended that no more states should adopt the initiative process, and those that have it should restrict its scope. How the task force reached its conclusion is a mystery since it presented no evidence, only mentioning that it listened to "expert testimony from a wide variety of witnesses." More revealing is the composition of the task force: its 11 members included representatives from chemical giant Monsanto, tobacco giant Philip Morris, pharmaceutical lobbying behemoth PhRMA, and Biotechnology Industry Organization, the world's largest biotech lobbying group, as well as sitting legislators and other government officials. The committee is almost a caricature of what direct democracy is designed to counteract—corporate capture of legislative processes—and it does not seem a coincidence that its recommended course of action likely would help big corporations.

In terms of the broad concerns that motivate this book, the main message is that direct democracy does appear to offer the people a tool to control interest group influence, as the progressives intended. Other issues remain to be considered in subsequent chapters, but it seems we can add controlling interest groups to the benefit column for direct democracy.

16

Protecting Minorities
from the Majority

EVERY DEMOCRACY MUST find a way to empower the majority while at the
same time protecting the rights of minorities. This issue preoccupied the framers of the US Constitution and led them to adopt their famous system of
"checks and balances." They hoped that by fragmenting political power it would
be difficult for a "tyrannical" majority to coalesce.

This problem is not the kind that has a definite solution. "It is impossible to
invent constitutional devices which will prevent the popular will from being
effective for wrong without also preventing it from being effective for right,"
observed former president Theodore Roosevelt.[1] Rather, it is one of finding the
right balance between majority rule and protection of minority rights, recognizing that neither will be fully achieved.

Direct democracy, by enhancing the power of the majority, skirts some of
the usual checks and balances in the legislative process. This raises questions
about its effect on minority rights. Are minorities endangered when ordinary
voters are allowed to put their hands directly on the levers of policy—and if so,
how serious is the threat? This chapter addresses these questions.

Two things should be acknowledged up front. The first is that we don't have
an extensive evidentiary record to go on. Minority-rights issues do arise in referendum elections, but much less often than tax and spending or government-
reform issues. Since we are forced to reason from anecdotes and isolated historical episodes that may be special cases, the conclusions should be viewed
as somewhat speculative.

Second, we have to employ *comparative* arguments—how direct democracy
compares with representative democracy—which might seem unsatisfying to
those seeking an unconditional evaluation. Because all forms of democracy are

imperfect, knowing that a particular form has defects is of little value on its own; to make assessments, we need to know if one form has more defects than another. The question we seek to answer is then: How well does direct democracy protect minority rights *compared with representative democracy*?

Constitutional Protections Apply to Direct Democracy, Too

The conventional strategy for protecting minority rights is to itemize them in a written constitution and then turn enforcement over to a body that is insulated from the public. In the United States, rights are listed in the Constitution's Bill of Rights (free speech, gun ownership, etc.) and several other amendments (e.g., voting rights for non-white Americans, women, and people younger than 21 years), and enforced by the US Supreme Court, which has the power to invalidate laws and regulations that violate these rights. There are other ways to do this: in the United Kingdom rights are provided by an act of Parliament, and in France rights are enforced by the Constitutional Council—a group of former high-ranking officeholders appointed for a nonrenewable nine-year term that can invalidate laws proposed by Parliament.

These protections remain in place for direct democracy. The rights protected in the US Constitution continue to apply to five of the six reform proposals listed in chapter 11, and those forms of direct democracy remain subject to court review. If a referendum was held that advised Congress to pass an impermissible law under reform #1 or #2 and Congress and the president passed such a law, it could be struck down by the Supreme Court as with any other law. The only case where judicial review would not apply is reform #6, initiated constitutional amendments, which is the case for representative democracy as well.

The Constitution's framers believed they could also protect minority rights by fragmenting power.[2] In the United States, laws must be approved by the House of Representatives and the Senate and signed by the president. These actors are all linked to the people through elections, but majorities cannot act through any one of them directly. Even if an intemperate majority were to gain control of one of them, the assumption is that it could not gain control of all three simultaneously. Procedures such as the Senate's supermajority (filibuster) rule and the power of committees to control the flow of legislation also blunt the power of majorities.[3]

These checks and balances remain in place for direct democracy when it takes the form of referendums (as opposed to initiatives). In a referendum, the electorate votes on a law proposed by the government, meaning the law was approved by both houses and signed by the executive. To the extent that minorities benefit from these checks and balances, referendums continue to provide this protection. Four of the six reforms proposed in chapter 11 involve referendums, and so fall into this category. Initiatives that create law—reforms #4 and #6—would bypass the traditional checks and balances of the legislative process.

The framers also hoped that minorities would be protected by the use of representatives. They believed that by filtering majority opinion through representatives, the allegedly narrow, intemperate passions of the masses would be "refined and enlarged" to reflect the public good and thereby protect minority interests.[4] The assumption was that the people would select wiser and more temperate men and women than itself, and those wiser men and women would refuse to advance unjust outcomes sought by the majority.

To the extent that representation protects minority rights, referendums offer the same degree of protection as representative government because the laws at issue in referendums are developed entirely by representatives. Whatever benefits may accrue from representation apply to referendums as well as ordinary legislation. Initiatives circumvent the legislature and thus do not receive the hypothesized benefits from filtering through representation.

The key thing to note here is that although direct democracy gives the majority a louder voice on policy matters, it does not bypass most conventional constitutional protections for minorities. *All* of the conventional protections apply to referendums, and many apply to initiatives as well. It is an unfortunate but common misimpression that direct democracy allows the majority to rule without any traditional constitutional restraints. This would be the case only if citizens were allowed to propose and approve constitutional amendments by initiative (reform #6), which I consider the least feasible of the reforms.

Parchment Protections Are Unreliable

In thinking about the connection between direct democracy and minority rights, it is worth mentioning that historically constitutional provisions have not given minorities reliable protection. I mention this to counteract a popular narrative that Americans have their rights primarily because they are encoded in the Constitution and protected by judges. Instead, as eminent political scientist Robert Dahl has noted:

Judging from the whole history of judicial review in the United States, judicial guardians do not in fact offer much protection for fundamental rights in the face of persistent invasion by the national demos and its representatives. The reputation of the U.S. Supreme Court for doing so rests mainly on a period of judicial activism beginning in 1954 when the Court was presided over by Chief Justice Earl Warren. . . . [D]espite its reputation, the U.S. Supreme Court has not regularly stood as a bulwark against violations of fundamental rights and interests by congressional legislation.[5]

The idea that our views about enumerated rights and judges rely too much on a few episodes from American history has been put on sound empirical footing by a remarkable series of papers by legal scholars Adam Chilton and Mila Versteeg.[6] Examining the constitutions of almost 200 countries, they found that governments were no more likely to respect individual rights when they were written down than when they weren't, and respect for rights did not depend on whether the country had an independent judiciary. All of which suggests that the "parchment barriers" of constitutions may be less effective than is sometimes believed.

The failures of constitutional protections in the United States are many and monumental. Allowing Jim Crow (segregation) and black disenfranchisement to prevail across the South for a century is the leading example.[7] Incarceration of American citizens of Japanese ancestry during World War II is another.[8] Black Americans were not protected by the 14th and 15th Amendments that allegedly guaranteed them equal protection of the law and the right to vote. Nor were written protections helpful to Japanese Americans: when the US attorney general objected to their relocation, the assistant secretary of war responded: "why the Constitution is just a scrap of paper to me."[9]

This is not to suggest that constitutional protections lack value. The fact that they do not always work does not mean that they *never* work. The point is that their effectiveness is limited; they should not be viewed as the complete solution, but rather as one tool among many in the democratic toolkit.

These violations of the civil rights of African Americans and Japanese Americans are also noteworthy because they happened under *representative* democracy. The rights of both groups were abridged by actions of Congress, the president, state legislators, and governors, and with approval of federal courts. Black Americans were not helped by the checks and balances within Southern legislatures or the "refinement" of popular opinion through Southern representatives. (In fact, the checks and balances in Congress probably hurt them, by allowing white supremacists in the US Senate to kill civil rights bills with filibusters.) Nor did the fragmentation of power stop the Japanese internment steamroller—all of the branches of government moved in unison to deny their rights.

The lesson is that the alternative to direct democracy—representative democracy—is far from perfect when it comes to protecting minorities (and these American examples could be multiplied if we looked at other countries). Direct democracy should be seen as a threat to minority rights only if it abridges them more than already happens under representative democracy, the status quo system. Whether or not this is the case can't be determined theoretically; we need to examine the historical record itself. I turn to that next.[10]

Lessons from 2,609 Initiatives in the States

The 2,609 state-level initiatives in the American states between 1904 and 2018 provide a rich historical record to gauge the threat to minority rights. Initiatives are the most undiluted form of direct democracy with the fewest checks and balances—if there is a problem it should rear its head there—and the data are available for more than a century, ample time to detect trends and patterns. The question to be answered is whether anti-minority initiatives are common or rare.

For this exercise, I started by flagging initiatives related to minority groups. "Minority groups" were defined in terms of race, ethnicity, primary language, immigration status, sexual orientation, and gender.[11] Based on each initiative's text and various supporting materials, each proposal was classified as "helping" or "hurting" the group. An initiative granting women the right to vote was classified as helping women, while an initiative prohibiting antidiscrimination laws based on sexual orientation was classified as hurting gays and lesbians. Initiatives that did not obviously help or hurt minorities were classified as "ambiguous." Examples in this class include civil rights initiatives considered by several states that declared: "The state shall not discriminate against, or grant preferential treatment to, any individual or group on the basis of race, sex, color, ethnicity, or national origin in the operation of public employment, public education, or public contracting."[12] On the face of it, these initiatives were racially neutral, and their language appears to protect minorities from discrimination. However, opponents argued that they hurt minorities by dismantling affirmative action programs intended to aid historically underrepresented groups, particularly in university admissions. Further complicating matters, some members of one minority group—Asian Americans—claim that university affirmative action programs discriminate against their children by holding them to higher standards.

Another example in the ambiguous category are initiatives pertaining to mandatory busing of students based on race. These initiatives were a response to federal court orders that attempted to force the integration of schools by requiring busing of students to schools outside their home neighborhoods. Forced busing was intended to overcome the effect of residential segregation on school segregation, but often required students as young as kindergartners to travel miles away to an unfamiliar neighborhood, and was not popular with white or black parents.[13]

Figure 16.1 shows the number and type of minority-related initiatives over time. Solid triangles indicate pro-minority initiatives; for example, the first panel shows a single pro-alien initiative, a 2008 Arizona proposal that would have made it easier for employers to hire immigrants. Open squares indicate anti-minority initiatives; the first panel shows six anti-alien initiatives, starting with a 1914 Arizona proposal requiring 80 percent of a company's employees to be American citizens. Initiatives classified as ambiguous are marked with plus signs.

Across all issues, initiatives related to sexual orientation were the most common. All 24 of them appeared in 1988 or later, and all but 3 proposed limiting the rights of gays and lesbians, mainly by prohibiting same-sex marriage. The next most common subject was race, with 16 initiatives. Most race-related initiatives are classified as ambiguous—the "preferential treatment" and busing initiatives discussed above—and the remainder are balanced between helpful and hurtful classifications. (The most blatantly discriminatory initiative was Oklahoma's State Question 17 in 1910, which established a literacy requirement for voting that applied only to descendants of slaves.)

The most positive picture is for issues related to women, where 11 of the 12 initiatives proposed to increase rights; most of these were pro-suffrage proposals in the early twentieth century. A more recent topic is the English language; 11 measures declared English to be the official language of the state or required school instruction to take place only in English.[14] Finally, seven initiatives concerned aliens and immigrants, some targeting legal aliens, such as laws prohibiting land ownership by noncitizens, and others targeting illegal aliens, such as laws denying government services to immigrants without proper documentation. Considering all initiatives together, anti-minority proposals outnumber pro-minority proposals 42 to 18.

Based on this information, we can draw a few conclusions. Anti-minority proposals are uncommon, comprising only 1.8 percent of all initiatives;

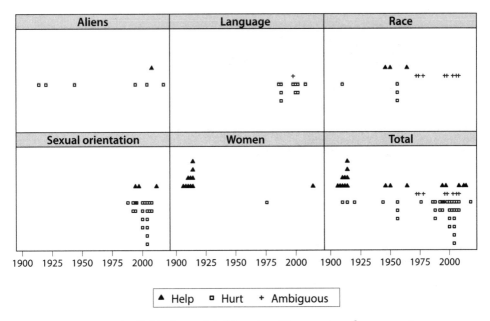

FIGURE 16.1. Initiatives related to minorities, proposed 1904–2018

pro-minority proposals are even rarer, just 0.7 percent of the total; and when a minority-related initiative does come to the ballot, most of the time (60 percent) it would have been harmful to minorities if approved.[15] Initiatives appear to provide a platform for anti-minority views, but such issues are a sideshow in initiative politics.

More important than the number of proposed initiatives is the number that were approved. Of 70 minority initiatives, voters approved 31 anti-minority laws and 5 pro-minority laws. At least 20 anti-minority initiatives were invalidated by courts within a few years of passage.[16] Of the 11 anti-minority initiatives that went into effect, 6 were largely symbolic measures declaring English the official language of the state; 2 required public schools to teach only in English; 1 denied public services to illegal immigrants; 1 revoked the governor's power to unilaterally ban discrimination based on sexual orientation in the executive branch; and 1 expanded an existing law limiting land ownership by Asian noncitizens.

That is the complete list for more than 100 years. I have not collected data on the number of anti-minority laws by legislatures during the same period, but the record for representative democracy during the same time period is surely worse—the rights violations from voter disenfranchisement and Jim Crow in the South and anti-Asian laws on the West Coast alone seem more heinous than the combined record of these initiatives.

Minority Policies in Initiative versus Noninitiative States

A related way to assess the impact of direct democracy on minority rights is to compare the policy choices of initiative and noninitiative states. Such comparisons, by focusing on the "bottom line," allow for the possibility that availability of initiatives alone might influence policy decisions—by providing a threat— without requiring an actual proposal. Inferring initiative effects by comparing outcomes in initiative and noninitiative states is a common research strategy in political economy; we can assemble findings from several studies to form a picture.[17]

Some of the best evidence concerns same-sex marriage. While most states had long taken it for granted that marriage involved only one man and one woman, gay marriage emerged as an issue in 1993 when the Hawaii Supreme Court ruled that same-sex marriage was protected under the state constitution. Hawaii legislators responded by placing a constitutional amendment on the ballot to define marriage as solely between one man and one women; other states followed over the next decade. In some states, legislators took the lead in amending the constitution, as in Hawaii; in other states, citizens took the lead with initiatives. The federal government adopted a "defense of marriage" law in 1996, supported by large majorities of both parties. The array of laws prohibiting same-sex marriage thus came about by a mixture of representative and direct democracy. The US Supreme Court's *Obergefell v. Hodges* decision in 2015 preempted all of these laws by declaring same-sex marriage a constitutional right.[18] Research shows that before the Supreme Court intervened, initiative states were about 12 percent more likely to adopt laws banning same-sex marriage than noninitiative states, reflecting the majority view at the time.[19] Prior to *Obergefell*, both representative and direct democracy were antagonistic toward same-sex marriage, but direct democracy somewhat more so.

Another type of law for which there is careful research is establishment of English as the official state language. The most recent wave of official-English laws can be traced to 1981, when US senator S. I. Hayakawa, a Republican from California, introduced an amendment to make English the nation's official language. Several states then passed their own laws making English the official state language, sometimes through legislatures and sometimes by initiatives.

Research shows that initiative states were about 30 percent more likely than noninitiative states to adopt official-English laws.[20]

For same-sex-marriage and official-English laws, the initiative pushed policy away from minority interests. Women's rights go in the other direction. Prior to ratification of the 19th Amendment, which prohibited denial of voting rights based on sex, several states adopted women's suffrage on their own, beginning with Wyoming in 1870. Initiatives played a role in advancing the issue—Arizona and Oregon adopted women's suffrage via initiatives, and unsuccessful initiatives in other states put pressure on legislators. By 1920, 68 percent of initiative states had given women the vote, compared with only 17 percent of noninitiative states, suggesting that the initiative may have helped advance the women's suffrage movement.

As mentioned at the outset of the chapter, the available evidence is thinner than we would like, but the research on the three issues just considered tends to reinforce the other evidence: initiatives worked to the disadvantage of minorities on two issues, and to their advantage on one issue. Initiatives do pose a threat to minority rights, but according to the data we have, the threat is not immense.

What Minorities Themselves Think about Direct Democracy

A different way to get a sense of direct democracy's risk to minority rights is to ask minorities themselves what they think about it—particularly those living in states that use it often. Those who live with direct democracy have a unique personal insight into how it impacts their lives. This is especially so in states with a long history of initiative use, where we would expect obvious problems to have come to light with the passage of time. Of course, the impressions of ordinary citizens are not in themselves conclusive—an underlying theme of this book is that direct democracy can have subtle effects that are not easily perceived—but they do constitute a piece of evidence that should be weighed along with the rest.

Again we focus on California, an excellent place to investigate, as I have argued earlier, because of the centrality of the initiative process in its government, but also because of its diverse population with numerous minority groups. Figure 16.2 shows what Californians think about the initiative process, by race. The survey, conducted in 2011 by the well-regarded Field Poll, asked: "Do you think that statewide ballot proposition elections are a good thing for California, a bad thing, or don't you think they make much of a difference?"[21]

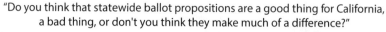

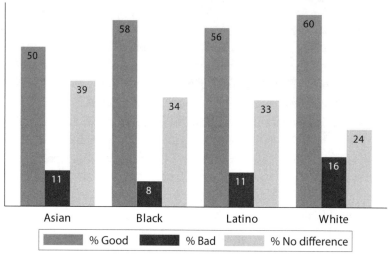

FIGURE 16.2. Public opinion in California on direct democracy

Several patterns jump out. Direct democracy is enormously popular among Californians: the good-to-bad ratio is about five to one. Most important for the purposes of this chapter, the positive assessment is shared across all racial/ethnic groups in the survey: Asians, blacks, Latinos, and whites. Most minorities living with direct democracy do not see it as a threat, or if they do, believe its benefits outweigh the dangers.

It might seem odd that racial minorities support a process that empowers the majority. But the support from minorities is surprising only if one assumes that the white majority is implacably intent on using initiatives to deprive minorities of their rights. In fact, as we saw earlier in the chapter, initiatives are usually focused on issues that do not involve race at all, issues that are likely to be important to every voter for reasons unconnected to race, such as taxes, term limits, campaign finance reform, environmental regulation, minimum-wage laws, and many others. Once we recognize that initiatives are mainly about issues that people do not see through the lens of race, there is no reason to think that minority voters will have a different attitude than anyone else.

This explanation for figure 16.2 is supported by a clever study conducted by three political scientists, Zoltan Hajnal, Elisabeth Gerber, and Hugh Louch. They examined exit poll data on 51 California ballot propositions to determine how often each person was on the winning side or the losing side.[22] If a proposition passed 60–40, or failed 40–60, then 60 percent of voters were on the winning side. Overall, they found that a typical voter was on the winning side about 60 percent of the time. African American, Asian American, and Latino voters were only about 1 percent less likely than white voters to be on the winning side of the vote. Essentially the same pattern emerged even when they focused on measures where minorities voted cohesively or on issues that minorities said they cared most about.[23]

In short, the issues that appear in initiatives generally do not divide citizens along racial lines. Minority voters react to initiatives as taxpayers, citizens concerned with the quality of government, consumers of public services, environmentalists worried about pollution, and so on, not primarily as representatives of their racial/ethnic groups.

Tentative Lessons: Proceed—but with Care

What lessons can we take away from this investigation? One is that we should not dismiss the threat to minorities associated with majority rule. Data are not as extensive as we might hope, but there is enough evidence from the historical record to reveal that initiatives, the most potent form of direct democracy, have sometimes targeted minorities.

Another lesson is that we have ways of managing the risks. Conventional constitutional protections—enumerated rights overseen by judges—should and usually do apply to direct democracy as much as ordinary legislation and seem to have been effective at preventing the most damaging anti-minority initiatives from going into effect. In terms of the reforms proposed in chapter 11, most involve referendums, and therefore legislators, so the full menu of factors that are alleged to protect minorities applies: filtering of mass opinion by representatives, checks and balances in lawmaking, as well as judicial review. The advisory referendums that I suggest as the first step in a reform agenda have exactly the same set of protections for minority rights as ordinary legislation.

While direct democracy creates risks for minority rights, there is little reason to believe that the risks are greater under direct democracy than representative democracy. A definitive conclusion is out of reach based on the available evidence, but it seems relevant that the worse infringements of minority rights in American history—Jim Crow, disenfranchisement of African Americans in the South, internment of Japanese Americans in World War II—were all produced by *representative* democracy. It is hard to come up with examples of anti-minority direct democracy laws that come close to stacking up. This does not constitute an affirmative case for direct democracy, of course, but as discussed at the outset of the chapter, evaluating governments is always about *comparisons* between imperfect alternatives because perfection is not attainable.

Moreover, the assumption that majorities constantly seek to undermine minority rights seems to neglect that majorities sometimes protect minorities from local oppressors. This happened during the Civil War when the Northern majority forced the South to end slavery; and during the 1960s when sentiment from the national majority prompted Congress to pass civil rights and voting rights laws that allowed the federal government to intervene and bring an end to segregation and black disenfranchisement. Direct democracy also played a role in the expansion of women's suffrage. On a smaller scale, in 2018 a solid majority of Floridians voted to restore voting rights to felons, not a particularly popular minority group, despite opposition from the sitting government. This may not be the normal case, but it illustrates that the people should not be stereotyped; they are more complex and nuanced than a simple majority-tyranny story suggests.

PART IV

Making Direct
Democracy Work

17

A Framework for Deciding Issues

IF WE ACCEPT the general point that direct democracy ought to be used from time to time, we come to a practical problem: Which issues should be decided by the public and which should be left to representatives? Voters do not have the time or inclination to be full-time legislators; they want to decide only select issues of particular importance. This chapter develops a framework to address the question, focusing on several key issue characteristics that determine whether an issue is best decided by direct or representative democracy, and then applies the framework to a number of concrete issues to show how it could be used in practice.

The Framework

Imagine there is a public policy to be decided, and we want to know whether to decide it using direct democracy or representative democracy. The issue is not what is the right *decision* for the policy, but what is the right *process* for making the decision. Each possible process has its advantages and disadvantages; we are looking for a set of principles that tells us which process is best for different classes of issues. To be useful, the principles have to be simple but at the same time applicable to a wide range of issues. The framework here treats direct democracy as a single "thing," although we have seen that it can take many forms.[1]

To assess whether one process is "better" than another, we need to specify an objective, the goal we are trying to achieve. The objective employed in this framework is to select the policy that would be favored by a majority of the people, if they were fully informed. While this is a natural starting point, it is not the only reasonable criterion; I offer some thoughts in its defense later in the chapter.

It is conceptually useful to distinguish two types of information pertinent to a decision: information about what outcomes would be produced by a policy (*technical information*) versus information about citizen preferences over outcomes (*preference information*). Suppose the issue was how to clean up a polluted lake. The policy "outcome" would be a level of cleanliness (parts per million of the pollutant that would remain in the lake) and the tax to be levied to fund the cleanup. The technical information would be the various technologies available for removing pollutants and what they would cost, while the preference information would be how much citizens value and are willing to pay for different levels of cleanliness. Both pieces of information are relevant for choosing the best policy; determining the best process for choosing a policy boils down to how effective different processes are in producing and applying different types of information. Representative democracy is better at producing technical information because of its access to experts in the bureaucracies, while direct democracy is better at accessing information about the public's own preferences. The best decision process is one that brings to bear the type of information necessary to decide the issue at hand.[2]

It follows, generally speaking, that "technical" issues should be decided by representatives while "values" issues should be decided directly, but we can say more than this. Let us think in more detail about the characteristics of issues that representatives are good at deciding. One characteristic of an issue is the degree to which underlying citizen preferences are aligned with one another, what we can call preference "homogeneity." Whether to site a nuclear waste dump near a population center or far from a population center is an issue with homogeneous preferences; everyone wants it far from the population center. Whether to limit abortion is an issue where preferences are heterogeneous. When an issue is homogeneous, representatives can make decisions effectively: they have the necessary technical knowledge and they can learn citizen preferences through introspection or by consulting a small sample of people or a group of legislators. When preferences are heterogeneous, even though legislators have technical information, they cannot be sure if their opinions, or the opinions of any small group, represent the general public's preferences, and they might not be able to select the policy favored by the majority.[3]

For representatives to be effective, they must also be willing to choose the right policy once they determine it. There are two reasons they might not do this. First, representatives may have a self-interest in the outcome. For example, even if representatives can discover what salaries voters would like to pay government officials, they will be tempted to vote themselves more. Second, representatives may be influenced by interest groups, which can offer them bribes, campaign contributions, future employment, and so forth, as discussed in chapter 15. In short, representatives might not choose the people's preferred policy on issues that present a conflict of interest or that impact powerful interest groups.

In order for representative decisions to be effective, then, three conditions must hold:

> Effective delegation: Representatives can decide an issue effectively if *all three* of the following conditions hold: (i) representatives understand voter preferences on the issue (homogeneous preferences), (ii) representatives do not have a personal stake in the issue, and (iii) there are no powerful interests concerned with the issue.

The condition for voters to make effective decisions is simpler conceptually. Unlike representatives, voters know their own preferences, but they lack technical information. Some issues are simple enough that they do not require technical information, and voters can decide them effectively. For other issues, voters need to overcome their limited technical information in order to make effective decisions. We saw in chapter 14 that the lack of technical information can be overcome through the use of information shortcuts, if they are available. In order for voters to be effective in deciding an issue, then, one of two conditions must hold:

> Effective voters: Voters can decide an issue effectively if *either* of two conditions hold: (i) the issue is nontechnical, or (ii) information shortcuts are available for the issue.

With these principles of effective delegation and voting in hand, we have a general decision framework, summarized in flowchart form in figure 17.1. If a decision can be effectively delegated, use representatives; if delegation is ineffective, use direct democracy if it can produce an effective outcome; if direct democracy is also ineffective, then no effective process is available.

Applications of the Framework

Whether an issue is best decided with representative or direct democracy depends on how it stacks up on the five issue characteristics just discussed: homogeneity of preferences, representative self-interest, interest group involvement, technical nature, and availability of information cues. Focusing on only

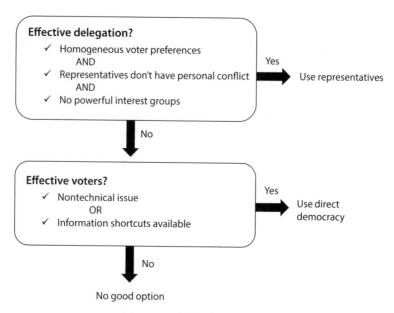

FIGURE 17.1. Framework for choosing decision process

five characteristics is an oversimplification, of course, and assigning issues to classes is somewhat subjective. The advantage is bringing some central trade-offs into sharper focus. Several examples follow that illustrate how to apply this framework; in each case the approach is to work down the flow chart, answering questions about the issue until we arrive at an answer.

Legislative term limits. Term limits restrict the amount of time an official can hold office. In the United States, the president is now limited to two four-year terms; most states currently restrict the terms of governors and about half restrict the terms of legislators; but there are no term limits on US senators and House members. In terms of the framework, because legislators have a strong self-interest in whether their terms are limited, this issue fails to satisfy the condition for effective representatives and should not be decided by representative democracy. As a nontechnical issue, it can be decided by voters directly, so the framework assigns this issue to direct democracy.

Government debt. Many representatives leave office after a few years because they jump to another position on the career ladder, lose an election, or leave politics. Because representatives hold office for

relatively short periods of time, they give too little weight to consequences that occur in the future, after they leave office. This might
cause them to think myopically, overweighting short-term benefits
and underweighting long-term costs of programs, and preferring
programs with front-loaded benefits and back-loaded costs.

Issuing debt in order to pay for a current program is a classic
example of a program with front-loaded benefits and back-loaded
costs that many elected officials cannot resist. Politicians can use debt
proceeds to deliver immediate benefits to their supporters; and it will
be someone else's problem when the debt comes due in 30 years. Because
of the conflict between what is good for politicians versus voters,
borrowing decisions fail the condition for effective representation. The
decision to borrow is nontechnical so it can be decided effectively by
voters. Therefore, the framework assigns this issue to direct democracy
(and provides a justification for the common practice of requiring
voter approval in order to issue government bonds).

Policy issues related to the *process* of issuing debt, such as
underwriting arrangements, on the other hand, are best left to
representatives. These decisions do not involve the temporal trade-offs
associated with the decision to issue in the first place, making representatives effective, and are technical in nature, making voters ineffective.

Public employee pension obligations are a form of debt. The government gains the services of public employees during their working years,
and promises to pay them a stream of benefits after they retire. As with
other forms of debt, there is a conflict in having politicians make these
decisions because they will be tempted to promise high pension benefits
to government workers today. As with conventional debt, this implies
that voters should decide whether to increase pension benefits.

Smoking laws. It has become common for states and cities to prohibit
smoking in indoor public spaces, such as restaurants, bars, and
workplaces. This issue does not meet the conditions for effective
representatives because of the presence of a powerful interest group—
the tobacco industry—that might influence legislators. The issue can
be decided effectively by voters because it is nontechnical. The
framework then implies that smoking laws are best decided by
referendums. The same argument would apply to liquor sales, partially
justifying the common practice of allowing voters to regulate liquor
sales in their communities.

Drug prices. The high price of prescription drugs is a recurring political issue in the United States. Two federal policies keep the prices higher than they would be otherwise: a prohibition on the Medicare system negotiating drug prices with manufacturers (unlike other countries) and a prohibition on reimporting drugs from countries where prices are cheaper. In terms of the framework, both policies fail the interest group condition for effective representatives because of the importance of the pharmaceutical industry and its lobbying arm PhRMA.

Could these issues be decided effectively by voters? This is not entirely clear because the issues have a technical component, involving questions about how prices are set, how prices affect innovation, and how importation would ripple through the market. It is not clear if adequate information shortcuts would appear for such referendums on these matters. Bottom line: these issues almost surely are not decided well by representatives, but they might not work well for direct democracy either.[4]

Capital punishment. The policy question is whether to use the death penalty as a punishment for certain crimes. In terms of the framework, there is no reason to expect that representatives have a personal stake in the issue, and there are not powerful interest groups involved. However, citizen preferences are heterogeneous on this matter because moral positions emanate from religious and ethical beliefs that vary from person to person. Because preferences are not homogeneous, this issue is not effectively decided by representatives. The issue involves little technical expertise, so it can be decided effectively by voters. The framework thus assigns the issue of capital punishment to direct democracy.

Immigration and trade. Immigration policy is an important political issue in the twenty-first century in the United States and Europe. In the United States, the questions include whether to provide a path to citizenship for persons who came to the country illegally when they were children (DREAM Act) and whether to build a border wall. In terms of the framework, there does not appear to be a problem with representatives having a personal stake or with powerful interest groups, but preference heterogeneity is a concern. The effect of immigration varies by community and occupation, and views on immigration may involve ethical and social considerations that vary from person to person. As such, representation may not be effective. In terms of voter effectiveness, the issues do not appear to be overly technical, so the framework suggests using direct democracy.

International trade agreements implicate the same set of concerns, so seem appropriate for referendums as well. International trade agreements can be complex and detailed, such as determining rules of origin, but the primary effects are evident to workers and firms: most people know if their business is going to be helped or hurt from a particular agreement. We might classify this issue as having "moderate" technical content, suggesting perhaps that broad trade agreements be approved by voters, but smaller agreements of a technical nature be left to representatives.

War. Operational decisions when fighting a war meet the conditions for effective delegation. In terms of the framework, citizen preferences are homogeneous: everyone prefers tactics, strategies, and technology that lead to victory. Representatives do not have a personal stake that conflicts with ordinary citizens, nor are there powerful interest groups involved (with the important exception of procurement decisions). Operational decisions in a war, then, are best delegated to representatives.

A more complicated case is the decision to initiate (or terminate) a military conflict. As we saw in chapter 11, in the 1930s the United States seriously considered requiring voter approval for the country to declare war. The decision to declare war does not seem at odds with any of the conditions for effective representation—when it comes to "defensive" conflicts such as World War II, which the United States entered after being attacked by Japan. But in the case of "discretionary" conflicts such as Iraq or Vietnam, citizen preferences may not be homogeneous. Such conflicts are not inherently technical, so they could be decided effectively by voters. Conceivably, the outcome of the US involvement in Vietnam and Iraq might have been better if preceded by an open public debate and formal approval (or not) by the people.[5]

Taxes. By and large, representatives do not have a conflict of interest on tax issues (except, perhaps, in that elected officials tend to be wealthier than most people). However, tax issues that relate to the amount of redistribution—how progressive income taxes are, or the size of estate taxes, for instance—fail the homogeneity condition. People have different preferences based on their economic situation and their normative views of what is a just distribution of income. As such, representatives cannot decide those issues effectively. Because they are nontechnical, they can be decided effectively by voters, and the framework suggests resolving them with direct democracy. Tax issues related to "loopholes"—exemptions, credits, and the like—can involve powerful interest groups, and thus these issues also create problems for representative democracy. Unless the loopholes are technical in nature, they could be decided effectively by voters. Tax issues related to compliance, such as auditing rules, violate none of the conditions for representation, and are best delegated to representatives, specifically to technocrats in the bureaucracy.

Monetary policy. Most countries delegate monetary policy to central banks. Such issues contain a technical component that would make them difficult for voters to decide effectively. They do not present personal conflicts of interest for representatives. However, in two respects they may create problems for delegation. First, there is the presence of a large, powerful interest group (the finance industry), which many believe influences decisions by "revolving doors" through which technocrats move back and forth between industry and government jobs. Second, monetary policy decisions concerning inflation have distributional implications—high inflation favors borrowers and hurts lenders—so the preference homogeneity condition might fail. By and large, the framework calls for delegating monetary policy to representatives, and thus provides a justification for independent central banks, but it suggests that they might not decide some monetary policy decisions effectively.[6]

Banking regulation. Finally, consider an issue that is problematic for both representative and direct democracy. Banking regulation fails the effective-delegation condition because it involves an apex interest group, the finance industry. This makes representative democracy a questionable option. However, banking regulation is also highly technical, which makes it challenging for direct democracy. It is possible that consumer groups could emerge to provide information shortcuts, in which case referendums would work. If information shortcuts are not available, the framework suggests that banking regulation will have an unsatisfactory outcome no matter how it is decided. The same argument suggests problems for regulations involving other financial services as well, such as insurance and securities markets.

Reasonable people could disagree about the technical nature, preference homogeneity, and so forth of any particular issue. The point here is not so much to make an argument for using direct democracy on any particular issue, but to highlight the questions that should be asked and show how the framework can organize thinking about when to use referendums.

Justifications for Majority Rule

The framework developed in this chapter seeks to produce policies consonant with majority opinion. Implicitly it assumes that the goal of democratic government is to choose policies favored by the majority. Because this is not an uncontested assumption, a few words in its defense are in order.

A potential concern with majority rule is that it counts everyone's opinion equally. While "one person, one vote" is a natural consequence of the premise that we are all equal under the law, it ignores intensity of preferences. In a case where 51 percent of the people want to take action X, but they don't care very much one way or the other, while 49 percent intensely prefer action Y, choosing Y seems reasonable. One approach to such issues is utilitarianism, which calls for choosing the policy that produces the greatest sum of "utilities" across the population. The utilitarian approach dominates economic analysis, but is less popular elsewhere.[7] For one thing, it is not self-evident that people with more intense preferences should count more—we would surely not want to give more weight to intensely held preferences for racial discrimination, for example. If racists have an intense preference to segregate public facilities, we would not defer to their strongly held preferences. A recurrent theme in democracy is the need to purge intemperate passions and temporary hysterias from public decisions. Far from wanting intense preferences to count for more, in many cases we want them to count for less. It may not be a shortcoming of majority rule that it ignores intensity of preferences.[8]

Another, perhaps deeper, concern stems from what is known as the "impossibility theorem" proved by economist Kenneth Arrow more than 50 years ago (for which he was awarded the Nobel Prize in economics). The impossibility theorem, roughly speaking, shows mathematically that there is no way to order policies from best to worst without either imposing an order independent of citizen preferences or having the preferences of one person entirely determine the order. This theorem has been interpreted to mean that no fully democratic decision process exists; every process must contain some undemocratic features. Political economists have also shown that democratic decisions often are unstable and prone to cycling, in the sense that option A will defeat B in an election, option B will defeat C, and option C will defeat A. If cycling is a possibility, policy outcomes are indeterminate, and final choices can vary arbitrarily with the order in which the options are decided.[9]

These and similar theorems are not criticisms of majority rule, per se, but of the possibility of designing a democratic process that is entirely free of undesirable features. In effect, they recast the question from whether majority rule has flaws to whether it has fewer flaws than other democratic processes. If the search for a perfect system is futile, we are left to choose from a set of imperfect processes. There is some theoretical basis for preferring majority rule when choosing between imperfect options. Mathematician Kenneth May proved a result, now called May's theorem, showing that majority rule is the only democratic process that satisfies a (limited) set of desirable conditions, such as basing outcomes on citizen preferences but not the identity of the person holding the preferences.[10]

Another concern is whether the will of the majority actually represents the public good or public interest. This raises the question of whether there is such a thing as the public good. The American Founders thought there was, and they believed that wise and educated men were able to perceive it. Today I think we take a more circumspect view. Most of us believe that there is something like the public good, but doubt that it can be objectively determined. We recognize that for some issues there is not a single outcome that is objectively "best" for society, but rather a set of policies about which reasonable people can disagree. If we believe the goal of government is to scientifically identify and implement an objective public good, then rule by technocrats or disinterested wise men has some appeal. If instead we recognize, as I believe is more realistic, that a substantial amount of policy making is about finding compromise and navigating through policy decisions for which there is not an objectively "optimal" decision, then our thoughts turn more toward mechanisms that can effectively resolve disputes, treating people fairly as far as possible.

At a practical level, majority rule has stood the test of time; from an evolutionary perspective it appears to have some desirable survival characteristics. It brings closure to issues and is fair in the sense of treating each person equally. It is not surprising that political thinkers through the ages—from Thomas Jefferson and James Madison to Joseph Schumpeter, F. A. Hayek, James Buchanan, and Gordon Tullock—have concluded that majority rule must be the basis for democracy. Abraham Lincoln put it well when he said, "rejecting the majority principle, anarchy or despotism in some form is all that is left."[11]

―――――

The framework in this chapter provides an intuitive and tractable way to think about whether an issue should be delegated to representatives or decided directly by voters. Its basic intuition is that delegation allows greater use of technical expertise, but exposes decisions to special-interest influence and the biases of representatives, and does not access the dispersed information of the population at large. A conceptual framework of this sort provides a path for winnowing down the issues that the people will decide to a manageable number.

Continuing in this more practical bent, the next chapter turns to describing more concretely how referendums should be implemented. It focuses on designing direct democracy that "works" by avoiding potential problems that can arise in practice.

18

Best Practices

THE PREVIOUS CHAPTERS range widely over various aspect of direct democracy, with an emphasis on identifying and evaluating the advantages and disadvantages of referendums. As we have seen, whether direct democracy achieves its potential depends on how it is implemented. With poor design choices, referendums can be disruptive rather than helpful. This chapter draws together a number of practical suggestions about the practice of direct democracy arising from the preceding discussion as an aid for designing well-functioning referendum processes.

Asking the Right Question

It matters how the question is asked. Brexit ran aground in part because it asked an ambiguous question: whether the United Kingdom should remain in or leave the European Union. The UK could leave the European Union in several different ways, each with distinct ramifications, but there was no connection between a vote to exit and a specific plan. This left voters unsure about exactly what they were voting for or against, and made it difficult for political leaders to implement the referendum because they were not sure what the people actually wanted. The first best practice is then:

1. *A ballot proposition should ask a specific question; ideally whether to approve a specific law.*

The virtue of voting on a specific law is that it allows voters—or their advisors—to parse the details and evaluate exactly what the proposal will do. This recommendation might seem counterintuitive, since few voters will read the legal fine print, but recall that many voters rely on information shortcuts. Organizations that provide shortcuts will read the text on behalf of voters and communicate their views about the details in their endorsements. And by asking a clear question, the meaning of the election outcome will be clear to those charged with implementing the referendum.

The only situation in which a broad question seems appropriate is if the government envisions a two-step process. In Brexit, a first referendum could have asked if voters favored negotiation of an exit treaty; and if they said yes, a second referendum would give them the opportunity to vote on the specific treaty that was negotiated.

The text describing the question should be written by a neutral party. The UK has a good system where an independent electoral commission formulates the question, giving both sides the opportunity to comment. Elected officials should not be the ones to draft the questions, to avoid tempting them to slant the language in favor of their own party or preferences. In 2018, an anti-tax group in California qualified an initiative to repeal a recent increase in fuel taxes that had given the state the highest diesel tax rate and second-highest gas tax rate in the country. The proponents wanted to title the initiative, "Prop 6. Gas Tax Repeal," which would have been to the point. The state's elected attorney general, who was charged to set the official title and opposed the repeal, instead chose to call it: "Prop 6. Eliminates Certain Road Repair and Transportation Funding." (The initiative failed.)

Giving Voters the Information They Need

Referendums can only reveal the public's preferences if voters have enough information to cast a vote that reflects their interests. Election officials should pay special attention to ensure that adequate information is available. In doing so, again, election administrators should recognize the importance of information shortcuts to voter decision making, especially for technical issues. One implication is immediate:

2. *Voters should be provided information on the individuals and groups that support and oppose a referendum.*

Since voters rely on the advice of experts, the campaign and electoral system should be designed to make that information widely and easily available. A natural approach is for the government to produce a voter guide that it mails to each citizen and posts online. In addition to routine information about voting mechanics (where to vote, when, what to bring, etc.), the guide could contain a neutral summary of the proposal, arguments by supporters and opponents, and, critically, a list of individuals and organizations on both sides.

Detailed factual information about a proposal, such as technical analysis by "independent" experts, is useful but likely to be of secondary importance for most voters. Since few experts are completely impartial, voters will be cautious about using expert analysis unless they understand the expert's interests. Voters might find it helpful to hear analysis from experts chosen by the campaigns themselves, in addition to an allegedly neutral analysis.

The discussion of interest groups in chapter 15 suggested that campaign spending has less of an effect than sometimes believed; a group cannot buy the outcome it wants simply by outspending its opponents. Restricting spending therefore is not necessary to ensure a fair outcome that accurately reflects voter preferences. However, if one side does not advertise or campaign at all, then voters may lack the information shortcuts they need to make a decision. To ensure that voters hear both sides of the argument:

> 3. *Public funds should be provided, if necessary, to ensure that both sides' arguments are publicly communicated.*

Implementing a public funding system would require a substantial administrative structure. It would take us too much into the weeds to lay out a specific plan here, but a few conceptual points can be noted. Perhaps most important, a program to provide public funding should not be used as leverage to restrict spending by one or more contestants. I mention this because public funding programs are often coupled with efforts to reduce spending overall, to equalize spending, or to reduce spending by one side.

The purpose of recommendation 3 is not to equalize funding; it is to ensure that each side is able to put its argument before the public, and that voters can find the information shortcut they need to decide. The amount of public funding that one side receives should not be calibrated to balance or offset spending by the other side; it should be targeted to ensure that each side has at least a minimum level of resources. The operating principle should be that spending communicates information to voters and that information is beneficial for producing an informed election outcome; the more informed the electorate is, the more likely it is to make a good decision. To implement such a plan would require designation of official campaigns on both sides—the UK system is a good example again—that are eligible to receive public funds.

Producing Outcomes that Settle Issues

Brexit also offers a lesson about approval procedures. The default rule is and ought to be that the majority rules. However, for issues of particular importance that contemplate a major change from existing practices, it may be wise to require more than a simple majority. This is Jefferson's point that "great innovations should not be forced on a slender majority."

Referendums that propose major changes from the status quo should be constructed to ensure that the change has substantial support. This can be accomplished by requiring supermajorities or requiring approval at multiple elections. Of course, determining what issues rise to this level of importance is tricky, and the principle could be manipulated to create roadblocks to change by parties that prefer the status quo. A natural place to consider applying this rule is for constitutional amendments. As discussed above, quorum requirements should be avoided as they incentivize citizens not to vote, which is undesirable in a democracy.

4. *Jefferson's principle: major changes in policy should not be based on a slender majority.*

In cases where ensuring broad popular support is important, supermajorities and double approval should be considered; minimum turnout and other quorum requirements should be avoided.

Choosing the Topics

The previous chapter discusses which public decisions are well suited for resolution by referendum, and which are not. The basic insight is that issues for which voters have homogeneous preferences and representatives can be trusted to do the right things are best delegated; issues for which voters disagree or where representatives might not pursue the public interest should be decided by referendums. The framework provides guidance for the type of referendums that the government might call, and the type that might be subject to a mandatory referendum.

The discussion of minority rights raises the question: Should certain topics be prohibited to limit the risk of majority tyranny? The state of Massachusetts, for example, does not allow initiatives on matters related to religion. In contrast, the state of California places no restrictions on the topics that can be brought to a vote, relying on courts to nullify unconstitutional proposals if they are approved. Experience shows that both systems can work.

The downside of prohibiting certain topics from even coming to a vote is that the rule could be abused by applying it too broadly. Because textual prohibitions are somewhat subjective and require interpretation, those charged to interpret the rules might use them as an excuse to exclude proposals they dislike. The state of Illinois, which is notorious for governmental corruption, provides a cautionary tale. Illinois's initiative process, adopted in 1970, restricts proposals to amending the "structural and procedural subjects contained in Article IV" of the state constitution. Article IV is titled "The Legislature" and lays out the powers, structure, selection, and procedures of the legislature and the process for passing laws. A series of state supreme court rulings have interpreted this provision so narrowly as to essentially kill the process, with only one initiative coming before the voters in the five decades that the process has been available. In 2016, the state supreme court struck from the ballot a proposal concerning redistricting and the powers of the attorney general, even though both topics are contained in article IV, on the grounds that they were not "structural and procedural." The court has also invalidated initiatives that would have imposed legislative term limits, prohibited legislators from being paid by other government entities while in office, and created an initiative process for statutes. The assumption underlying direct democracy is that the people are capable of judging their own interests; this suggests that subject-matter restrictions ought to be minimal or nonexistent, leaving it to the people to decide at the polls whether or not an issue is appropriate.

Petitioning Requirements

An important design element for the initiative and petition referendum processes is the petition process itself. The required number of signatures must be specified and the process for soliciting signatures must be regulated. Petition rules usually require proposals to be registered with an election authority and given an official title before the signature collection process begins. It is common to use paid petitioners to collect signatures. Although the practice is controversial, there is little convincing evidence (perhaps none) that paid petitioners undermine the integrity of the process. Other rules include the amount of time that petitions may circulate, the means of signing (in person or online), and the process for verifying signature validity.

A critical feature of the petition process is the number of signatures that are required. The signature requirement should not be so onerous as to preclude successful petition campaigns, and should not be so easy that the ballot ends up cluttered with trivial matters. There is no formula that prescribes the optimal number of signatures, but examining the practices of states that use initiatives provides an indication of the range that is reasonable.

Table 18.1 lists the signature requirements of select nations and states. Sometimes signature requirements are stated in absolute numbers; other times they take the form of a percentage of the electorate. A percentage formulation allows for the requirements to automatically evolve as the population changes in size. As can be seen, requirements range from about 1 to 10 percent of the electorate, with numbers in the middle of that range most common. Research indicates that signature requirements in excess of 10 percent create a substantial hurdle that can make petitioning prohibitively costly and cause the process to atrophy.[1]

It is common, but not universal, to require a geographic distribution of signatures so that petitioners cannot focus on only one populous region. The EU's Citizens' Initiative requires one million signatures in total, with a designated minimum number from each of seven countries. The state of Florida requires signatures from 8 percent of the electorate including 8 percent of the electorate in half of the state's congressional districts to initiate constitutional amendments. The idea behind distributional requirements is to ensure that one region does not dominate the petition process. It is a contestable point whether proposals that rely heavily on signatures from a particular geographic region are inherently less democratic or otherwise harmful to the people.

Finally, it is worth noting that the harm from making a mistake and sending a proposal to the voters without a sufficient number of valid signatures is likely to be small. Unlike an election, where votes directly determine whether or not a law goes into effect, initiative petitions do not make law; they only send a proposal to the voters. If the proposal is undesirable, voters can reject it. When it comes to petition signatures there should be a presumption toward accepting signatures, and not invalidating them on technical grounds. This is a real concern because the record is replete with examples of election administrators invalidating petitions on the most technical of pretexts, such as the presence of coffee stains or ink scribbles on the petition forms. In the spirit of self-government, final decisions should be left to the people where possible; they should not be "protected" from a referendum election by administrative decisions.

5. *Petition rules should be interpreted liberally, with a preference for allowing voters to make the final judgment.*

TABLE 18.1 Initiative Petition Signature Requirements

	Process	# Signatures Required
European Union	European Citizens' Initiative	1 million, of which a specified number in 7 member nations
Italy	Petition referendum	500,000
Switzerland	Initiative amendment	100,000
Switzerland	Petition referendum	50,000
Taiwan	Initiative statute	1.5% of electorate
Uruguay	Initiative amendment	10% of citizens
California	Initiative amendment	8% of votes cast in previous gubernatorial election
California	Initiative statute	5% of votes cast in previous gubernatorial election
Florida	Initiative amendment	8% of votes cast in previous presidential election, overall and in half of congressional districts
North Dakota	Initiative amendment	4% of population
North Dakota	Initiative statute	2% of population
Oregon	Initiative amendment	8% of votes cast in previous gubernatorial election
Oregon	Initiative statute	6% of votes cast in previous gubernatorial election
Wyoming	Initiative statute	15% of votes cast in previous general election, overall and in two-thirds of counties

The Path of Reform

Finally, in terms of the broad reform agenda, chapter 11 lays out specific forms of direct democracy that could be adopted. The proposals are formulated with the US federal government in mind, where the starting point is zero, but could be adapted to other countries or subnational governments depending on how far they are along the direct democracy path. The proposals are organized in terms of feasibility and potential impact, from least to most, and it would make sense to implement them in roughly that order.

Given that adding or expanding direct democracy is essentially a form of experimentation, it seems natural to start with smaller controlled experiments and proceed to bigger experiments later. Starting small allows for learning and customization. As this chapter suggests, using direct democracy requires making a number of operational decisions, some of great import. Operationalizing in the wrong way could result in referendums that do more harm than good. This is not a one-size-fits-all situation; each country and government needs to customize the processes to mesh with its other democratic institutions and political culture. Experience suggests that small experiments will create a demand for larger experiments, leading to a natural progression up the reform ladder. Like democracy in general, the more people have the more they want.

19

Final Thoughts

ACROSS THE GLOBE, in country after country, voter frustration is boiling over into populist politics. From the Brexit referendum in the UK to American presidential campaigns, the message that government has slipped away from "the people" and into the hands of elites is finding a receptive audience. This development is troubling. It is one thing if voters are angry with elected officials—they can simply replace them with another batch—but when they come to believe that the system is "rigged" against them, they may turn against the system itself. Why do people feel like this? And what, if anything, can be done about it? These are the questions that animate this book.

On the first question, we have seen that people feel like they are losing control of government because they *are* losing control of it. Over the past several decades, perhaps as long as a century, lawmaking has gradually drifted out of the reach of voters and into the hands of unelected administrative agencies and courts. Government needed technocratic expertise to manage the increasingly complex and dynamic world that grew out of industrialization, urbanization, and globalization—and while this evolution was a rational response to changing times, it had the unintended side effect of making policy decisions increasingly difficult for ordinary people to understand and control, and opened the door for greater influence by special interests with the resources to navigate the bureaucracies.[1]

As for what we can do about it, this book has argued for giving the people more control over policy by expanding the use of referendums. I have presented an array of evidence suggesting that many fears about direct democracy are misplaced. Referendums have a long history and have been road tested in American states and cities and in nations across the world, giving us a good understanding of their strengths and shortcomings. Direct democracy promises to bring

policies into greater alignment with majority preferences, to diminish the influence of special interest groups, and to reduce political polarization by allowing
the centrist majority to override the partisan extremes.

———

These days we have a tendency to evaluate reform proposals based on their perceived partisan implications, rather than on how they would affect the performance of democracy in the abstract. Democratic Party support for dismantling
the Electoral College is connected to the party's defeat in two recent presidential
elections that it would have won with a popular vote; Republican opposition
stems from the same fact.[2] In contrast, my argument for expanding direct democracy is not based on its partisan implications, but on its potential to make
policy more responsive to the people. Direct democracy could shift policy to
the left or the right depending on the issue and orientation of the electorate,
but that is incidental to my argument.

Evaluating reform proposals without regard to their partisan implications
is a deliberate choice. I believe we have become too ready to see the world
through a partisan lens and need to guard against the inclination to seek partisan advantage from changes in the basic structure of government. Shifting
power toward actors that are not under popular control—such as technocrats
and judges—in the hope that they will override the people and impose decisions favorable to the partisan side we support is not only undemocratic but
short-sighted. Eventually, unaccountable actors will fall under the control of
the "other side" and be used against us.

If anything is certain in politics, it is that the other party will have its turn
in power. During the Democratic Obama administration, some progressives
argued that the executive branch should be given more power over public decisions as a way to overcome opposition from the Republican-controlled Congress; they had second thoughts once the Trump administration took office.
Similarly, some conservatives favor enhancing the power of federal courts, where
they are currently influential; but they would regret it when the courts next have
a liberal majority. We would be wiser to build up the democratic parts of government and trust the people to govern themselves.

This point applies to direct democracy, but I believe it is important more
generally. In thinking about addressing the challenges of populism, we
should take a long-run perspective and shape our democratic institutions to

promote the underlying value of self-government rather than seek to enhance the nondemocratic power of the branch that our side currently controls.[3]

———

My argument for direct democracy goes against the grain of several other proposals for addressing the challenges of populism. Most fundamentally, unlike others, I argue that we must take steps to *enhance* the power of the people.

This thinking pushes against the view that populism is a passing storm, triggered by the financial crisis and a few idiosyncratic election outcomes, and we should temporize until it passes. My take is closer to that of legal scholar Samuel Issacharoff, that "a percentage or two change in the Brexit vote, or a few tens of thousands votes cast differently in a few key U.S. states would certainly have postponed the confrontation," but it would not have removed the underlying political tensions.[4] Tectonic shifts in the foundation of democracy over the past century, described at length in the book, have created policy disconnects that are increasingly noticeable. This is not an issue that we can wait out, hoping it will go away on its own.

Some agree that populism is a response to democratic drift, but argue that the solution is to improve the performance of technocrats—or, going further, to give technocrats even more power, freeing them from the encumbrances of democratic accountability. This book lays out the reasons we should doubt that technocrats are capable of functioning as neutral arbiters in pursuit of some objective notion of the public good, like Plato's philosopher-king. Like all people, they are influenced by their own interests and their subjective sense of what is right, which can diverge sharply from the preferences of the general public. Giving technocrats more power would only compound the underlying problem.

Finally, some argue that the solution is already in the hands of the people themselves. They need to assert more control over their elected representatives, become more involved in protests and political campaigns, and learn about and exercise their civic duty.[5] I have emphasized and substantiated the competence of ordinary people as political actors, but am skeptical of a solution that asks the people, in effect, to pull themselves up by their bootstraps. Ordinary citizens would have to climb a mountain in order to overturn a decision of a federal regulatory agency or a federal court. Instead of assigning the people an insurmountable task, we should give them tools that they can realistically employ—tools that are readily available.

———

A growing number of influential voices believe the pressures of populism are propelling us toward having to choose between two unpalatable options: we can give up on technocratic government or we can give up on rule by the people.

Elite opinion increasingly leans toward technocracy over the people, fueled by skepticism about the judgment and capabilities of ordinary men and women. The people themselves still believe in and support democracy, in the United States and across the world, according to opinion surveys. But if democracy continues to drift out of popular control, how long will it be until the people lose faith in the enterprise and turn toward populist strong men, as has happened too often around the world? If government is going to be autocratic, the people might decide it is better to have *their* autocrats running it than the autocrats of elites.

Fortunately, I believe there is a third option, and it is the only viable choice: we must retain a government administered by experts *and* expand government by the people. We can neither return to a preindustrial government without agencies and experts, nor weaken our commitment to the idea of self-rule. Our path forward must include greater public consultation via referendums, overlaid on existing institutions of representative democracy.

For Americans, this means considering a radical shift in the nature of the national government, which so far has excluded the people from participation in policy decisions. That we consider it radical to allow the people a say in important public matters affecting their lives is an unfortunate testament to the undemocratic nature of US government and something that is overdue for remediation.

In the end, self-rule means that each generation must design its own government to meet its own needs. Successive generations of Americans have done just this, adapting the Founders' framework to make it more democratic, expanding suffrage, bringing more offices under popular control, and making elections more competitive. Nothing more befits a democracy than the people updating its rules where history and evidence tell them they can do things better. We now know enough about direct democracy to be confident about doing it right. It is time to let the people rule.

NOTES

Notes to Introduction

1. Donald Trump, speech in Charlotte, North Carolina, August 19, 2016, quoted in Blake (2016); emphasis added.

2. Bernie Sanders, "The Political Revolution Continues," speech, June 16, 2016, quoted in *Politico* staff (2016); emphasis added.

3. Nigel Farage, speech to the European Parliament, June 28, 2016, transcript in UKPol (2016); emphasis added.

4. The *Oxford Dictionaries Online* defines "populism" as a political approach that appeals to "ordinary people who feel that their concerns are disregarded by established elite groups."

5. Specifically, I used the ANES Time Series Cumulative Data File (1948–2012) and the ANES 2016 Time Series Study, survey variables VCF0613 and V162216, respectively. The survey structure changed in a potentially material way in 1988, when respondents were allowed to answer "neither agree or disagree" instead of being forced into either "agree" or "disagree." The downward trend in feelings about government responsiveness appears even after adjusting for this change. A related question asked by the Pew Research Center (2015; "Most elected officials don't care what people like me think") shows a similar pattern from 1994 to 2015.

6. The percentage is an average of country-specific percentages (Zapryanova and Christiansen 2017).

7. Dalton (2004, 191). On recent trends, see, for example, European Commission Directorate-General for Communication (2018).

8. For examples of the economics view, see Algan et al. (2017), Becker, Fetzer, and Novy (2017), and Rodrick (2017). Economics-based studies tend to focus on short-run causal explanations, perhaps because of the nature of available data. For examples of the cultural view, see Inglehart and Norris (2016) and Sullivan (2017).

9. Wike et al. (2017). This is a common finding—e.g., see the 2013 Gallup survey summarized in Jones (2013). Waters (2003, 477–78) reports survey data on support for initiatives in American states.

10. India and Israel are the other established democracies that have never held a national referendum. One might include Japan, since its 1946 referendum on changing the country's official name predated adoption of its democratic constitution; Prime Minister Shinzo Abe has announced that Japan will hold a referendum on article 9, in which the country renounces war forever, no later than 2020. If we consider only democracies established before World War II, the United States stands alone in never having held a national vote on an issue.

11. FARC, the Revolutionary Armed Forces of Colombia—People's Army.

12. Polling data from Wike et al. (2017). List of nations that have held national referendums from International Institute for Democracy and Electoral Assistance, Direct Democracy Database, https://www.idea.int/data-tools/data/direct-democracy.

13. Based on a careful analysis of polling data, political scientist Morris Fiorina observed that "pro-life and pro-choice activists may believe that all questions are settled by a pronouncement that life begins at conception or at birth, but 80 percent of Americans either aren't sure when life begins or don't believe that an answer settles all questions. Whether the typical American is pro-life or pro-choice all depends on why the abortion is needed and when it will take place." See Fiorina (2009, ch. 2, quote p. 35).

14. Fineman (2015).

15. First quote from Weiss (2012); second from Heagney (2013).

16. *Economist* (2003).

17. Khanna (2017, 1). Khanna also calls for more consultation of the people.

18. Blinder (1997) and Howell and Moe (2016) develop arguments that boil down to increasing the power of unelected experts in the bureaucracies in order to avoid what they see as inefficiencies associated with democratic accountability.

19. Elmendorf and Wood (2018, 577). One of the more convincing studies is Broockman and Skovron (2018), which finds that state legislators overestimated how conservative their constituents were in 2014.

20. Fiorina (2009, 47).

21. Pew Research Center (1998).

22. Madison or Hamilton ([1788a] n.d.).

Chapter 1: Disconnected by the Administrative State

1. Samuel Alito, remarks at Claremont Institute, February 11, 2017 (Alito 2017).

2. See Postell (2012) for a conservative critique (from the Heritage Foundation), and Wallach (2016) for a liberal critique (from the Brookings Institution). Strauss (1984) is a classic scholarly article and Vermeule (2015) provides a recent overview of legal issues.

3. Substantial power has also been transferred to the judicial branch, as discussed in the next chapter.

4. "The modern state is, by any conceivable measure, largely an administrative state" (Vermeule 2015, 1).

5. This summary glosses over some details. While Congress did not specify rates, it did outright prohibit rebates and "pooling," a practice whereby railroads divided business in a region and set common rates. Also, the original Interstate Commerce Act (1887) did not authorize the ICC to set rates directly; that power came in a 1906 amendment to the act.

6. Interstate Commerce Act of 1887.

7. Vermeule (2015, 4). In addition to rationalizing the administrative state, the APA was influenced by political fighting over the fate of the New Deal (Sheperd 1996; McNollgast 1999).

8. According to the *Unified Agenda of Federal Regulatory and Deregulatory Actions*, published by the Office of Management and Budget in the Executive Office of the President, there were 70 cabinet, executive, and independent agencies in spring 2019 (Office of Information and

Regulatory Affairs, 2019, "Spring 2019 Agenda Agency Preambles," Reginfo.gov, https://www
.reginfo.gov/public/do/eAgendaMain?operation=OPERATION_GET_PREAMBLE
_LIST&currentPub=true). The *United States Government Manual*, the official handbook of the
federal government, lists 83 executive agencies, departments, independent establishments, and
government corporations in 2019 ("Organizational Chart of the US Government," *The United
States Government Manual*, n.d., accessed August 9, 2019, https://www.usgovernmentmanual.gov/).
FOIA.gov, the website for Freedom of Information Act requests from the federal government lists
117 agencies as of 2017. According to the *Federal Register*, the official journal of the federal government, there were 449 departments, agencies, and subagencies in August 2019 (search on "all
agencies" at https://www.federalregister.gov/agencies).

9. This summary oversimplifies a bit to avoid becoming too granular. For example, the Safe
Drinking Water Act calls on the EPA administrator specifically to consider arsenic, sulfate, and
radon, although it does not require a particular regulatory action.

10. Clean Air Act of 1970, 42 U.S.C. § 7411(b)(1) (1970).

11. Safe Drinking Water Act Amendments of 1986, 42 U.S.C. § 300g-1(b)(1) (1986).

12. By this, I am not taking a position on the contested issue of whether the Obama EPA or
the Trump EPA was better aligned with public opinion. The point is that the significant swing
in policy was not the result of a dramatic swing in the public's policy preferences, contrary to
how we hope that democracy would work.

13. Quoted in Kovacic and Winerman (2015, 2092–93).

14. The dramatic change in antitrust in the 1980s is often associated with Robert Bork's *The
Antitrust Paradox* (1978), among other writings in the Chicago School tradition.

15. U.S. Const. art. I, § 8.

16. This history of trade policy draws on C. Lewis (2016).

17. Tariff Act of 1930, § 338(d).

18. Trade Expansion Act of 1962, §§ 201(a) and 232(b); Trade Act of 1974, §§ 122(a) and 501;
North American Free Trade Agreement Implementation Act of 1993, § 201(b); Bipartisan Congressional Trade Priorities and Accountability Act of 2015, § 3(a).

19. Richman (1988).

20. Lowande, Jenkins, and Clarke (2018).

21. U.S. Const. art. II, § 2 states that the president "shall have the power, by and with the
consent of the Senate, to make treaties, provided two thirds of the Senators present concur."

22. As late as 1898, at the conclusion of the Spanish-American War, President William
McKinley sent a five-man delegation to Paris to conclude a peace treaty, including three senators
from the Foreign Relations Committee. President Woodrow Wilson's administration broke the
pattern by negotiating the Treaty of Versailles (which ended World War I and created the League
of Nations) without involving the Senate (J. Smith 2007, ch. 9), which may have contributed to
the Senate's decision to reject the treaty, the first time that happened in US history.

23. Data and quote (p. 1) from Peake (2018).

24. Data and quotes (p. 3) from Peake (2018). For a general discussion, see Krutz and Peake
(2009).

25. U.S. Const. art. IV, § 3.

26. Yosemite was first protected as the Yosemite Grant in 1864, later converted to Yosemite
National Park in 1890.

244 NOTES TO CHAPTER 2

27. McCann and Shipan (2018), covering 1947–2016, based on "major law" designations by David Mayhew. Eighty percent of the laws delegated to more than one agency.

28. Appelbaum (2010).

29. Both quoted in Copeland (2010a, first quote n.p., second quote 2).

30. Barack Obama (October 24, 2011), quoted in White House (n.d.).

31. Remarks during Senate hearing on September 4, 2018—see Sasse (2018; ellipsis in original). The senator was not being facetious; I checked and there actually is a position in the Department of Agriculture called the "deputy administrator, plant protection and quarantine," whose job is to safeguard animals and plants from destructive pests and diseases.

32. The limitations of elections as a tool to incentivize politicians have been explored in a stream of theoretical research, beginning with Barro (1973) and Ferejohn (1986).

33. Quoted in Holthaus (2017).

34. Breyer (1993).

35. Gailmard and Patty (2007).

36. Clinton and Lewis (2007); Richardson, Clinton, and Lewis (2018).

37. Surveys also show that federal workers are much more likely to identify as liberal than conservative (D. E. Lewis 2017).

38. Howard (2012).

39. Boehmke, Gailmard, and Patty (2013, 3).

40. Bentley ([1908] 1995) contains an early statement of the idea that democracy is facilitated by competition between interest groups. Lowi (2009) offered a view of American democracy as the confluence of interest groups and the administrative state. G. Becker (1983) developed a model showing how competition between interest groups could lead to efficient policy choices.

41. See, for example, the series of papers by Mat McCubbins, Roger Noll, and Barry Weingast (1987; McNollgast 1989, 1999).

42. The classic formulation of regulatory capture theory is Stigler (1971), which grounded the idea in an economic framework of demand and supply. Peltzman (1976) extended the theory in significant ways. The basic idea that regulatory agencies could become servants of the industries they regulated was understood even at the time of the ICC's creation. See Novek (2014) for a history of capture theory, and Carpenter and Moss (2014) for a wide-ranging collection of articles related to the theory.

43. Huntington (1952) provides a detailed analysis of rate-setting actions taken by the ICC to help the railroad industry through the middle of the twentieth century.

Chapter 2: Disconnected by Courts

1. See discussion in Posner (2010, 78).

2. Posner (2010, 5): "American antitrust law is far more the creation of judicial decisions than of antitrust legislation: the most important antitrust laws are . . . skimpy and vague."

3. Data until 2016 from "Acts of Congress Held Unconstitutional in Whole or in Part by the Supreme Court of the United States" and "State Constitutional and Statutory Provisions and Municipal Ordinances Held Unconstitutional or Held to Be Pre-Empted by Federal Law,"

Congressional Research Service (analysis of cases decided through June 27, 2016), at congress
.gov. More recent data updated from law.justia.com.

4. I am not aware of an explanation for the decline in nullification of state laws in the late
twentieth and early twenty-first centuries.

5. For example, see Google's Ngram Viewer with keywords "supreme court nominee" and
"supreme court nomination." The battle over the nomination of Robert Bork in 1987 is seen by
many as an important turning point.

6. See Shlaes (2013, 324). On the evolution of the confirmation process, see Collins and Ringhand (2016).

7. The more recent nomination of Brett Kavanaugh took even longer and was more of a
spectacle, but in part that was due to allegations that he had sexually assaulted another student
while in high school.

8. See "Supreme Court Nominations: Present–1789," United States Senate website, n.d., accessed August 4, 2019, https://www.senate.gov/pagelayout/reference/nominations/Nominations
.htm.

9. Exit poll by consortium of five networks and Associated Press on election day (Bowman
2017).

10. Dinan (2016).

11. Lincoln ([1861] n.d.). The United States is anomalous in this regard; no other democracy
gives judges such power (Dahl 1989).

12. Posner (2010, 371).

13. Posner (2010).

14. For a variety of systematic evidence on the emergence of the norm of appointing judges
with prior judicial experience, see Epstein, Knight, and Martin (2003). A similar trend toward
appointment of professional judges and away from practitioners and lawyers with other backgrounds also has been documented for district court judges (Wheeler 2010).

15. Frankfurter (1957, 795).

16. Epstein, Landes, and Posner (2013).

Chapter 3: Disconnected by Legislatures?

1. Madison or Hamilton ([1788b] n.d.).

2. Downs (1957); Hotelling (1929). The intuition is this: Suppose candidate A stakes out a
policy position at the median. If the other candidate, B, were to take a position to the (say) left
of the median, we can infer that candidate B would receive less than 50 percent of the vote, because
the 50 percent of voters to right of the median will stick with candidate A, while the 50 percent
of voters to left will sort between the two candidates according to whether they are closer to
candidate A or B. It follows that candidate B would be best off choosing the median position as
well. Therefore, both candidates find it optimal to choose the median policy position.

3. Much of this material is drawn from Matsusaka (2017), which describes the data and empirical methods in more detail.

4. Matsusaka (1992) and Matsusaka and McCarty (2001) explored the idea of "honest
mistakes" theoretically. Broockman and Skovron (2018) provided evidence that state legislators

misperceive constituent views, typically erring by 10 percentage points or more. Daniel Butler and Nickerson (2011) showed that state legislators adjust their voting behavior in response to new information about constituent preferences. Elmendorf and Wood (2018) surveyed the evidence.

5. I used the updated ideology estimates of Shor and McCarty (2011): a legislator was classified as a conservative if his or her NPAT score is positive, and liberal if it is negative. NPAT scores are based on the entire history of roll-call votes by each legislator. See Matsusaka (2017) for more background.

6. Poole and Rosenthal (1991); Poole (2007). This characterization fits the citizen-candidate model of Osborne and Slivinsky (1996) and Besley and Coate (1997). The conclusion is not at odds with the large political economy literature showing a cross-sectional correlation between roll-call votes and district characteristics; we expect district opinion to predict votes through selection of candidates with aligned preferences.

7. For a review of evidence and a discussion of competition-increasing reform proposals, see the various chapters in McDonald and Samples (2006).

8. The figure is based on 3,555 roll-call votes. Competition is measured by vote margin, the difference in votes received by the top two candidates divided by their combined votes; I rescaled so that electoral competition = 1 − vote margin. Legislators and voters *agree* if they prefer the same policy; otherwise they *disagree*. The lines are kernel regressions using the Epanechnikov kernel function with bandwidth of 0.15.

9. I do not want to overstate the case: the evidence in this chapter is not "causal" in the sense that it does not show that changing competition changes congruence; the evidence is what scholars call "correlational." Having said that, the evidence gives reason to be cautious about assuming that more competition will improve representation.

10. Again, these are not causal estimates; I use causal language for ease of exposition. Even interpreted purely as correlations, I believe the relations pose a question for stories that emphasize the role of money in causing noncongruence.

11. I collected data on campaign contributions raised by each legislator in the two-year period before the previous election. To account for the fact that contributions vary across legislators simply because of their state or the time period (for example, contributions are usually higher in California than in Alaska), I normalized each legislator's contributions by adjusting for mean contributions in the legislator's state, chamber, and time period. Specifically, I calculated the mean and variance in total contributions for each year-state-chamber, and then for each legislator subtracted the mean and divided by the variance. This forces the contributions for each election year-state-chamber into a distribution with a mean of zero and a variance of one. The figure is based on 1,622 roll-call votes. The lines are kernel regressions using the Epanechnikov kernel function with bandwidth of 1.0.

12. The basic patterns in figures 3.3 and 3.4 are robust to a variety of statistical controls, such as issue type and state. These relations clearly cannot support a causal interpretation.

13. For evidence and links to the literature, see Matsusaka (2010b).

14. See McCarty, Poole, and Rosenthal (2016) and Fiorina (2009) for evidence and discussion of causes.

15. DeSilver (2018).

Chapter 4: How Disconnected Is Government?

1. This exercise is restricted to policies with only two outcomes, such as whether or not a state uses capital punishment. For policies with a multiplicity of outcomes, such as the income tax rate, there may not be an outcome that commands majority support.

2. An aside for researchers seeking to put this evidence in context: Researchers have attempted to measure the connection between policy and preferences in several ways, only recently converging on a common set of terms. "Congruence" is whether the policy conforms to popular preferences. Another concept, "responsiveness," is whether policy choices are correlated with preferences, either over time or in the cross-section. Although the two terms seem related, "responsiveness" is not logically connected to "congruence" (Achen 1977; Romer and Rosenthal 1979; Matsusaka 2001). The inference issues are subtle and not critical for the present purposes, but can briefly be explained by analogy: Suppose one wishes to know if the content of movies is congruent with the wishes of the film-going public. One could document that when the public become more interested in, say, romances then the number of romance movies increases (positive time-series correlation). But even if such a correlation exists, it could still be the case that the number of romance movies overall is much lower or much higher than the public would prefer. So finding that policy responds at the margin to changes in public opinion does not imply that the policy choices overall are congruent with public opinion. For a conceptual discussion, see Golder and Stramski (2010) and Matsusaka (2010b, 2017).

3. Matsusaka (2010b). The study includes all policies for which state-level opinion data are available during 1988–2004.

4. Lax and Phillips (2012). Lax and Phillips imputed public opinion using multilevel regression and poststratification, allowing them to expand the analysis beyond policies for which state-specific polling data are available. I thank Jeffery Lax for providing the original data from his study.

5. There is one other study in this vein that focuses on a single issue, the state-level minimum wage (Simonovits, Guess, and Nagler 2019). It found that the minimum wage in 2016 was $2.26 an hour less on average than what the median voter wanted. Since minimum wage rates ranged from $7.25 to $10.10 an hour, this also indicates a big deviation from congruence.

6. Gilens and Page (2014).

7. This discussion skirts the issue of whether citizens have meaningful preferences over policy issues. Certainly, some citizens lack well-formed views over unfamiliar issues. While a valid concern in the abstract, it is less troubling for the issues considered in figure 4.1, which are prominent, have been in the public eye for some time, and for which citizens can be expected to have well-formed opinions.

8. Sullivan (2016). Other offerings in this vein include *Against Democracy* by Jason Brennan (2016), *Democracy for Realists: Why Elections Do Not Produce Responsive Government* by Christopher H. Achen and Larry M. Bartels (2016), and *The People Have Spoken (and They Are Wrong)* by David Harsanyi (2014). This line of thinking often concludes that we should move away from democracy; as shown in chapter 10, this is opposite to how the country has reacted in response to previous populist surges.

9. Pitkin (1967) contains one of the most thorough theoretical discussions of representation. She ultimately concludes that legitimate representation should include both trustee and agent

components, but the views of the represented cannot be routinely ignored. Lincoln quote from Pitkin (1967, 277).

10. Galston (2017) contains a nice discussion of these issues. Fortunately, opinion surveys give no reason to believe that voters are turning their backs on democracy.

11. Madison or Hamilton (n.d.).

Chapter 5: Direct Democracy Defined

1. Wallach (2016, 22).

2. Wike et al. (2017).

3. Broder (2000, 1).

4. Somewhat confusingly, "referendum" is occasionally used as a catchall term for any proposal on the ballot (that is, as a synonym for "ballot proposition"), a practice I sometimes follow in the book. The term "plebiscite" is seldom used today, but stands for a vote by the people on a policy proposal, whether in person or by ballot.

5. Also called a "compulsory" or "obligatory" referendum.

6. Also called an "optional" or "veto" referendum.

7. On subject-matter restrictions and other rules for initiatives and petition referendums, see Matsusaka (2004, appendix A) and the website of the Initiative and Referendum Institute (www .iandrinstitute.org).

8. See Matsusaka and McCarty (2001) on determinants of initiative use.

9. The legislature approved a law in 1916 that allowed signatures to be collected, but in a manner that was practically infeasible; see Schmidt (1989, 270).

10. E. Gerber et al. (2001).

Chapter 6: Direct Democracy in the United States

1. On adoption of state constitutions by referendum, see Dodd ([1910] 1970), especially chapter 1, and Oberholtzer (1911), especially chapter 4.

2. On the history of amendment of state constitutions by referendum, see Dodd ([1910] 1970), especially chapter 4, and Oberholtzer (1911), especially chapter 6.

3. Tarr (2002) contains an extensive discussion of this point.

4. For more details, see Oberholtzer (1911), chapters 7 and 8.

5. Oberholtzer (1911, ch. 7).

6. See Moss (2017, ch. 6) for a rich case study of the New York episode.

7. Oberholtzer (1911, ch. 7).

8. Quoted in Ford (1912, 72).

9. Henry Loucks, as quoted in Piott (2003, 25).

10. Piott (2003) provides state-by-state histories of initiative and referendum adoption. Ballotpedia (https://ballotpedia.org/History_of_initiative_and_referendum_in_the_U.S.) gives additional information. Mississippi's adoption in 1914 was invalidated by the state supreme court in 1922. Delaware (1906) and Illinois (1902, 1910) voted in favor of adoption in advisory referendums, but their legislatures ignored the will of the people and took no action.

11. See Bradford (1911, ch. 19) and Matsusaka (2009).

12. Twenty-three states currently allow petition referendums: all of the initiative states except Florida, Illinois, and Mississippi, and the noninitiative states Maryland and New Mexico.

13. This information is from Matsusaka (2009) and the Legal Landscape Database collected by the Initiative and Referendum Institute. Table 6.1 was compiled from state constitutions, statutes, and city charters.

14. Data on the number of initiatives over time and by state are from the Initiative and Referendum Institute. For more historical data, see Initiative and Referendum Institute (2019).

15. Historical data on noninitiative propositions are patchy going back in time. Table 6.2 reports complete data for 1998–2018 that I collected by hand from official state election documents. Legislative propositions include constitutional amendments and bond issues proposed by the legislature, legislative proposals to modify initiatives (California), proposals from special commissions (Arizona), advisory votes on legislative tax increases (Washington), and mandatory votes on calling a constitutional convention.

16. Data from 2009–19 of Gallup's "Trust in Government" poll, available at https://news .gallup.com/poll/5392/trust-government.aspx. Surveys by other organizations report similar findings. The reported number for the federal government concerns trust in solving domestic problems; the comparable number for solving international problems is 51 percent.

Chapter 7: Direct Democracy in Europe

1. Vote share data from P. Lewis et al. (2018). First quote from Mikelionis (2018); second quote from *Economist* (2018).

2. Berman (2017).

3. Wike, Fetterolf, and Fagan (2019, 2).

4. Quoted in Keohane (2018).

5. Data from Wike et al. (2017). The precise question was: "I'm going to describe various types of political systems and ask what you think about each as a way of governing our country. For each one, would it be a very good, somewhat good, somewhat bad or very bad way of governing this country? (a) A democratic system where citizens, not elected officials, vote directly on major national issues to decide what becomes law." Figure 7.1 reports the proportion who responded "very good" or "somewhat good," as a percentage of all responses other than "don't know"/"refused."

6. International Institute for Democracy and Electoral Assistance (2008, table 8.4). See also Kaufmann, Büchi, and Braun (2010).

7. Topaloff (2017) discusses the connection between elite objectives and European referendums.

8. Treaty of Lisbon, art. 24.

9. For a detailed discussion of the European Citizen Initiative, see Kaufmann, Büchi, and Braun (2010, 209–17). For current developments, see the ECI's official website: http://ec.europa.eu /citizens-initiative. One innovation of the ECI is that it permits signatures to be gathered online, something that many governments have been hesitant to allow.

10. Herold (1963) and Blanning (2007, quote 347).

11. As an aside, the Weimar Constitution was ahead of its time in its direct democracy provisions, permitting initiatives and referendums at the national and subnational levels.

Unfortunately, the implementation procedures were so cumbersome that only two initiatives reached the ballot, and neither was approved.

12. Kobach (1993) contains a detailed history of the development of Swiss direct democracy institutions. Matsusaka (2018a) lists direct democracy institutions in the cantons.

13. Data from Swiss Federal Chancellery. Ballot propositions include initiatives and referendums.

14. On the Five Star Movement, see Loucaides (2019).

Chapter 8: Direct Democracy in Unexpected Places

1. The data were collected by the International Institute for Democracy and Electoral Assistance, and are available at https://www.idea.int/data-tools/data/direct-democracy. Latin American includes Central America (including Mexico), South America, and the Caribbean.

2. Wike et al. (2017). GDP per capita in 2018 US dollars, PPP-adjusted, were taken from the International Monetary Fund, available at https://knoema.com/pjeqzh/gdp-per-capita-by-country-statistics-from-imf-1980–2024. I used data for 2017 for Venezuela because its 2018 GDP was not available.

3. Surveys of direct democracy across the world: David Butler and Ranney (1994), Kaufmann, Büchi, and Braun (2010), and International Institute for Democracy and Electoral Assistance (2008). Hwang (2006) and Lee and Kaufmann (2009) are especially good for Asia. Altman (2011) is especially good for Latin America.

4. Quoted in Kaufmann (2018).

5. See Roy (2003) on the democratic transition of Taiwan, and Taiwan Foundation for Democracy (2004), Hwang (2009), and Kaufmann (2018) on direct democracy in Taiwan. Quote from Kaufmann (2018).

6. Japan took some tentative steps toward democracy during the Taisho period (1912–26), such as expanding suffrage, but the legislature was secondary government decisions.

7. In 1947, under its provisional government, Japan held a national referendum to change the country's official name.

8. For a detailed discussion of direct democracy in Japan, see Hwang (2009).

9. For a detailed description of South Korean law and practice, see Ha (2009).

10. For more, see Kaufmann, Büchi, and Braun (2010, 222–24); Rissotto and Zovatto (2008); and Altman (2011, ch. 6).

11. According to the *Economist* Intelligence Unit's democracy index, in 2018 Uruguay ranked top in Latin America, and #15 of 167 nations worldwide (above the United States at #25): "Democracy Index 2018," *Economist* Intelligence Unit, n.d., accessed August 4, 2019, https://www.eiu.com/topic/democracy-index.

12. For more on Bolivia, see Altman (2011, ch. 4); Kaufmann, Büchi, and Braun (2010, 227–30); and Casey (2018).

Chapter 9: The American Anomaly

1. Wike et al. (2017).
2. Wood ([1969] 1998, 513).
3. Madison or Hamilton (n.d.).

4. Quotes: Adams from J. Adams ([1763] n.d.); Rush from Rush ([1789] n.d.); Marshall from Marshall ([1838] 2006). In his speech to the Pennsylvania ratifying convention, James Wilson, the Constitution's leading architect after Madison, listed the disadvantages of pure democracy as "dissensions, the delay and disclosure of public counsels, the imbecility of public measures retarded by the necessity of a numerous consent" (J. Wilson [1787] 2009).

5. For a discussion of the sense of crisis in the 1780s, see Wood (2009, ch. 1).

6. Richard (1994, 12).

7. Richard (1994, 10).

8. Hamilton quote from Hamilton ([1788] n.d.).

9. For a description of political institutions of the Roman Republic, see Lintott (1999) and Mouritsen (2017).

10. The word "republic" itself comes from the Latin *res publica*, meaning "the public's things"—that is, public affairs. The text describes the formal structure of government. Historians debate how close practice came to the formal structure, and in particular, how much influence the people actually had. Most agree that citizen assemblies became sideshows during the final decades of the Republic, when internal strife was common. Recent scholarship suggests that the citizen assemblies otherwise were not simply rubber stamps. And they clearly retained symbolic value as evidenced by the fact that Julius Caesar and especially Augustus took care to secure popular approval for their assumption of autocratic powers (Mouritsen 2017, ch. 1). See Lintott (1999) more generally.

11. There were three assemblies, whose membership and powers varied over time: *Comitia Centuriata*, *Comitia Tributa*, and *Consilium Plebis*.

12. Originally, different assemblies were responsible for approving different policies, but in 287 BCE the plebeian assembly became the primary decision maker for all policies; its laws were called *plebiscita*—hence the modern "plebiscite." The change came about through the *Lex Hortensia*.

13. The *Lex Sempronia Agraria*.

14. Dickinson ([1788] n.d.). Two other examples illustrate the Founders' mindset: "In the ancient republics, where the whole body of the people assembled in person, a single orator, or an artful statesman, was generally seen to rule with as complete a sway as if a sceptre had been placed in his single hand" (Madison, n.d.). "The Romans never discovered the secret of representation—the whole body of citizens assembled for the purposes of legislation—a circumstance that exposed their government to frequent convulsions, and to capricious measures" (Webster [1787] n.d.).

15. Richard (1994), especially chapters 3 and 4.

16. One well-known example occurred in 406 BCE when six Athenian generals who had won an important and unexpected naval victory over the Spartans off the Arginusae islands were tried before a citizen assembly on a charge of having allowed some sailors to drown. Demagogues, so the story goes, inflamed the people so that they convicted and executed the generals, an action they regretted shortly thereafter, and followed by bringing charges against the initial instigators. The chief historical source is Xenophon's *Hellenica*.

17. On the structure of Athenian government, see Rhodes (1985) and Ober (2008), especially chapter 4. The structure of government evolved over time; the text is a snapshot of the most successful period.

18. The following description of the status of Athens and the referenced statistical information comes from chapter 2 of Ober (2008).

19. On the causal role of democracy, see chapter 2 of Ober (2008). This begs the question of how Athens happened to adopt the democratic institutions it did; Fleck and Hanssen (2006) offer one theory based on terrain and type of agricultural land, and Fleck and Hanssen (2013) stress the role of short-run dictatorships in laying the groundwork.

20. This paragraph is based on chapter 4 in Ober (2008). Fleck and Hanssen (2012) give related evidence on how Athenian courts brought out information while controlling harmful self-interested behavior.

21. Ober notes in passing that the idea of assemblies being dominated by elite experts may have a commonsense (albeit spurious) appeal "because of the limited experience most modern individuals have with participatory processes of self-government" (2008, 164). This would have been true for the Founders as well, who had little experience with direct democracy.

22. Webster ([1787] n.d.).

23. This description of education in the early American republic is based on Wood (2009, ch. 13) and Urban and Wagoner (2014, ch. 3).

24. Information on communication and newspapers is taken from Wood (2009, ch. 13) and John (1998).

25. James Madison, de facto leader of the House in the early republic, was regarded by his peers as "a thorough master of almost every public question that can arise." See Wood (2009, 58–62, quote 62).

26. Madison ([1787] n.d.).

27. Dahl (2006, 141).

28. Indeed, as much as Americans venerate their Constitution, few countries have chosen to follow its model. Legal scholars Mila Versteeg and Emily Zackin (2014, 1641) show that the US Constitution is "a global outlier," far shorter, less adaptable, and with a shorter list of rights and less popular participation than the constitutions of other countries.

29. Or, more precisely, what we presume would have been their negative views. There is no indication that the Founders ever considered using referendums. All of their writing against direct democracy pertained to citizen assemblies. In the famous *Federalist* No. 10 that is usually cited as an argument against direct democracy, Madison explicitly considered only "a society consisting of a small number of citizens, who assemble and administer the government in person"— that is, a citizen assembly (Madison [1787] n.d.).

30. The objection that the United States is "a republic and not a democracy," which in my experience invariably comes up in any discussion of direct democracy, is an example of this sort of slavish adherence to the Founders. In fact, the United States is both a republic and a democracy, something that was recognized by most Americans of the founding era, and the Founders themselves, and is obvious to most people today. For those curious about this largely semantic point, see Dahl (2003, appendix A; 2006, 155–58) for a careful discussion of why it is ahistorical and the role it plays in discussions.

Chapter 10: A Work in Progress

1. See Middlekauf (1982, 132–34) for discussion. Essay 91, "How Exclusive Companies Influence and Hurt Our Governments," in Trenchard and Gordon's *Cato's Letters: Essays on Liberty*, first published in 1711, focused on the dangers of monopolies to politics.

2. The Intolerable Acts, passed in 1774, blockaded the port of Boston, preventing imports and exports; revoked the Massachusetts charter, removing all institutions of self-government; allowed royal officials to be tried in Great Britain; and allowed British troops to be billeted in private homes and public buildings. The Quebec Act had a different origin, but was also considered one of the Intolerable Acts.

3. Calabresi and Leibowitz (2013) and Zingales (2012, ch. 3) discuss the role of "crony capitalism" in the Tea Act and other British laws, and the influence this had on the American revolutionaries.

4. Both the terms "aristocratic" and "democratic" were considered pejoratives at the time, and used to describe one's opponents in these debates. The contestants on both sides would have characterized themselves as "republicans." Direct democracy was not seriously considered at the time because it was deemed infeasible for such a large nation.

5. *Letters from the Federal Farmer*, October 12, 1787, quoted in Storing (1985, 60).

6. On the Democratic-Republican Societies, see Wood (2009, ch. 4) and Wilentz (2005a, ch. 2).

7. Wilentz (2005a, xx).

8. On the inauguration, coaches, and other stylistic changes in the culture, see Bernstein (2003, ch. 8) and Wood (2009, ch. 8).

9. Thomas Jefferson, "To Samuel Kercheval Monticello, July 12, 1816," American History, from Revolution to Reconstruction and Beyond, n.d., accessed August 9, 2019, http://www.let.rug .nl/usa/presidents/thomas-jefferson/letters-of-thomas-jefferson/jefl246.php.

10. "The mass of the citizens is the safest depository of their own rights. . . . [T]he evils flowing from the duperies of the people are less injurious than those from the egoism of their agents." Thomas Jefferson, "To John Taylor Monticello, May 28, 1816," American History, from Revolution to Reconstruction and Beyond, n.d., accessed August 12, 2019, http://www.let.rug.nl/usa /presidents/thomas-jefferson/letters-of-thomas-jefferson/jefl245.php.

11. These reforms were not simple, direct consequences of populist pressure. They had multiple causes, such as the need to empower the common men who were asked to carry arms for the country, and in the western states, a desire to attract settlers.

12. Turnout and eligibility numbers in the early republic are necessarily rough estimates. Pasley (2004) calculates that turnout in 1790 in Massachusetts and Pennsylvania was less than 30 percent of eligible white males, which would be roughly 10 percent of the adult population. The traditional English justification for linking voting rights to property was that landholders had a stake in the community, were not dependent on another person, and were more likely to be competent about public matters (Keyssar 2009, 4–5).

13. Keyssar (2009, tables A.2 and A.3). The 5 states (out of 21) with significant requirements in 1824 were New Jersey, North Carolina (state senate only), Rhode Island, South Carolina, and Virginia. Several states required property but provided exceptions: Connecticut exempted

taxpayers and militiamen; New York exempted white men; Tennessee exempted persons who had resided in the county for six months or more.

14. Lutz (1979, tables 5, 6).

15. Wilentz (2005a, 125, 303).

16. Calhoun quote from Wilentz (2005a, 251).

17. Howe (2007, 143).

18. "Thomas Jefferson to George Logan, November 12, 1816," Founders Online, National Archives, n.d., accessed August 12, 2019, https://founders.archives.gov/documents/Jefferson/03-10 -02-0390. He also wrote that "banking establishments are more dangerous than standing armies" (Jefferson, "To John Taylor"). This was not an entirely new concern for Jefferson—during the late 1780s he had argued that the Constitution's Bill of Rights should include a restriction on government-created monopolies.

19. The first quote is from Wilentz (2005a, 4), attributed to a letter from Andrew Jackson to Francis Blair on August 22, 1836, but I have not found the quote in that letter, so the citation may be in error. The second quote is from Jackson's first state of the nation address (Jackson ([1829] n.d.).

20. In the presidential election of 1824, Jackson received the most popular votes and the most electoral-college votes. But because of the Constitution's byzantine selection rules, the winner was chosen by the House of Representatives, and they selected John Quincy Adams, a former Federalist and son of the second president. Taking office with a stain of illegitimacy, Adams made matters worse in his first message to Congress when he urged legislators not to be "palsied by the will of [your] constituents" (J. Q. Adams [1825] n.d.).

21. For discussions of Jackson and the BUS, see Wilentz (2005a, ch. 12; 2005b, ch. 4).

22. Quoted in Wilentz (2005b, 77).

23. Campbell (2016).

24. Jackson ([1832] n.d.).

25. Quote from Wilentz (2005a, 253).

26. Data adapted from Keyssar (2009), especially table A.2.

27. Lutz (1979, table 3).

28. Ferguson (2006); Seifter (2017).

29. Wilentz (2005a, 246).

30. See Keyssar (2009, 54–56).

31. Theodore Roosevelt, speech to the Ohio Constitutional Convention, February 21, 1912 (Roosevelt [1912] n.d.).

32. The discussion of populism in this section is informed by Chambers (2000), Cherny (1997), Edwards (2006), McGuire (1981), McMath (1993), and Postel (2007).

33. Cherny (1997, 98).

34. White (2017, 518).

35. Holding for the sugar trust: *United States v. E. C. Knight,* 156 U.S. 1 (1895). Holding that strikes were an unlawful restraint of trade: *United States v. Debs,* 158 U.S. 564 (1895).

36. White (2017, 530–31).

37. "Populist Party Platform of 1892," The American Presidency Project (Gerhard Peters and John T. Woolley), UC Santa Barbara (July 4, 1892) n.d., https://www.presidency.ucsb.edu /documents/populist-party-platform-1892.

38. Taft ([1911] n.d.).

39. Roosevelt ([1912] 2018).

40. For historical background and evidence that the 17th Amendment made senators more responsive, see Gailmard and Jenkins (2009).

41. On women's right to vote, see Keyssar (2009), especially chapter 6 and tables A.17–A.20.

42. States also began to adopt the recall process during the Progressive Era.

43. Interestingly, proponents justified the act on the grounds that it would *protect* corporations—from being extorted by politicians and parties.

44. Keyssar (2009, ch. 4). The role of populists in disenfranchisement remains in dispute; removing black voting rights was not a central part of their agenda in the South but it appears they lent the effort support. During this period, Southern states also adopted white-only primary elections.

45. While there was no nationwide populist movement, there were populist politicians such as Huey Long (Louisiana) in the 1930s and George Wallace (Alabama) in the 1960s. It may not be a coincidence that these populist politicians emerged in the least democratic part of the country, the South, which had become a one-party state under control of the Democratic Party.

46. One important democratizing reform took place during the war, when the Magnuson Act (1943) allowed Chinese persons to become citizens. This was followed by the McCarran-Walter Act of 1952, which, although primarily an anti-immigration law, permitted people of Asian ancestry to become citizens.

47. Keyssar (2009, ch. 8).

Chapter 11: Six Reforms

1. The last serious attempt to amend the US Constitution to allow initiatives was in the late 1970s, when a bipartisan group of 55 senators and House members sponsored SJR 33, the Voter Initiative Constitutional Amendment. A Senate committee held hearings and the national media weighed in, but the effort went nowhere (Schmidt 1989, ch. 8).

2. DREAM, in the title of the DREAM Act of 2001, is an acronym for "Development, Relief, and Education for Minor Aliens."

3. This level of support holds across numerous polls, and for different question wordings (Nichols 2017).

4. In addition to breaking gridlock, an auxiliary benefit would be to reduce the executive branch's temptation to step in and solve the problem on its own, slowing the shift in power from the legislative to the executive branch discussed in part I. The phenomenon appeared in this case when President Obama, impatient with Congress's failure to act, attempted to implement the DREAM Act through executive actions, some of which the courts invalidated as beyond the scope of his presidential authority (President Trump rescinded other parts).

5. Peake (2018).

6. Video available at Edward Everitt, "Governor Reagan as Guest with Johnny Carson—03/15/75," YouTube, December 28, 2013, https://www.youtube.com/watch?v=SHoT561u1zY.

7. The requirement to give voters a "say on pay" originates in the Dodd-Frank Act of 2010. Ertimur, Ferri, and Stubben (2010) show that directors lose votes if they ignore shareholder recommendations.

8. A modest reform would be to require states to hold a referendum to ratify an amendment proposed by Congress, instead of allowing legislatures to ratify. This would require a constitutional amendment.

Chapter 12: A Tale of Two Referendums

1. Quoted in Mehta and Finnegan (2014).

2. "Revenue from own sources" data are from the Census Bureau's *State and Local Government Finances* (published annually). The numbers exclude transfers from the federal government, and are expressed in 2018 dollars.

3. Reagan quote from "The Kid vs. the Old Champ: Moretti, Reagan Put Careers on Line in Tax Initiative Battle," *Los Angeles Times*, October 1, 1973, 3A.

4. Jesse Unruh quote from "Gaining Attention by Snubbing Tradition: Brown: Image Is Carefully Cultivated," *Los Angeles Times*, October 17, 1978, 1.

5. Quote from "Calbuzz Dustbin: When Jarvis Stormed the Capitol," Calbuzz, May 24, 2009, http://www.calbuzz.com/2009/05/calbuzz-dustbin-of-history-when-howard-jarvis-stormed-the-capitol/. See D. Smith (1998) for a detailed description of Howard Jarvis and the Proposition 13 campaign.

6. The American Federation of Labor and Congress of Industrial Organizations.

7. Quotes from "Brown's Political Future May Hinge on How He Handles Proposition 13," *Atlanta Constitution*, June 18, 1978, 11C; and "Tries to Get Ahead of Movement He Opposed," *Washington Post*, June 8, 1978, A3. See also "How California Business Views Tax Revolt: Why Many Firms Decide to Oppose Proposition 13," *Christian Science Monitor*, June 2, 1978, 11.

8. Jarvis quote from "Foes Get Down to Business on Proposition 13: Major Contributions Sought from Firms to Stock Campaign Chest," *Los Angeles Times*, April 16, 1978, B1.

9. "Grass Roots on Airwaves to Push 13," *Los Angeles Times*, May 28, 1978, A1.

10. William Schneider, "Punching through the Jarvis Myth: Prop. 13's Biggest Booster Was Inflation, Not Anger against Government," *Los Angeles Times*, June 11, 1978, I1.

11. Quoted in "Los Angeles Times Poll: Brown Gets High Marks on Handling of Prop. 13," *Los Angeles Times*, July 10, 1978, B1.

12. Quoted in "Brown Seeks Spending Limit: Legislature OKs Prop. 13 Relief Bill," *Los Angeles Times*, June 24, 1978, 1.

13. One challenge, that Proposition 13 violated the 14th Amendment of the US Constitution by assessing different taxes based on the amount of time property had been owned, eventually made its way to the US Supreme Court, where it was rejected in *Nordlinger v. Hahn*, 505 U.S. 1 (1992).

14. "California Taxpayers to Get $1 Billion in Rebates," *New York Times*, July 8, 1987.

15. Quote from California Secretary of State, 1988, *Voter Information Guide for 1988, General Election* (UC Hastings Scholarship Repository) http://repository.uchastings.edu/ca_ballot_pamphlets/. The Gann Limits apply only to certain categories of spending; as time has passed, voters have approved more exceptions.

16. The following discussion is pieced together from various news stories, and the detailed accounts in Shipman (2017) and Qvortrup (2018).

17. Countries that held a referendum on joining the EU: Austria, Croatia, Czech Republic, Estonia, Finland, Hungary, Latvia, Lithuania, Malta, Poland, Slovakia, Slovenia, Sweden. Countries that joined without a referendum: Bulgaria, Cyprus, Romania.

18. Indeed, parliament institutionalized the referendum process in 2000 when it adopted the Political Parties, Elections and Referendums Act, establishing national referendum procedures and creating a national electoral commission to administer referendum elections.

19. "This will be a once-in-a-generation moment to shape the destiny of our country." David Cameron, speech, February 19, 2016 (Prime Minister's Office, "PM Statement Following European Council Meeting: 19 February 2016," Gov.uk, February 20, 2016, https://www.gov.uk/government/speeches/pms-statement-following-european-council-meeting-19-february-2016). The other quotes in this and the next paragraph are from the same speech.

20. Quote from Theresa May's speech launching her candidacy for leadership of the Conservative Party, reported in "Theresa May's Tory Leadership Launch Statement: Full Text," *Independent*, June 30, 2016.

21. I discuss this polling evidence in more detail in the next chapter.

22. The idea of asking voters a general question should not be dismissed altogether. One could imagine a two-step process for Brexit. In step one, voters would have been asked if they would like the government to negotiate an exit treaty, and in step two, they would have been asked to approve an actual treaty. This approach might be practical when specifying the law requires a lot of work, and the government wishes to determine how much interest there is in the general idea before starting down the path.

23. "From Thomas Jefferson to John Armstrong, Jr., 2 May 1808," Founders Online, National Archives, n.d., accessed August 9, 2019, https://founders.archives.gov/documents/Jefferson/99-01-02-7944.

24. Several observers raised this possibility following Brexit; for example, Rogoff (2016). For reasons I do not quite understand, countries seldom require supermajorities on referendums.

25. A different approach to ensuring a broad consensus is to require a minimum level of turnout, called a "turnout quorum." Turnout quorums do not solve the slender-majority problem, and as discussed later can even compound problems by encouraging opponents to abstain instead of showing up and voting "no." For a theoretical analysis of quorum rules, see Aguiar-Conraria and Magalhães (2010).

26. House of Lords Select Committee on the Constitution, *Referendums in the United Kingdom: Report with Evidence*, 12th report of the session 2009–10, H.L. paper 99, p. 51. See sections 180–89 on turnout thresholds and supermajorities, and sections 195–96 on voting for specific laws.

27. The double referendum is discussed in Shipman (2017, 51, 162, 168, 182).

28. "On the Referendum #6: Exit Plans and a Second Referendum," Dominic Cummings's Blog, June 23, 2015, https://dominiccummings.com/2015/06/23/on-the-referendum-6-exit-plans-and-a-second-referendum/.

29. Cameron aide quoted in Elvey (2015).

Chapter 13: Potential Benefits of Referendums

1. Some would argue that giving people what they want is actually a cost, not a benefit, because the people do not know what they want, and the things they want are bad for them. I discuss this at length in the next chapter. We have surprisingly little statistical evidence on the degree to which direct democracy brings policy into alignment with preferences. For the 43 state-level issues discussed in chapter 4, where policy was aligned with majority preferences only 50 percent of the time, congruence was 4 percent higher in states that permitted initiatives than in other states. This difference remains after controlling for issue-specific effects and size of the majority, but it not a causal estimate.

2. Duncan (2016).

3. David Butler and Ranney (1994, 262).

4. Polling data from the Field Poll (Mark DiCamillo, "Voters Inclined to Support Many of This Year's Statewide Ballot Propositions," The Field Poll, release #2555, UC Berkeley, Institute of Governmental Studies, November 4, 2016, https://igs.berkeley.edu/igs-poll/berkeley-igs-poll). The figure shows the percentage of survey respondents in favor (excluding those with no opinion) for September and October, and the percentage of voters in favor for the November election.

5. The pattern of support declining over time appears to be a general phenomenon. Considering 242 California propositions between 1958 and 2014, support dropped 6 percent on average from the first poll to the election outcome (Matsusaka 2016).

6. Huder, Ragusa, and Smith (2011); Kogan (2016).

7. The idea that direct democracy helps by allowing voters to "unbundle" issues is explored theoretically in Besley and Coate (2008) and Matsusaka (2008). Matsusaka (2008) provides evidence that unbundling allows voters to send clearer preference signals in gubernatorial elections.

8. "Los Angeles Times Poll: Voters Perceive Brown as High in Imagination," Los Angeles Times, October 8, 1978, A1.

9. For a contemporary account of the budget deal, see Young (2009). Schwarzenegger appointed two Republicans who broke ranks to support the deal, Anthony Adams and Roy Ashburn, to the California Board of Parole Hearings and California Unemployment Insurance Appeals Board, respectively; both positions paid more than six figures per year, with minimal responsibilities. Schwarzenegger also appointed Abel Maldonado to fill a vacancy in the Office of the Lieutenant Governor. See Jon Fleischman, "Did the Six GOP Legislators Who Voted for Big Taxes in 2009 Pay a Political Price? Or Not?" Flashreport (blog), February 28, 2011, http://www.flashreport.org/blog/2011/02/28/did-the-six-gop-legislators-who-voted-for-big-taxes-in-2009-pay-a-political-price-or-not-63/; and Jon Coupal, "Betrayal," Howard Jarvis Taxpayers Association website, December 13, 2010, https://www.hjta.org/california-commentary/betrayal/.

10. Republican Kevin Jeffries, quoted in "Legislature Finally Passes Budget," Orange County Register, February 19, 2009.

11. Reactions to the budget deal were widely reported. Examples include: Rau, Halper, and McGreevy (2009); Song and Blume (2009); and "Thousand Protest Taxes," Orange County Register, March 8, 2009.

12. The minority could still block tax increases under Proposition 13's two-thirds rule.

13. Jerry Brown campaign advertisement: Brown for Governor, "JB401" YouTube, September 2, 2010, https://www.youtube.com/watch?v=plWquvOBt5A.

14. A large theoretical literature in economics and political science explores the formation of legislative coalitions. Accommodating individual members can help or hurt, depending on the particulars of the situation. Classic references include Weingast, Shepsle, and Johnsen (1981) and Baron and Ferejohn (1989).

15. Another example that may be familiar to some readers is the side deals that were struck in order to secure passage of President Obama's health-care plan in 2009. One of the most notorious was the "cornhusker kickback" that Democratic senator Ben Nelson from Nebraska extracted, specifying that the federal government would cover the cost of all new Medicaid expenses in the state forever.

16. See Curtis and Roberts (2017). Data from *YouGov Survey Results* (YouGov: 2017) https://d25d2506sfb94s.cloudfront.net/cumulus_uploads/document/9pum7c5c4j/AnthonyResults_170613_Brexit_W.pdf. "Don't know" responses omitted. A survey in October 2017 found the same pattern.

17. First quote from "'Brexit Devastated Me, but Now I Back the Tories': Re-Leavers on How They Will Vote," *Guardian*, May 18, 2017. Second quote from Parker (2017).

18. At a general level, people care about "procedural justice"—they view some decision processes as more legitimate than others (Tyler 2004). Survey evidence indicates that Americans would prefer processes with more direct decision making by the people (Hibbing and Theiss-Morse 2001). Johnson, Tipler, and Camarillo (2019) conducted a survey experiment regarding removal of a Confederate monument from a park in an American city, finding that respondents considered the decision fairer and more legitimate if made by referendum than by elected officials, even if they were on the losing side of the issue. In a field experiment in Indonesia, Olken (2010) found that villagers reported higher satisfaction when development projects were chosen by referendum rather than by their representatives, even though the projects chosen were similar under the two decision processes.

19. Skelton (1978).

20. *Economist* (2003).

21. The importance of multiple gatekeepers in creating policy inertia is a common feature in spatial models of lawmaking; for example, Krehbiel (1996, 1998). Boehmke, Osborne, and Schilling (2015) show theoretically that initiatives can increase and decrease stability.

22. The idea that elections can aggregate information efficiently is called the Condorcet jury theorem. Lupia (2001) contains an illuminating nontechnical discussion. Li and Suen (2009) and Nitzan and Paroush (2017) survey the technical literature. I discuss the wisdom of crowds again in chapter 14.

23. Ober (2008, 2, 20). He calls this the *epistemic function* of democratic institutions.

24. There is a large literature on the determinants of political trust. The foundational study related to direct democracy is D. Smith and Tolbert (2004), which found a positive relation between initiative use and trust in government. Dyck (2009) questioned whether those findings are robust to minor variations in specification. Existing research, which focuses on variation across states, is limited in several ways: (1) with one exception, previous research examines responses to a general question about trust in government, which respondents likely interpret as

applying to the federal government, rather than trust in *state* government; (2) the studies use data from national surveys to estimate state-level effects, but the surveys are not representative at the state level; (3) the regressions include numerous explanatory variables that arguably are influenced by the initiative (such as legislative professionalism, divided government, or partisanship), possibly biasing the key coefficients.

25. Jones (2014). This is one of the very few studies that provide state-level data on how much respondents trust their state government.

26. The difference in trust between initiative and noninitiative states is statistically significant at about the 5 percent level, although again these should not be interpreted as causal estimates. Illinois is coded as a noninitiative state because its initiative process has been effectively nullified by courts.

27. Bourne (1912, 8).

28. The most comprehensive exploration of educative effects remains D. Smith and Tolbert (2004). Much of the existing literature was produced before the causal inference revolution, and scholars are revisiting the findings using updated methods; see Seabrook, Dyck, and Lascher (2015).

29. The idea was proposed as early as 1967, by US senator Lee Metcalf, according to law professor Richard Hasen, who has advocated for the idea since the 1990s in a series of scholarly and popular publications. See Hasen (1996).

30. Kiff (2018).

31. For a more extensive discussion of competition in direct democracy and policy entrepreneurs, see Matsusaka (2004, ch. 9). Kobach (1993, ch. 5) discusses policy entrepreneurs in Switzerland.

Chapter 14: Are Voters Up to the Task?

1. Delli Carpini and Keeter (1996) report at length what voters do and not know.

2. Quote from Sabato, Ernst, and Larson (2001, xi). A string of ominously titled books explore aspects of the skeptics' view: *Democratic Delusions* (Ellis 2002), *Democracy Derailed* (Broder 2000), *Dangerous Democracy?* (Sabato, Ernst, and Larson 2001), and *Paradise Lost* (Schrag, 2004).

3. What I am calling "competence" here is sometimes called "rationality." The reader who prefers to think in terms of "rational" voting can substitute that language throughout the chapter. I have avoided the term "rationality" because its connotation of deliberate calculation can cause confusion.

4. I mention this explicitly because public discourse today sometimes goes down precisely this path by assuming that those on the other side are incompetent (ill-informed, selfish, irrational), rather than granting that they have a principled and reasoned disagreement.

5. Downs (1957).

6. Popkin (1991) and Lupia and McCubbins (1998) analyze in depth the use of information cues in voting.

7. Even campaign commercials, which are much maligned, can provide an information shortcut from their tone, positioning, and arguments, and the identity of their sponsors.

8. This condition is known in the literature as the case of "common values."

9. See the debate between James S. Fishkin, Benjamin Ginsburg, and Benjamin I. Page in Abrams (2002).

10. The original study is Page and Shapiro (1992). The quote is from Page (2002, 84).

11. Peltzman (1987, 1990, 1992). The quote is from Peltzman (1998, 155).

12. Research has found that voters respond appropriately to economic performance (Kramer 1971; Lenz 2012), candidate ideology (Hirano et al. 2014; A. Hall 2015), and candidate quality (Hirano and Snyder 2009; Fowler 2016).

13. We also found that voters could see through misleading ballot titles and deceptive campaign arguments. Two initiatives promised to protect forests, "Forests Forever" (Proposition 130) sponsored by conservation groups, which would have restricted timber harvests in state parks, and the "Forests Improvement" initiative (Proposition 138) sponsored by the timber industry, which, despite appearances, would have allowed more trees to be cut. Counties with high employment in forestry and construction, which would have suffered from logging restrictions, voted against 130 and in favor of 138, while counties with high employment in white-collar jobs (tending to be pro-environment) voted in favor of 130 and against 138.

14. Deacon and Shapiro (1975) was the pioneering study of this sort. Kahn and Matsusaka (1997) and Kahn (2002) study voting on environmental issues. Other studies: Dubin, Kiewiet, and Noussair (1992) on growth control, Filer and Kenny (1980) on city-county consolidation, and Schroeder and Sjoquist (1978) on public transit.

15. The flurry of counterinitiatives was designed to take advantage of a provision of California law that if two propositions approved in the same election contain conflicting provisions, the one that received the most votes prevails.

16. In addition to the 5 insurance initiatives, the ballot contained 24 other ballot measures, races for US president, US senator, member of Congress, state senator, state assembly member, and various local offices and issues.

17. The ballot contained only the summary information in table 14.1. The complete text of each initiative along with a neutral analysis by the state Legislative Analyst and arguments for and against were printed in the state's voter pamphlet and mailed to each registered voter before the election.

18. Quote from Lupia (2001, 66).

19. Bowler and Donovan (1998, 168), one of the more extensive studies, concludes that although voters are not "fully informed" about the details of most propositions, they "appear able to figure out what they are for and against in ways that make sense in terms of their underlying values and interests." Lau and Redlawsk (2001) suggest that shortcuts might be more useful for political experts than ordinary people, based on responses to hypothetical campaigns in laboratory experiments. Burnett, Garrett, and McCubbins (2010) contains a general, somewhat skeptical discussion.

20. Lupia and McCubbins (1998).

21. Hamilton's speech to the Constitutional Convention, June 18, 1787, quoted in Yates ([1787] n.d.).

22. Specifically, I estimated a regression of state and local direct general expenditure as a fraction of income on initiative-state × year dummies, log of population, federal aid as a fraction of income, a dummy for Southern states, and year dummies. The figure reports the coefficients on the initiative-state × year dummies. Alaska and Wyoming, two well-known outliers whose

revenue is driven by fluctuations in mineral prices, are excluded as usual in the literature. Data cover 1957–2016 except that data are unavailable for 2001 and 2003. Data came from the Bureau of Economic Analysis at the US Census Bureau.

23. Matsusaka (1995, 2004) studies spending and tax differences between US states with and without the initiative. Funk and Gathmann (2011) study spending in Swiss cantons. The negative relation between state/canton spending and the initiative process is one of most consistent findings in the literature. The pattern appears to run the other way for cities, although the evidence is limited. Only a handful of studies exploit plausibly exogenous variation in direct democracy to produce causal estimates, but they tend to point in the same direction as the reduced-form estimates. See Matsusaka (2018a) for a survey.

24. See Matsusaka (1995, 2004). Funk and Gathmann (2013) find that Swiss cantons with more direct democracy are more conservative, but this alone does not account for the spending differences.

25. According to this interpretation, if it happened that voters were more fiscally *liberal* than legislators, spending would be *higher* in initiative than noninitiative states. In fact, initiative states spent more on average than noninitiative states in the early twentieth century, when voters probably were more fiscally liberal than legislators. Massive migration from farms to cities around the turn of the century transformed the population from rural to urban, but because states did not redistrict their legislatures to adjust for population change—this was before the one-person-one-vote principle—rural areas came to be significantly overrepresented in state legislatures. Rural interests were not sympathetic to the new programs favored by city dwellers, such as old-age insurance, welfare programs for the poor, public transit, and other urban infrastructure such as clean-water systems. Voters in initiative states used the initiative to override their legislatures and drive up spending. See Matsusaka (2000).

26. A different interpretation is that voters are too stingy to tax themselves for necessary public services. This argument is mainly a difference of opinion about the desired scope of government, not a claim that voters behave irresponsibly in any objective sense. Moreover, although voters choose lower spending levels than legislators choose, the differences are not enormous—certainly in the same ballpark—so the differences do not imply fundamentally different scales of government.

27. These estimates control for other factors that might influence spending, such as income. Feld and Matsusaka (2003).

28. See Matsusaka (2018a) for a summary of the literature from which these findings are drawn. The connection between a mandatory referendum and lower spending is not mechanical; there are game-theoretic reasons it could go the other way (Marino and Matsusaka 2005).

29. Issacharoff, Karlan, and Pildes (2007, 957), citing DuVivier (1995). DuVivier in turn cites an article by a British journalist in the *Financial Times* that does not provide a reference.

30. Matsusaka (2005) lists articles making these claims.

31. I ignored initiatives that were no longer in effect, and when faced with uncertainty about the amounts involved, I took the largest reasonable number supplied by the nonpartisan Legislative Analyst, so that the final number I came up with would be an upper bound. See Matsusaka (2010a) for more details.

32. I mention this last fact because some would paint a picture of California as suffering from an accumulation of incompatible initiatives that have built up over the years. If there is a problem, it is not due to an accumulation but rather to a single initiative, Proposition 98.

33. The only restriction on the income tax was that it be indexed to inflation. The only restriction on the sales tax was that it not be applied to food.

34. A 1 percent personal income tax surcharge for millionaires, a minimum tobacco tax of 75 cents a pack, and a state lottery.

35. I owe this observation about the virtue of binary choices to Lupia (2001).

36. Bowler and Donovan (1998), especially chapter 3, considers voting *no* and abstention; Matsusaka (1992) considers abstaining in order to let more-informed voters make the decision.

37. Claiming that voters are influenced by irrelevant events: Achen and Bartels (2016; shark attacks and droughts); Healy, Malhotra, and Mo (2010; college football games); Healy and Malhotra (2010; tornadoes—although they argue voters might be responding rationally to a failure to take mitigating actions). Criticisms: Fowler and Montagnes (2015; college football); Fowler and Hall (2018; shark attacks). Graham et al. (2019) suggest a way to make the findings in this literature more credible.

Chapter 15: The Challenge of Interest Groups

1. Classic statements of the pluralist view include Bentley ([1908] 1995) and Truman (1951).

2. References for the reader interested in the underlying scholarly literature: On vote buying—Snyder (1991); Grossman and Helpman (1994); Besley and Coate (2001). Dal Bó (2007) for theory. Ansolabehere, de Figueiredo, and Snyder (2003) and Dal Bó (2006) for surveys. Strattmann (1992, 1998, 2002) for evidence. On revolving doors—Che (1995) and Kwak (2014). On lobbying—R. Hall and Deardorff (2006); de Figueiredo and Silverman (2006); Richter, Samphantharak, and Timmons (2009); Kang (2016); de Figueiredo and Richter (2014); and Lambert (2019).

3. W. Wilson (1912). One historian of the Progressive Era (Goebel 2002, 10–11) summarizes: "reading of [reformer] arguments clearly reveals that the initiative, referendum, and recall were primarily intended to abolish oppressive monopolies and artificial trusts in America by removing the legislative basis for their existence."

4. Broder (2000, 243).

5. Lohmann (1998) develops a model of interest group influence in mass elections. Bawn et al. (2012) argues that interest groups influence the candidate-nomination process.

6. Initiatives that cut across multiple industries, such as a change in the sales tax, were excluded, as were initiatives that involved an intra-industry dispute (such as a proposal to authorize a new casino that was opposed by existing casino operators and supported by out-of-state gaming interests) because they cannot be classified as pro- or anti-business. For more details on the raw data, data collection, and data cleaning, see Matsusaka (2018b).

7. Businesses were worse off as a result of 20, 16, and 41 percent of initiatives in the energy, finance, and tobacco industries, respectively. The tobacco industry's particularly dismal record is not for lack of trying; as will be seen later, the industry invests heavily in ballot measure campaigns. Three-quarters of initiatives had no effect one way or the other because they were not approved.

8. A potential limit of this exercise is that it does not take into account the importance of the different laws. It is conceivable that business interests rarely win, but their victories produce huge benefits while their defeats produce only minor setbacks. For the finance and tobacco industries this is not possible because they scored zero wins. For the energy industry, perusing the initiatives does not give the impression that the pro-business winners were unusually consequential.

9. This is not an apples-to-apples comparison. While we observe all initiatives, we only observe those legislative acts that go to a referendum. It is possible that the business orientation of legislative acts that go to a referendum is different from those that do not go to a referendum. For this reason, we should not draw strong conclusions from the comparison between initiatives and legislative referendums.

10. For each ballot measure, I aggregated all contributions by a given individual/organization to produce a total contribution amount by that individual/organization on that measure. Contributions to multiproposition campaigns were apportioned equally to each campaign. For example, a $100 contribution to the Committee in Support of Propositions 1 and 2 was treated as a $50 contribution in support of Proposition 1 and a $50 contribution in support of Proposition 2. For more details on data construction and cleaning, see Matsusaka (2018b).

11. The "other" category consists of activist groups, such as the American Civil Liberties Union, Howard Jarvis Taxpayers Organization, and Sierra Club, and ad hoc campaign committees not clearly linked to the other groups.

12. One could argue that businesses actually lost even when the initiative failed because of the money they spent defeating it. Here I am focusing on gains and losses from the law itself, not from the campaigning.

13. The 100 percent benefit rate for tribes and "other" is based on only 9 and 32 observations, respectively.

14. The three large-scale studies are A. Gerber et al. (2011) on the 2006 Texas gubernatorial primary election (finding that valence information improved a candidate's favorability rating in the short term); Kendall, Nannicini, and Trebbi (2015) on an Italian mayoral election (finding that mail and phone information on candidate valence shifted votes); and Rogers and Middleton (2015) on 12 Oregon ballot measures (finding that mailed information on endorsements and issue content shifted votes). See Kendall, Nannicini, and Trebbi (2015) for references to several related studies.

15. The first study to reach this conclusion was Lowenstein (1982). The conclusion is contested by some: see Garrett and Gerber (2001); Stratmann (2006); and de Figueiredo, Ji, and Kousser (2010) for discussion. Estimating the effect of campaign spending on votes is the subject of an enormous literature, and complicated by the fact that spending is not distributed randomly as would be needed to produce causal estimates. I am not making any causal claims about spending here, only noting that deep pockets are not enough to ensure victory in a ballot measure campaign.

16. E. Gerber (1999, 82).

17. Matsusaka (2009).

18. NCSL Initiative and Referendum Task Force (2002).

Chapter 16: Protecting Minorities from the Majority

1. Roosevelt ([1912] n.d., 5).

2. Of course, the Founders were not concerned about protecting the rights of the minority groups we think of today that are defined in terms of race, ethnicity, language, gender, and sexual orientation; they were concerned about protecting the property rights of the numerically few property holders from expropriation by the masses.

3. While the conventional view is that checks and balances protect minority rights, this conclusion is not a theoretical necessity. Checks and balances would actually *hurt* minorities under the following scenario: the majority would like to expand minority rights, but because of fragmented power an anti-minority group can block the expansion. This is the story of how white Southerners in the US Senate blocked civil rights laws for decades.

4. James Madison ([1787] n.d.): "The effect of [representation] is, on the one hand, to refine and enlarge the public views, by passing them through the medium of a chosen body of citizens, whose wisdom may best discern the true interest of their country, and whose patriotism and love of justice will be least likely to sacrifice it to temporary or partial considerations." It is not clear that Madison fully endorsed this view; he followed it by noting that, on the other hand, "men of factious tempers, of local prejudices, or of sinister designs, may, by intrigue, by corruption, or by other means, first obtain the suffrages, and then betray the interests, of the people."

5. Dahl (1989, 189–90).

6. Chilton and Versteeg (2016, 2017, 2018).

7. The white "Redeemer" backlash to Reconstruction and the origins of Jim Crow are chronicled in Brands (2010) and White (2017). Woodward ([1955] 2001) is a classic history of Jim Crow. Patterson (1996) contains an even-handed history of the postwar civil rights movement. See also Thernstrom and Thernstrom (1997, ch. 1).

8. Daniels (2004) and Reeves (2015) describe Japanese internment.

9. Quoted in Daniels (2004, 40).

10. An aside: Majority rule is not always detrimental to minority rights—in the case of discrimination against African Americans, the activation of majority opinion outside the South by civil rights activists played an important role in prodding Congress to dismantle segregation and restore voting rights. If direct democracy bypasses some of the standard checks and balances of legislatures, history suggests that it might sometimes help minority groups.

11. Women are included although they are not a numerical minority. I flagged initiatives concerning religion, but there were too few and their impact was ambiguous. I also searched for initiatives targeting the rights of political minorities, such as communists, but found only two initiatives of that type.

12. This is the text of California's Prop. 209 (1996), Washington's I-200 (1998), Michigan's Proposal 2 (2006), Arizona's Prop. 107 (2010), Colorado's Amendment 46 (2008), and Nebraska's Initiative 424 (2008).

13. A 1971 Gallup poll found a majority of black people against busing (Patterson 1996, 732).

14. I classified California's Proposition 227 in 1998 as ambiguous because although it proposed to end bilingual education, it was supported by 60 percent of Asian Americans, 52 percent of Latinos, and 48 percent of African Americans, according to pollsters (DeBare 1998).

15. It would be useful to have similar information for local governments because some notable cases involve gay-rights initiatives in cities, but I am not aware of such information having been assembled.

16. Invalidated: 13 same-sex marriage bans invalidated by the US Supreme Court's *Obergefell v. Hodges* decision; three Arkansas segregation measures; Arizona's measure requiring native employees; California Proposition 187 limiting government services to illegal immigrants; Colorado's 1992 ban on local laws protecting gays and lesbians from discrimination; Oklahoma's black disenfranchisement law.

17. For the interested reader, the studies (referenced below) generally estimate cross-sectional or panel regressions, controlling for a variety of state-specific factors, and sometimes public opinion. The estimates generally do not support a causal interpretation.

18. *Obergefell v. Hodges,* 576 U.S. (2015).

19. See Hume (2011), D. C. Lewis (2011), and Matsusaka (2018a).

20. The evidence in the text is from Schildkraut (2001); Matsusaka (2018a) provides supporting evidence.

21. The figure reports weighted responses from question Q31 in the California Poll 11-03, administered September 1–12, 2011, available at UC Berkeley, "Field Polls in SDA 3.5," UC Data, n.d., accessed August 6, 2019, http://ucdata.berkeley.edu/data_record.php?recid=58.

22. Hajnal, Gerber, and Louch (2002).

23. A follow-up study using an expanded data set of 65 propositions but otherwise similar methods reached similar conclusions, that black, Latino, and Asian voters were about 1–3 percent less likely than white voters to be on the winning side, and 4–5 percent less likely to be on the winning side for minority-targeted propositions (Moore and Ravishankar 2012).

Chapter 17: A Framework for Deciding Issues

1. This framework is designed to apply to *public* issues, not to private issues that are best left to the market or private individuals, such as most individual consumption, employment, and investment decisions. There is also a small set of issues that are constitutionally protected and not subject to legislation, typically issues that implicate fundamental rights, such as (in the United States) freedom of speech or religious choice. The question of which issues should be decided collectively, and which should be off the table, is important but too broad for the present purposes; the goal here is to understand how to decide issues that we have already determined are in the public sphere.

2. This information-theoretic approach to direct versus representative democracy draws from and extends the analysis in Matsusaka (1992). Maskin and Tirole (2004) is related. Alesina and Tabellini (2007) emphasize how the allocation of decision authority affects the effort of representatives. Buchanan and Tullock (1962), Olson (1965), and Arrow (1974) are foundational for thinking about optimal decision making. Tucker (2018) contains a wealth of interesting ideas about delegation, some synthesizing the literature and others based on his years as a central banker.

3. Formally, one can think of this in terms of a model in which a policy x must be selected that applies to a population of $i = 1, \ldots, N$ people, and individual i has a utility function

$u_i = -H|x—\theta| - (1-H)|x—\phi_i|$, where θ is a common random variable, ϕ_i is a person-specific parameter, and H is a parameter. The parameter H captures homogeneity of effects, where $H = 1$ is the case of complete homogeneity (identical preferences). The technical nature of an issue is captured by the variance in θ, assuming that an expert can perceive the realization while non-experts know only the distribution.

4. Potter and Penniman (2016, ch. 5) discusses the influence of big pharma on American drug policy.

5. Considering these examples brings out an important dimension that is missing from the framework: decision speed. Representative democracy can be faster than direct democracy. This is clearly important if a country is under attack, responding to a natural disaster, or dealing with other issues for which delay is costly. One reason for delegating command of the army is the need for quick decisions. When it comes to declarations of war, speed might be valuable, but on the other hand, delay could be desirable to allow tempers to cool before making a decision.

6. The argument here echoes and is inspired by a similar argument questioning central-bank independence by Paul Tucker, former deputy governor of the Bank of England, in Tucker (2018).

7. Economic analysis also makes use of the Pareto principle, which says that policy X is better than policy Y if all people are at least as well off under X as under Y. However, real policy choices seldom present such obvious trade-offs (which is why we find people on both sides of any issue of consequence). Therefore, when economists speak of Pareto efficiency they typically mean Kaldor-Hicks efficiency, which prescribes choosing X over Y if it would be possible hypothetically to redistribute resources so that everyone would prefer X to Y after redistribution—even if the redistribution does not take place (it also assumes that resources can be redistributed at no cost). Policy makers and the general public are seldom persuaded by economic arguments based on Kaldor-Hicks efficiency.

8. It should also be noted that there is no reason to believe that representative democracy takes preference intensity into account more than direct democracy. Both systems pivot on an election in which each person has one vote regardless of preference intensity.

9. The classic reference for Arrow's theorem is Arrow (1950); it has been extended and generalized many times over the years. Black ([1958] 1987) and Riker (1961) are classic references on cycling. Mueller (2003) provides a good overview of these theorems and their implications.

10. The conditions are anonymity (the outcome depends on the underlying preferences but not the identity of the person holding the preferences), neutrality (if a given set of citizen preferences leads to the choice of X instead of Y on some issue, then the same set of preferences on a different issue also leads to choice of X instead of Y), and responsiveness (if a person's preference shifts in favor of an outcome, then that outcome is more likely to be chosen). May's theorem implicitly assumes that preference intensity is not taken into account. See May (1952). Mueller (2003) provides a good discussion of May's theorem and the related Rae-Taylor theorem.

11. Lincoln ([1861] n.d.).

Chapter 18: Best Practices

1. Matsusaka (2004).

Chapter 19: Final Thoughts

1. This evolution of democracy likely has also contributed to the growth of "crony capitalism," the tendency of government to tilt the playing field in favor of corporations, by shifting policy decisions to parts of the government that are vulnerable to special-interest influence. See Zingales (2012) for an extended discussion of crony capitalism. An implication of my analysis is that in order to correct the problems of crony capitalism, we first need to correct the root problems in democracy that allow corporate influence to flourish.

2. According to a 2019 survey, 79 percent of Democrats would like to replace the Electoral College with a direct popular vote, while 74 percent of Republicans want to keep the Electoral College (Easley 2019).

3. My emphasis on separating the choice of decision process from the choice of policies follows a line of thinking in philosophy and political economy represented by Buchanan and Tullock (1962) and Rawls (1971). This approach imagines people choosing their constitution—decision process—before they know exactly the issues they will face and their position on those issues. From behind this "veil of ignorance," they will choose a process that is "neutral" and thus fair in some sense.

4. Issacharoff (2018, 486).

5. An example in this vein is Mounk (2018).

REFERENCES

Abrams, Elliott, ed. 2002. *Democracy: How Direct?* Lanham, MD: Rowman and Littlefield.

Achen, Christopher H. 1977. "Measuring Representation: Perils of the Correlation Coefficient." *American Journal of Political Science* 21, no. 4 (November): 805–15.

Achen, Christopher H., and Larry M. Bartels. 2016. *Democracy for Realists: Why Elections Do Not Produce Responsive Government.* Princeton, NJ: Princeton University Press.

Adams, John. (1763) n.d. "VII. An Essay on Man's Lust for Power, with the Author's Comment in 1807." Founders Online, National Archives. Accessed August 9, 2019. https://founders .archives.gov/documents/Adams/06-01-02-0045-0008.

Adams, John Quincy. (1825) n.d. "First Annual Message." The American Presidency Project (Gerhard Peters and John T. Woolley), UC Santa Barbara (December 6, 1825), accessed August 13, 2019. https://www.presidency.ucsb.edu/node/206789.

Aguiar-Conraria, Luis, and Pedro C. Magalhães. 2010. "How Quorum Rules Distort Referendum Outcomes: Evidence from a Pivotal Voter Model." *European Journal of Political Economy* 26, no. 4 (December): 541–57.

Alesina, Alberto, and Guido Tabellini. 2007. "Bureaucrats or Politicians? Part I: A Single Policy Task." *American Economic Review* 97, no. 1 (March): 169–79.

Algan, Yann, Sergei Guriev, Elias Papaioannou, and Evgenia Passari. 2017. "The European Trust Crisis and the Rise of Populism." *Brooking Papers on Economics Activity* (Fall): 309–82.

Alito, Samuel. 2017. "Justice Samuel Alito's Remarks at the Claremont Institute, 2/11/2017." Scotus. February 13, 2017; last updated February 22, 2017. https://www.scotusmap.com /posts/2.

Altman, David. 2011. *Direct Democracy Worldwide.* New York: Cambridge University Press.

Ansolabehere, Stephen, John M. de Figueiredo, and James M. Snyder Jr. 2003. "Why Is There So Little Money in U.S. Politics?" *Journal of Economic Perspectives* 17, no. 1 (Winter): 105–30.

Appelbaum, Binyamin. 2010. "On Finance Bill, Lobbying Shifts to Regulations." *New York Times,* June 26, 2010, A1.

Arrow, Kenneth J. 1950. "A Difficulty in the Concept of Social Welfare." *Journal of Political Economy* 58, no. 4 (August): 328–46.

———. 1974. *The Limits of Organization.* New York: W. W. Norton.

Baron, David P., and John A. Ferejohn. 1989. "Bargaining in Legislatures." *American Political Science Review* 83, no. 4 (December): 1181–206.

Barro, Robert J. 1973. "The Control of Politicians: An Economic Model." *Public Choice* 14, no. 1 (Spring): 19–42.

Bawn, Kathleen, Marty Cohen, David Karol, Hans Noel, Seth Masket, and John Zaller. 2012. "A Theory of Political Parties: Groups, Policy Demands, and Nominations in American Politics." *Perspectives on Politics* 10, no. 3 (September): 571–97.

Becker, Gary S. 1983. "A Theory of Competition among Pressure Groups for Political Influence." *Quarterly Journal of Economics* 98, no. 3 (August): 371–400.

Becker, Sascha O., Thiemo Fetzer, and Dennis Novy. 2017. "Who Voted for Brexit? A Comprehensive District-Level Analysis." *Economic Policy* 32, no. 92: 601–50.

Bentley, Arthur F. (1908) 1995. *The Process of Government: A Study of Social Pressures*. New Brunswick, NJ: Transaction.

Berman, Sheri. 2017. "Populism Is a Problem. Elitist Technocrats Aren't the Solution." *Foreign Policy*, December 20, 2017. https://foreignpolicy.com/2017/12/20/populism-is-a-problem-elitist-technocrats-arent-the-solution/.

Bernstein, R. B. 2003. *Thomas Jefferson*. New York: Oxford University Press.

Besley, Timothy, and Stephen Coate. 1997. "An Economic Model of Representative Democracy." *Quarterly Journal of Economics* 112, no. 1 (February): 85–114.

———. 2001. "Lobbying and Welfare in a Representative Democracy." *Review of Economic Studies* 68, no. 1 (January): 67–82.

———. 2008. "Issue Unbundling by Citizens' Initiatives." *Quarterly Journal of Political Science* 3, no. 4 (December): 379–97.

Black, Duncan. (1958) 1987. *The Theory of Committee and Elections*. Norwell, MA: Kluwer Academic.

Blake, Aaron. 2016. "Donald Trump's Best Speech of the 2016 Campaign, Annotated." *Washington Post*, August 19, 2016. https://www.washingtonpost.com/news/the-fix/wp/2016/08/19/donald-trumps-best-speech-of-the-2016-campaign-annotated/?noredirect=on.

Blanning, Tim. 2007. *The Pursuit of Glory: Europe 1648–1815*. New York: Viking.

Blinder, Alan S. 1997. "Is Government Too Political?" *Foreign Affairs* 76, no. 6 (November/December): 115–26.

Boehmke, Frederick J., Sean Gailmard, and John W. Patty. 2013. "Business as Usual: Interest Group Access and Representation across Policy-Making Venues." *Journal of Public Policy* 33, no. 1 (April): 3–33.

Boehmke, Frederick J., Tracy L. Osborne, and Emily U. Schilling. 2015. "Pivotal Politics and Initiative Use in the American States." *Political Research Quarterly* 68, no. 4 (December): 665–77.

Bourne, Jonathan, Jr. 1912. "Functions of the Initiative, Referendum and Recall." *Annals of the American Academy of Political and Social Science* 43, no. 1 (September): 3–16.

Bowler, Shaun, and Todd Donovan. 1998. *Demanding Choices: Opinion, Voting, and Direct Democracy*. Ann Arbor: University of Michigan Press.

Bowman, Karlyn. 2017. "Reading the Polls: Supreme Court Nominations, Public Opinion and Litmus Tests." *Forbes*. January 30, 2017. https://www.forbes.com/sites/bowmanmarsico/2017/01/30/reading-the-polls-supreme-court-nominations-public-opinion-and-litmus-tests/.

Bradford, Ernest S. 1911. *Commission Government in American Cities*. New York: Macmillan.

Brands, H. W. 2010. *American Colossus: The Triumph of Capitalism, 1865–1900*. New York: Doubleday.

Brennan, Jason. 2016. *Against Democracy*. Princeton, NJ: Princeton University Press.

Breyer, Stephen. 1993. *Breaking the Vicious Circle: Toward Effective Risk Regulation.* Cambridge, MA: Harvard University Press.

Broder, David S. 2000. *Democracy Derailed: Initiative Campaigns and the Power of Money.* New York: Harcourt.

Broockman, David E., and Christopher Skovron. 2018. "Bias in Perceptions of Public Opinion among Political Elites." *American Political Science Review* 112, no. 3 (August): 542–63.

Buchanan, James M., and Gordon Tullock. 1962. *The Calculus of Consent: Logical Foundations of Constitutional Democracy.* Ann Arbor: University of Michigan Press.

Burnett, Craig M., Elizabeth Garrett, and Mathew D. McCubbins. 2010. "The Dilemma of Direct Democracy." *Election Law Journal* 9, no. 4 (December): 305–24.

Butler, Daniel M., and David W. Nickerson. 2011. "Can Learning Constituency Opinion Affect How Legislators Vote? Results from a Field Experiment." *Quarterly Journal of Political Science* 6, no. 1 (August): 55–83.

Butler, David, and Austin Ranney, eds. 1994. *Referendums around the World: The Growing Use of Direct Democracy.* Washington, DC: AEI.

Calabresi, Steven G., and Larissa C. Leibowitz. 2013. "Monopolies and the Constitution: A History of Crony Capitalism." *Harvard Journal of Law and Public Policy* 36, no. 3 (Summer): 983–1097.

Campbell, Stephen W. 2016. "Funding the Bank War: Nicholas Biddle and the Public Relations Campaign to Recharter the Second Bank of the U.S., 1828–1832." *American Nineteenth Century History* 17, no. 3 (August): 273–99.

Carpenter, Daniel, and David A. Moss, eds. 2014. *Preventing Regulatory Capture: Special Interest Influence and How to Limit It.* New York: Cambridge University Press.

Casey, Nicholas. 2018. "Bolivia Tells President His Time Is Up. He Isn't Listening." *New York Times,* January 28, 2018, A6.

Chambers, John Whiteclay, II. 2000. *The Tyranny of Change: America in the Progressive Era, 1890–1920.* 2nd ed. New Brunswick, NJ: Rutgers University Press.

Che, Yeon-Koo. 1995. "Revolving Doors and the Optimal Tolerance for Agency Collusion." *RAND Journal of Economics* 26, no. 3 (Autumn): 378–97.

Cherny, Robert W. 1997. *American Politics in the Gilded Age: 1868–1900.* Chichester, UK: Wiley-Blackwell.

Chilton, Adam S., and Mila Versteeg. 2016. "Do Constitutional Rights Make a Difference?" *American Journal of Political Science* 60, no. 3 (July): 575–89.

———. 2017. "Rights without Resources: The Impact of Constitutional Social Rights on Social Spending." *Journal of Law and Economics* 60, no. 4 (November): 713–48.

———. 2018. "Courts' Limited Ability to Protect Constitutional Rights." *University of Chicago Law Review* 8, no. 2 (March): 293–336.

Clinton, Joshua D., and David E. Lewis. 2007. "Expert Opinion, Agency Characteristics, and Agency Preferences." *Political Analysis* 16, no. 1 (April): 3–20.

Collins, Paul M., Jr., and Lori A. Ringhand 2016. "The Institutionalization of Supreme Court Confirmation Hearings." *Law and Social Inquiry* 41, no. 1 (Winter): 126–51.

Copeland, Curtis W. 2010a. "Regulations Pursuant to the Patient Protection and Affordable Care Act (P.L. 111-148)." Congressional Research Service Report for Congress, Report R41180.

———. 2010b. "Rulemaking Requirements and Authorities in the Dodd-Frank Wall Street Reform and Consumer Protection Act." Congressional Research Service Report for Congress, Report R41472.

Curtis, Chris, and Marcus Roberts. 2017. "Forget 52%. The Rise of the 'Re-Leavers' Mean the Pro-Brexit Electorate is 68%." YouGov. May 12, 2017. https://yougov.co.uk/topics/politics/articles-reports/2017/05/12/forget-52-rise-re-leavers-mean-pro-brexit-electora.

Dahl, Robert A. 1989. *Democracy and Its Critics*. New Haven, CT: Yale University Press.

———. 2003. *How Democratic Is the American Constitution?* 2nd ed. New Haven, CT: Yale University Press.

———. 2006. *A Preface to Democratic Theory*. Expanded Ed. Chicago: University of Chicago Press.

Dal Bó, Ernesto. 2006. "Regulatory Capture: A Review." *Oxford Review of Economic Policy* 22, no. 2 (July): 203–25.

———. 2007. "Bribing Voters." *American Journal of Political Science* 51, no. 4 (October): 789–803.

Dalton, Russell J. 2004. *Democratic Challenges, Democratic Choices: The Erosion of Political Support in Advanced Industrial Democracies*. New York: Oxford University Press.

Daniels, Roger. 2004. *Prisoners without Trial: Japanese Americans in World War II*. Rev. ed. New York: Hill and Wang.

Deacon, Robert, and Perry Shapiro. 1975. "Private Preference for Collective Goods Revealed Through Voting on Referenda." *American Economic Review* 65, no. 5 (December): 943–55.

DeBare, Ilana. 1998. "Voter Support for Prop. 226 Ebbs, Polls Says/61% Back 227 to End Bilingual Education." *San Francisco Chronicle*, May 29, 1998. https://www.sfgate.com/politics/article/Voter-Support-For-Prop-226-Ebbs-Poll-Says-61-3004873.php.

de Figueiredo, John M., Chang Ho Ji, and Thad Kousser. 2010. "Financing Direct Democracy: Revisiting the Research on Campaign Spending and Citizen Initiatives." *Journal of Law, Economics, and Organization* 27, no. 3 (September): 485–514.

de Figueiredo, John M., and Brian Kelleher Richter. 2014. "Advancing the Empirical Research on Lobbying." *Annual Review of Political Science* 17: 163–85.

de Figueiredo, John M., and Brian S. Silverman. 2006. "Academic Earmarks and the Returns to Lobbying." *Journal of Law and Economics* 49, no. 2 (October): 597–625.

Delli Carpini, Michael X., and Scott Keeter. 1996. *What Americans Know about Politics and Why It Matters*. New Haven, CT: Yale University Press.

DeSilver, Drew. 2018. "U. S. Population Keeps Growing, but House of Representatives Is Same Size as in Taft Era." Pew Research Center. May 31, 2018. https://www.pewresearch.org/fact-tank/2018/05/31/u-s-population-keeps-growing-but-house-of-representatives-is-same-size-as-in-taft-era/.

Dickinson, John. (1788) n.d. *The Letters of Fabius, in 1788, on the Federal Constitution*. Edited by Paul. L. Ford. Online transcript of 1797 reprint by W. C. Smith, office of the Delaware Gazette, Wilmington. Internet Archive. Accessed August 13, 2019. https://archive.org/stream/lettersoffabiusioodickuoft/lettersoffabiusioodickuoft_djvu.txt.

Dinan, John. 2016. "State Constitutional Developments in 2015." In *The Book of the States*, edited by The Council of State Governments, vol. 48, chapter 1, "State Constitutions," 3–8. Lexington, KY: The Council of State Governments.

Dodd, Walter Farleigh. (1910) 1970. *The Revision and Amendment of State Constitutions*. New York: Da Capo.

Downs, Anthony. 1957. *An Economic Theory of Democracy*. New York: Harper and Row.

Dubin, Jeffery A., D. Roderick Kiewiet, and Charles Noussair. 1992. "Voting on Growth Control Measures: Preferences and Strategies." *Economics and Politics* 4, no. 2 (July): 191–213.

Duncan, Pamela. 2016. "How the Pollsters Got It Wrong on the EU Referendum." *Guardian*, June 24, 2016. https://www.theguardian.com/politics/2016/jun/24/how-eu-referendum-pollsters-wrong-opinion-predict-close.

DuVivier, K. K. 1995. "By Going Wrong All Things Come Right: Using Alternative Initiatives to Improve Citizen Lawmaking." *University of Cincinnati Law Review* 63: 1185–221.

Dyck, Joshua J. 2009. "Initiated Distrust: Direct Democracy and Trust in Government." *American Politics Research* 37, no. 4 (July): 539–68.

Easley, Jonathan. 2019. "Poll: Most Voters Support Abolishing Electoral College." *Hill*, May 6, 2019. https://thehill.com/homenews/campaign/442276-poll-most-voters-support-abolishing-electoral-college.

Economist. 2003. "Abortion in America: The War that Never Ends." January 16, 2003. https://www.economist.com/special-report/2003/01/16/the-war-that-never-ends.

———. 2018. "Dancing with Danger: Europe's Populists Are Waltzing into the Mainstream." February 3, 2018. https://www.economist.com/briefing/2018/02/03/europes-populists-are-waltzing-into-the-mainstream.

Edwards, Rebecca. 2006. *New Spirits: Americans in the Gilded Age, 1865–1905*. New York: Oxford University Press.

Ellis, Richard J. 2002. *Democratic Delusions: The Initiative Process in America*. Lawrence: University of Kansas Press.

Elmendorf, Christopher S., and Abby K. Wood. 2018. "Elite Political Ignorance: Law, Data, and the Representation of (Mis)Perceived Electorates." *UC Davis Law Review* 52, no. 2 (December): 571–636.

Elvey, Suz. 2015. "Leave MEANS Leave: David Cameron Vows Britain Will NOT Have a Second Vote on EU Exit." *Express*, October 25, 2015. https://www.express.co.uk/news/uk/614500/Cameron-no-mean-no-EU-vote.

Epstein, Lee, Jack Knight, and Andrew D. Martin. 2003. "The Norm of Judicial Experience and Its Consequences for Career Diversity on the U. S. Supreme Court." *California Law Review* 91, no. 4 (July): 903–65.

Epstein, Lee, William M. Landes, and Richard A. Posner. 2013. *The Behavior of Federal Judges: A Theoretical and Empirical Study of Rational Choice*. Cambridge, MA: Harvard University Press.

Ertimur, Yonca, Fabrizio Ferri, and Stephen R. Stubben. 2010. "Board of Directors' Responsiveness to Shareholders: Evidence from Shareholder Proposals." *Journal of Corporate Finance* 16, no. 1 (February): 53–72.

European Commission Directorate-General for Communication. 2018. *Public Opinion in the European Union*. Standard Eurobarometer 89, Annex. Brussels: European Commission Directorate-General for Communication.

Ferejohn, John. 1986. "Incumbent Performance and Electoral Control." *Public Choice* 50, no. 1/3: 5–25.

Ferguson, Margaret R. 2006. "Introduction to State Executives." Chapter 1 in *The Executive Branch of State Government: People, Process and Politics,* edited by Margaret R. Ferguson. Santa Barbara, CA: ABC-CLIO.

Feld, Lars P., and John G. Matsusaka. 2003. "Budget Referendums and Government Spending: Evidence from Swiss Cantons." *Journal of Public Economics* 87, no. 12 (December): 2703–24.

Filer, John E., and Lawrence W. Kenny. 1980. "Voter Reaction to City-County Consolidation Referenda." *Journal of Law and Economics* 23, no. 1 (April): 179–90.

Fineman, Howard. 2015. "Why U.S. Politics Is Obsessed with Abortion: The Issue Isn't a Priority for Most Americans, yet It's Helped Shape—and Ruin—U.S. Politics. Here's How." *Huffington Post,* December 2, 2015. https://www.huffpost.com/entry/us-politics-abortion_n _565e66f1e4b072e9d1c40a72.

Fiorina, Morris P. 2009. *Disconnect: The Breakdown of Representation in American Politics.* Norman: University of Oklahoma Press.

Fleck, Robert K., and Andrew Hanssen. 2006. "The Origins of Democracy: A Model with Application to Ancient Greece." *Journal of Law and Economics* 49, no. 1 (April): 115–46.

———. 2012. "On the Benefits and Costs of Legal Expertise: Adjudication in Ancient Athens." *Review of Law and Economics* 8, no. 2 (October): 367–99.

———. 2013. "How Tyranny Paved the Way to Democracy: The Democratic Transition in Ancient Greece." *Journal of Law and Economics* 46, no. 2(May): 389–416.

Ford, Henry. 1912. "Direct Legislation and the Recall." *Annals of the American Academy of Political and Social Science* 43, no. 1 (September): 65–77.

Fowler, Anthony. 2016. "What Explains Incumbent Success? Disentangling Selection on Party, Selection on Candidate Characteristics, and Office-Holding Benefits." *Quarterly Journal of Political Science* 11, no. 3: 313–38.

Fowler, Anthony, and Andrew B. Hall. 2018. "Do Shark Attacks Influence Presidential Elections? Reassessing a Prominent Finding on Voter Competence." *Journal of Politics* 80, no. 4 (October): 1423–37.

Fowler, Anthony, and B. Pablo Montagnes. 2015. "College Football, Elections, and False-Positive Results in Observational Research." *Proceedings of the National Academy of Sciences of the United States* 112, no. 45 (November): 12800–12804.

Frankfurter, Felix. 1957. "The Supreme Court in the Mirror of Justices." *University of Pennsylvania Law Review* 105, no. 2 (April): 781–96.

Funk, Patricia, and Christina Gathmann. 2011. "Does Direct Democracy Reduce the Size of Government? New Evidence from Historical Data, 1890–2000." *Economic Journal* 121, no. 557 (December): 1252–80.

———. 2013. "Voter Preferences, Direct Democracy and Government Spending." *European Journal of Political Economy* 32: 300–319.

Gailmard, Sean, and Jeffrey A. Jenkins. 2009. "Agency Problems, the 17th Amendment, and Representation in the Senate." *American Journal of Political Science* 53, no. 2 (April): 324–42.

Gailmard, Sean, and John W. Patty. 2007. "Slackers and Zealots: Civil Service, Policy Discretion, and Bureaucratic Expertise." *American Journal of Political Science* 51, no. 4 (October): 873–89.

Galston, William A. 2017. "The Populist Moment." *Journal of Democracy* 28, no. 2 (April): 21–33.

Garrett, Elizabeth, and Elisabeth R. Gerber. 2001. "Money in the Initiative and Referendum Process: Evidence of Its Effects and Prospects for Reform." Chapter 5 in *The Battle over Citizen Lawmaking*, edited by M. Dane Waters. Durham, NC: Carolina Academic.

Gerber, Alan S., James G. Gimpel, Donald P. Green, and Daron Shaw. 2011. "How Large and Long-Lasting Are the Persuasive Effects of Televised Campaign Ads? Results from a Randomized Field Experiment." *American Political Science Review* 105, no. 1 (February): 135–50.

Gerber, Elisabeth R. 1999. *The Populist Paradox: Interest Group Influence and the Promise of Direct Legislation*. Princeton, NJ: Princeton University Press.

Gerber, Elisabeth R., Arthur Lupia, Mathew D. McCubbins, and D. Roderick Kiewiet. 2001. *Stealing the Initiative: How State Government Responds to Direct Democracy*. Upper Saddle River, NJ: Prentice-Hall.

Gilens, Martin, and Benjamin I. Page. 2014. "Testing Theories of American Politics: Elites, Interest Groups, and Average Citizens." *Perspectives on Politics* 12, no. 3 (September): 564–81.

Goebel, Thomas. 2002. *A Government by the People: Direct Democracy in America 1890–1940*. Chapel Hill: University of North Carolina Press.

Golder, Matt, and Jacek Stramski. 2010. "Ideological Congruence and Electoral Institutions." *American Journal of Political Science* 54, no. 1 (January): 90–106.

Graham, Matthew H., Gregory A. Huber, Neil Malhotra, and Cecilia Hyunjung Mo. 2019. "Observational Open Science: An Application to the Literature on Irrelevant Events and Voting Behavior." Working paper, Yale University, Stanford University, and UC-Berkeley, March 18, 2019.

Grossman, Gene M., and Elhanan Helpman. 1994. "Protection for Sale." *American Economic Review* 84, no. 4 (September): 833–50.

Ha, Seung-Soo. 2009. "Korea: Challenges toward Direct Democratization." Chapter 9 in *Global Citizens in Charge: How Modern Direct Democracy Can Make Our Representative Democracies Truly Representative*, edited by Jung-Ok Lee and Bruno Kaufmann. Seoul: Korea Democracy Foundation.

Hajnal, Zoltan L., Elisabeth R. Gerber, and Hugh Louch. 2002. "Minorities and Direct Legislation: Evidence from California Ballot Proposition Elections." *Journal of Politics* 64, no. 1 (February): 154–77.

Hall, Andrew B. 2015. "What Happens when Extremists Win Primaries?" *American Political Science Review* 109, no. 1 (February): 18–42.

Hall, Richard L., and Alan V. Deardorff. 2006. "Lobbying as Legislative Subsidy." *American Political Science Review* 100, no. 1 (February): 69–84.

Hamilton, Alexander. (1788) n.d. "The Federalist Papers: No. 34." The Avalon Project, Yale Law School, Lillian Goldman Law Library. (January 4, 1788), accessed August 13, 2019. https://avalon.law.yale.edu/18th_century/fed34.asp.

Harsanyi, David. 2014. *The People Have Spoken (and They Are Wrong): The Case Against Democracy*. Washington, DC: Regnery.

Heagney, Meredith. 2013. "Justice Ruth Bader Ginsburg Offers Critique of Roe v. Wade during Law School Visit." University of Chicago Law School. May 15, 2013. https://www.law.uchicago.edu/news/justice-ruth-bader-ginsburg-offers-critique-roe-v-wade-during-law-school-visit.

Healy, Andrew, and Neil Malhotra. 2010. "Random Events, Economic Losses, and Retrospective Voting: Implications for Democratic Competence." *Quarterly Journal of Political Science* 5, no. 2: 193–208.

Healy, Andrew J., Neil Malhotra, and Cecilia Hyunjung Mo. 2010. "Irrelevant Events Affect Voters' Evaluations of Government Performance." *Proceedings of the National Academy of Sciences of the United States of America* 107, no. 29 (July): 12804–9.

Herold, J. Christopher. 1963. *The Age of Napoleon*. New York: American Heritage.

Hibbing, John R., and Elizabeth Theiss-Morse. 2001. "Process Preferences and American Politics: What the People Want Government to Be." *American Political Science Review* 95, no. 1 (March): 145–53.

Hirano, Shigeo, Gabriel S. Lenz, Maksim Pinkowsky, and James M. Snyder Jr. 2014. "Voter Learning in State Primary Elections." *American Journal of Political Science* 59, no. 1 (January): 91–108.

Hirano, Shigeo, and James M. Snyder Jr. 2009. "Using Multimember District Elections to Estimate the Sources of the Incumbency Advantage." *American Journal of Political Science* 53, no. 2 (April): 292–306.

Holthaus, Eric. 2017. "'We Will Never Stop': An EPA Employee Blasts the Trump Administration." *Mother Jones*. February 22, 2017. https://www.motherjones.com/environment/2017/02/donald-trump-scott-pruitt-epa-employee-resist/.

Hotelling, Harold. 1929. "Stability in Competition." *Economic Journal* 39, no. 153 (March): 41–57.

Howard, Alex. 2012. "Rethinking Regulatory Reform in the Internet Age." *Radar*, July 25, 2012. http://radar.oreilly.com/2012/07/rethinking-regulatory-reform-in-the-internet-age.html.

Howe, Daniel Walker. 2007. *What Hath God Wrought: The Transformation of America, 1815–1848*, New York: Oxford University Press.

Howell, William G., and Terry M. Moe. 2016. *Relic: How Our Constitution Undermines Effective Government and Why We Need a More Powerful Presidency*. New York: Basic Books.

Huder, Joshua, Jordan Michael Ragusa, and Daniel A. Smith. 2011. "Shirking the Initiative? The Effects of Statewide Ballot Measures on Congressional Roll Call Behavior." *American Politics Research* 39, no. 3 (May): 582–610.

Hume, Robert J. 2011. "Comparing Institutional and Policy Explanations for the Adoption of State Constitutional Amendments: The Case of Same-Sex Marriage." *American Politics Research* 39, no. 6 (November): 1097–126.

Huntington, Samuel P. 1952. "The Marasmus of the ICC: The Commission, the Railroads, and the Public Interest." *Yale Law Journal* 61, no. 4 (April): 467–509.

Hwang, Jau-Yuan, ed. 2006. *Direct Democracy in Asia: A Reference Guide to the Legislations and Practices*. Taipei: Taiwan Foundation for Democracy.

———. 2009. "Nice Ideas, Difficult Realities: Examples of Recent Direct Democracy in Asia." Chapter 5 in *Global Citizens in Charge: How Modern Direct Democracy Can Make Our Representative Democracies Truly Representative*, edited by Jung-Ok Lee and Bruno Kaufmann. Seoul: Korea Democracy Foundation.

Inglehart, Ronald F., and Pippa Norris. 2016. "Trump, Brexit, and the Rise of Populism: Economic Have-Nots and Cultural Backlash." Harvard Kennedy School Faculty Research Working Paper Series RWP16-026, August 2016.

Initiative and Referendum Institute. 2019. *Overview of Initiative Use, 1900–2018.* Los Angeles: Initiative and Referendum Institute. www.iandrinstitute.org.

International Institute for Democracy and Electoral Assistance (IDEA). 2008. *Direct Democracy: The International IDEA Handbook.* Stockholm: IDEA.

Issacharoff, Samuel. 2018. "Democracy's Deficits." *University of Chicago Law Review* 85, no. 2 (March): 484–519.

Issacharoff, Samuel, Pamela S. Karlan, and Richard H. Pildes. 2007. *The Law of Democracy: Legal Structure of the Political Process.* 3rd ed. New York: Foundation.

Jackson, Andrew. (1829) n.d. "State of the Nation 1829: Washington, DC, 8 December 1829." American History, from Revolution to Reconstruction and Beyond. Accessed August 12, 2019. http://www.let.rug.nl/usa/presidents/andrew-jackson/state-of-the-nation-1829.php.

———. (1832) n.d. "President Jackson's Veto Message Regarding the Bank of the United States; July 10, 1832." The Avalon Project, Yale Law School, Lillian Goldman Law Library. Accessed August 13, 2019. https://avalon.law.yale.edu/19th_century/ajveto01.asp.

John, Richard R. 1998. *Spreading the News: The American Postal System from Franklin to Morse.* Rev. ed. Cambridge, MA: Harvard University Press.

Johnson, Tyler, Kathleen Tipler, and Tyler Camarillo. 2019. "Monumental Decisions: How Direct Democracy Shapes Attitudes in the Conflict over Confederate Memorials." *PS: Political Science and Politics* 52, no. 3 (July): 1–5.

Jones, Jeffrey M. 2013. "Americans in Favor of National Referenda on Key Issues." *GALLUP News*, July 20, 2013. https://news.gallup.com/poll/163433/americans-favor-national-referenda-key-issues.aspx.

———. 2014. "Illinois Residents Least Trusting of Their State Government." *GALLUP News*, April 4, 2014. https://news.gallup.com/poll/168251/illinois-residents-least-trusting-state-government.aspx.

Kahn, Matthew E. 2002. "Demographic Change and the Demand for Environmental Regulation." *Journal of Policy Analysis and Management* 21, no. 1 (Winter): 45–62.

Kahn, Matthew E., and John G. Matsusaka. 1997. "Demand for Environmental Goods: Evidence from Voting Patterns on California Initiatives." *Journal of Law and Economics* 40, no. 1 (April): 137–74.

Kang, Karam. 2016. "Policy Influence and Private Returns from Lobbying in the Energy Sector." *Review of Economic Studies* 83, no. 1 (January): 269–305.

Kaufmann, Bruno. 2018. "How Taiwan Got One of the World's Best Direct Democracy Laws." SWI swissinfo.ch. March 9, 2018. https://www.swissinfo.ch/eng/-ddworldtour-notebook-from-taichung_how-taiwan-got-one-of-world-s-best-direct-democracy-laws/43958776.

Kaufmann, Bruno, Rolf Büchi, and Nadja Braun. 2010. *Guidebook to Direct Democracy: In Switzerland and Beyond.* Marburg, Germany: Initiative and Referendum Institute—Europe.

Kendall, Chad, Tommaso Nannicini, and Francesco Trebbi. 2015. "How Do Voters Respond to Information? Evidence from a Randomized Campaign." *American Economic Review* 105, no. 1 (January): 322–53.

Keohane, David. 2018. "Emmanuel Macron Vows to Press Ahead with French Economic Reforms." *Financial Times*, December 31, 2018. https://app.ft.com/content/4f009528-0d37-11e9-a3aa-118c761d2745.

Keyssar, Alexander. 2009. *The Right to Vote: The Contested History of Democracy in the United States.* Rev. ed. New York: Basic Books.

Khanna, Parag. 2017. *Technocracy in America: Rise of the Info-State.* Self-published, CreateSpace.

Kiff, Sarah. 2018. "Seattle's Radical Plan to Fight Big Money in Politics." *Vox*, November 5, 2018. https://www.vox.com/2018/11/5/17058970/seattle-democracy-vouchers.

Kobach, Kris W. 1993. *The Referendum: Direct Democracy in Switzerland.* Brookfield, VT: Ashgate.

Kogan, Vladimir. 2016. "When Voters Pull the Trigger: Can Direct Democracy Restrain Legislative Excess?" *Legislative Studies Quarterly* 41, no. 2 (May): 297–325.

Kovacic, William E., and Marc Winerman. 2015. "The Federal Trade Commission as an Independent Agency: Autonomy, Legitimacy, and Effectiveness." *Iowa Law Review* 100, no. 5 (May): 2085–113.

Kramer, Gerald H. 1971. "Short-Term Fluctuations in U.S. Voting Behavior, 1896–1964." *American Political Science Review* 65, no. 1 (March): 131–43.

Krehbiel, Keith. 1996. "Institutional and Partisan Sources of Gridlock: A Theory of Divided and Unified Government." *Journal of Theoretical Politics* 8, no. 1 (January): 7–40.

——. 1998. *Pivotal Politics: A Theory of U.S. Lawmaking.* Chicago: University of Chicago Press.

Krutz, Glen S., and Jeffrey S. Peake. 2009. *Treaty Politics and the Rise of Executive Agreements: International Commitments in a System of Shared Powers.* Ann Arbor: University of Michigan Press.

Kwak, James. 2014. "Cultural Capital and the Financial Crisis." Chapter 4 in *Preventing Regulatory Capture: Special Interest Influence and How to Limit It,* edited by Daniel Carpenter and David Moss. New York: Cambridge University Press.

Lambert, Thomas. 2019. "Lobbying on Regulatory Enforcement Actions: Evidence from U.S. Commercial and Savings Banks." *Management Science* 65, no. 6 (June): 2545–72.

Lau, Richard R., and David P. Redlawsk. 2001. "Advantages and Disadvantages of Cognitive Heuristics in Political Decision Making." *American Journal of Political Science* 45, no. 4 (October): 951–71.

Lax, Jeffrey R., and Justin H. Phillips. 2012. "The Democratic Deficit in the States." *American Journal of Political Science* 56, no. 1 (January): 148–66.

Lee, Jung-Ok, and Bruno Kaufmann, eds. 2009. *Global Citizens in Charge: How Modern Direct Democracy Can Make Our Representative Democracies Truly Representative.* Seoul: Korea Democracy Foundation.

Lenz, Gabriel S. 2012. *Follow the Leader?: How Voters Respond to Politicians' Policies and Performance.* Chicago: University of Chicago Press.

Lewis, Caitlain Devereaux. 2016. "Presidential Authority over Trade: Imposing Tariffs and Duties." Congressional Research Service Report R44707.

Lewis, Daniel C. 2011. "Direct Democracy and Minority Rights: Same-Sex Marriage Bans in the U.S. States." *Social Science Quarterly* 92, no. 2 (June): 364–83.

Lewis, David E. 2017. "'Deep State' Claims and Professional Government." *Regulatory Review,* December 5, 2017. https://www.theregreview.org/2017/12/05/lewis-deep-state-professional-government/.

Lewis, Paul, Seán Clarke, Caelainn Barr, Josh Holder, and Niko Kommenda. 2018. "Revealed: One in Four Europeans Vote Populist." *Guardian*, November 20, 2018.

Li, Hao, and Wing Suen. 2009. "Decision-Making in Committees." *Canadian Journal of Economics* 42, no. 2 (May): 359–92.

Lincoln, Abraham. (1861) n.d. "First Inaugural Address of Abraham Lincoln." The Avalon Project, Yale Law School, Lillian Goldman Law Library. Accessed August 12, 2019. https://avalon .law.yale.edu/19th_century/lincoln1.asp.

Lintott, Andrew. 1999. *The Constitution of the Roman Republic*. New York: Oxford University Press.

Lohmann, Susanne. 1998. "An Information Rationale for the Power of Special Interests." *American Political Science Review* 92, no. 4 (December): 809–27.

Loucaides, Darren. 2019. "What Happens When Techno-Utopians Actually Run a Country." *Wired*, February 14, 2019.

Lowande, Kenneth S., Jeffrey A. Jenkins, and Andrew J. Clarke. 2018. "Presidential Particularism and US Trade Politics." *Political Science Research and Methods* 6, no. 2 (April): 265–81.

Lowenstein, Daniel H. 1982. "Campaign Spending and Ballot Propositions: Recent Experience, Public Choice Theory and the First Amendment." *UCLA Law Review* 29: 505–641.

Lowi, Theodore J. 2009. *The End of Liberalism: The Second Republic of the United States*. 40th Anniversary Ed. New York: W. W. Norton.

Lupia, Arthur. 1994. "Shortcuts versus Encyclopedias: Information and Voting Behavior in California Insurance Reform Elections." *American Political Science Review* 88, no. 1 (March): 63–76.

———. 2001. "Dumber than Chimps? An Assessment of Direct Democracy Voters." In *Dangerous Democracy?: The Battle over Ballot Initiatives in America*, edited by Larry J. Sabato, Howard R. Ernst, and Bruce A. Larson, 66–70. Lanham, MD: Rowman and Littlefield.

Lupia, Arthur, and Mathew D. McCubbins. 1998. *The Democratic Dilemma: Can Citizens Learn What They Need To Know?* Cambridge: Cambridge University Press.

Lutz, Donald S. 1979. "The Theory of Consent in the Early State Constitutions." *Publius* 9, no. 2 (Spring): 11–42.

Madison, James. (1787) n.d. "The Federalist Papers: No. 10." The Avalon Project, Yale Law School, Lillian Goldman Law Library. (November 23, 1787), accessed August 13, 2019. https://avalon .law.yale.edu/18th_century/fed10.asp.

———. n.d. "The Federalist Papers: No. 58." The Avalon Project, Yale Law School, Lillian Goldman Law Library. Accessed August 13, 2019. https://avalon.law.yale.edu/18th_century/fed58 .asp.

Madison, James, or Alexander Hamilton. (1788a) n.d. "The Federalist Papers: No. 51." The Avalon Project, Yale Law School, Lillian Goldman Law Library. (February 8, 1788), accessed August 13, 2019. https://avalon.law.yale.edu/18th_century/fed51.asp.

———. (1788b) n.d. "The Federalist Papers: No. 52." The Avalon Project, Yale Law School, Lillian Goldman Law Library. (February 8, 1788), accessed August 13, 2019. https://avalon.law .yale.edu/18th_century/fed52.asp.

———. (1788c) n.d. "The Federalist Papers: No. 55." The Avalon Project, Yale Law School, Lillian Goldman Law Library. (February 15, 1788), accessed August 13, 2019. https://avalon.law .yale.edu/18th_century/fed55.asp.

———. n.d. "The Federalist Papers: No. 63." The Avalon Project, Yale Law School, Lillian Goldman Law Library. Accessed August 13, 2019. https://avalon.law.yale.edu/18th_century/fed63 .asp.

Marino, Anthony M., and John G. Matsusaka. 2005. "Decision Processes, Agency Problems, and Information: An Economic Analysis of Capital Budgeting Procedures." *Review of Financial Studies* 18, no. 1 (Spring): 301–25.

Marshall, John. (1838) 2006. *The Life of George Washington*. Urbana, IL: Project Gutenberg. https://www.gutenberg.org/files/28859/28859-h/28859-h.htm.

Maskin, Eric, and Jean Tirole. 2004. "The Politician and the Judge: Accountability in Government." *American Economic Review* 94, no. 4 (September): 1034–54.

Matsusaka, John G. 1992. "Economics of Direct Legislation." *Quarterly Journal of Economics* 102, no. 2 (May): 541–71.

———. 1995. "Fiscal Effects of the Voter Initiative: Evidence from the Last Thirty Years." *Journal of Political Economy* 103, no. 3 (June): 587–623.

———. 2000. "Fiscal Effects of the Voter Initiative in the First Half of the Twentieth Century." *Journal of Law and Economics* 43, no. 2 (October): 619–50.

———. 2001. "Problems with a Methodology Used to Test the Responsiveness of Policy to Public Opinion in Initiative States." *Journal of Politics* 63, no. 4 (November): 1250–56.

———. 2004. *For the Many or the Few: The Initiative, Public Policy, and American Democracy*. Chicago: University of Chicago Press.

———. 2005. "Direct Democracy and Fiscal Gridlock: Have Voter Initiatives Paralyzed the California Budget?" *State Politics and Policy Quarterly* 5, no. 3 (Fall): 248–64.

———. 2008. "Direct Democracy and the Executive Branch." Chapter 7 in *Direct Democracy's Impact on American Political Institutions*, edited by Shaun Bowler and Amihai Glazer. New York: Palgrave Macmillan.

———. 2009. "Direct Democracy and Public Employees." *American Economic Review* 99, no. 5 (December): 2227–64.

———. 2010a. "A Case Study on Direct Democracy: Have Voter Initiatives Paralyzed the California Budget?" In *The Book of the States*, edited by The Council of State Governments, 2010, chapter 6, "Elections," 324–29. Lexington, KY: The Council of State Governments.

———. 2010b. "Popular Control of Public Policy: A Quantitative Approach." *Quarterly Journal of Political Science* 5, no. 2 (August): 133–67.

———. 2016. "Ballot Order Effects in Direct Democracy Elections." *Public Choice* 167, nos. 3–4 (June): 257–76.

———. 2017. "When Do Legislators Follow Constituent Opinion? Evidence from Matched Roll Call and Referendum Votes." Working paper, USC Marshall School of Business.

———. 2018a. "Public Policy and the Initiative and Referendum: A Survey with Some New Evidence." *Public Choice* 174, nos. 1–2 (January): 107–43.

———. 2018b. "Special Interest Influence under Direct vs. Representative Democracy." Working paper, USC Marshall School of Business.

Matsusaka, John G., and Nolan M. McCarty. 2001. "Political Resource Allocation: The Benefits and Costs of Voter Initiatives." *Journal of Law, Economics, and Organization* 17, no. 2 (October): 413–48.

May, Kenneth O. 1952. "A Set of Independent Necessary and Sufficient Conditions for Simpler Majority Decisions." *Econometrica* 20, no. 4 (October): 680–84.

McCann, Pamela J. Clousser, and Charles R. Shipan. 2018. "How Many Major U.S. Laws Delegate to Federal Agencies? (Almost) All of Them." Working paper, University of Southern California and University of Michigan.

McCarty, Nolan M., Keith T. Poole, and Howard Rosenthal. 2016. *Polarized America: The Dance of Ideology and Unequal Riches.* 2nd ed. Cambridge, MA: MIT Press.

McCubbins, Mathew D., Roger G. Noll, and Barry R. Weingast. 1987. "Administrative Procedures as Instruments of Political Control." *Journal of Law, Economics, and Organization* 3, no. 2 (Autumn): 243–77.

McDonald, Michael P., and John Samples, eds. 2006. *The Marketplace of Democracy: Electoral Competition and American Politics.* Washington, DC: Brookings Institution.

McGuire, Robert A. 1981. "Economic Causes of Late-Nineteenth Century Agrarian Unrest: New Evidence." *Journal of Economic History* 41, no. 4 (December): 835–52.

McMath, Robert C., Jr. 1993. *American Populism: A Social History, 1877–1898.* New York: Hill and Wang.

McCubbins, Matthew D., Roger G. Noll, and Barry R. Weingast. 1989. "Structure and Process, Politics and Policy: Administrative Arrangements and the Political Control of Agencies." *Virginia Law Review* 75, no. 2 (March): 431–82.

———. 1999. "The Political Origins of the Administrative Procedure Act." *Journal of Law, Economics, and Organization* 15, no. 1 (April): 180–217.

Mehta, Seema, and Michael Finnegan. 2014. "An Experienced Jerry Brown Vows to Build on What He's Already Done." *Los Angeles Times,* October 19, 2014.

Middlekauf, Robert. 1982. *The Glorious Cause: The American Revolution, 1763–1789.* New York: Oxford University Press.

Mikelionis, Lukas. 2018. "From Italy to Hungary to France, How Populist Movements in 2018 Enveloped Europe." *Fox News,* December 18, 2018. https://www.foxnews.com/world/from-italy-to-hungary-to-france-how-populist-movements-in-2018-enveloped-europe.

Moore, Ryan T., and Nirmala Ravishankar. 2012. "Who Loses in Direct Democracy?" *Social Science Research* 41, no. 3 (May): 646–56.

Moss, David A. 2017. *Democracy: A Case Study.* Cambridge, MA: Belknap Press of Harvard University Press.

Mounk, Yascha. 2018. *The People vs. Democracy: Why Our Freedom Is in Danger and How to Save It.* Cambridge, MA: Harvard University Press.

Mouritsen, Henrik. 2017. *Politics in the Roman Republic.* New York: Cambridge University Press.

Mueller, Dennis C. 2003. *Public Choice III.* Cambridge: Cambridge University Press.

NCSL Initiative and Referendum Task Force. 2002. *Initiative and Referendum in the 21st Century.* Denver, CO: NCSL. http://www.ncsl.org/research/elections-and-campaigns/task-force-report.aspx.

Nichols, Chris. 2017. "Do Three-Quarters of Americans Support the DREAM Act? Nancy Pelosi Says So." *Politifact,* September 19, 2017. https://www.politifact.com/california/statements/2017/sep/19/nancy-pelosi/nancy-pelosi-claims-three-quarters-americans-suppo/.

Nitzan, Shmuel, and Jacob Paroush. 2017. "Collective Decision-Making and Jury Theorems." Chapter 24 in *The Oxford Handbook of Law and Economics,* vol. 1, edited by Francesco Parisi. Oxford: Oxford University Press.

Novek, William J. 2014. "A Revisionist History of Capture Theory." Chapter 1 in *Preventing Regulatory Capture: Special Interest Influence and How to Limit It*, edited by Daniel Carpenter and David A. Moss. New York: Cambridge University Press.

Ober, Josiah. 2008. *Democracy and Knowledge: Innovation and Learning in Classical Athens*. Princeton, NJ: Princeton University Press.

Oberholtzer, Ellis Paxson. 1911. *The Referendum in American (Together with Some Chapters on the Initiative and the Recall)*. New York: Charles Scribner's Sons.

Olken, Benjamin A. 2010. "Direct Democracy and Local Public Goods: Evidence from a Field Experiment in Indonesia." *American Political Science Review* 104, no. 2 (May): 243–67.

Olson, Mancur. 1965. *The Logic of Collective Action: Public Goods and the Theory of Groups*. Cambridge, MA: Harvard University Press.

Osborne, Martin J., and Al Slivinski. 1996. "A Model of Political Competition with Citizen-Candidates." *Quarterly Journal of Economics* 111, no. 1 (February): 65–96.

Page, Benjamin I. 2002. "Response: Refined and Enlarged Public Opinion." In *Democracy: How Direct?* edited by Elliott Abrams, 82–86. Lanham, MD: Rowman and Littlefield.

Page, Benjamin I., and Robert Y. Shapiro. 1992. *The Rational Public: Fifty Years of Trends in American Policy Preferences*. Chicago: University of Chicago Press.

Parker, George. 2017. "'Re-Leavers' Reluctantly Get in Tune on Brexit: Remain Towns Such as Lewes Want a Good EU Deal Rather than a Re-run of Referendum." *Financial Times*, May 16, 2017.

Pasley, Jeffrey L. 2004. "The Cheese and the Words: Popular Political Culture and Participatory Democracy in the Early American Republic." Chapter 1 in *Beyond the Founders: New Approaches to the Political History of the Early American Republic*, edited by Jeffrey L. Pasley, Andrew W. Robertson, and David Waldstreicher. Chapel Hill: University of North Carolina Press.

Patterson, James T. 1996. *Grand Expectations: The United States, 1945–1974*. New York: Oxford University Press.

Peake, Jeffrey S. 2018. "The Decline of Treaties? Obama, Trump, and the Politics of International Agreements." Working paper, Clemson University.

Peltzman, Sam. 1976. "Toward a More General Theory of Economic Regulation." *Journal of Law and Economics* 19, no. 2 (August): 211–40.

———. 1987. "Economic Conditions and Gubernatorial Elections." *American Economic Review Papers and Proceedings* 77, no. 2 (May): 293–97.

———. 1990. "How Efficient Is the Voting Market?" *Journal of Law and Economics* 33, no. 1 (April): 27–63.

———. 1992. "Voters as Fiscal Conservatives." *Quarterly Journal of Economics* 107, no. 2 (May): 327–61.

———. 1998. *Political Participation and Government Regulation*. Chicago: University of Chicago Press.

Pew Research Center. 1998. "Washington Leaders Wary of Public Opinion." Pew Research Center, U.S. Politics & Policy. April 17, 1998. http://www.people-press.org/1998/04/17/washington-leaders-wary-of-public-opinion/.

———. 2015. "Beyond Distrust: How Americans View Their Government." Part 6, "Perceptions of Elected Officials and the Role of Money in Politics." Pew Research Center, U.S. Politics

& Policy. November 23, 2015. http://www.people-press.org/2015/11/23/6-perceptions-of
-elected-officials-and-the-role-of-money-in-politics/.

Piott, Steven L. 2003. *Giving Voters a Voice: The Origins of the Initiative and Referendum in America*. Columbia: University of Missouri Press.

Pitkin, Hanna Fenichel. 1967. *The Concept of Representation*. Berkeley: University of California Press.

Politico staff. 2016. "Transcript: Bernie Sanders Speech in Burlington, Vermont." *Politico*, June 16, 2016. https://www.politico.com/story/2016/06/transcript-bernie-sanders-speech-in
-burlington-vermont-224465.

Poole, Keith T. 2007. "Changing Minds? Not in Congress!" *Public Choice* 131, nos. 3–4 (June): 435–51.

Poole, Keith T., and Howard Rosenthal. 1991. "Patterns of Congressional Voting." *American Journal of Political Science* 35, no. 1 (February): 228–78.

Popkin, Samuel L. 1991. *The Reasoning Voter: Communication and Persuasion in Presidential Elections*. Chicago: University of Chicago Press.

Posner, Richard A. 2010. *How Judges Think*. Cambridge, MA: Harvard University Press.

Postel, Charles. 2007. *The Populist Vision*. New York: Oxford University Press.

Postell, Joseph. 2012. *From Administrative State to Constitutional Government*. Washington, DC: The Heritage Center. https://www.heritage.org/political-process/report/administrative-state
-constitutional-government.

Potter, Wendell, and Nick Penniman. 2016. *Nation on the Take: How Big Money Corrupts Our Democracy and What We Can Do about It*. New York: Bloomsbury.

Qvortrup, Matt. 2018. *Government by Referendum*. Manchester, UK: Manchester University Press.

Rau, Jordan, Evan Halper, and Patrick McGreevy. 2009. "The State Budget Crisis: Far-Reaching Consequences; Budget's Fate in Voters' Hands; Governor to Sign Bill Today, but Much Hinges on Ballot Measures." *Los Angeles Times*, February 20, 2009, A1.

Rawls, John. 1971. *A Theory of Justice*. Cambridge, MA: Harvard University Press.

Reeves, Richard. 2015. *Infamy: The Shocking Story of the Japanese Internment in World War II*. New York: Picador.

Rhodes, P. J. 1985. *The Athenian Boule*. New York: Oxford University Press.

Richard, Carl J. 1994. *The Founders and the Classics: Greece, Rome, and the American Enlightenment*. Cambridge, MA: Harvard University Press.

Richardson, Mark D., Joshua D. Clinton, and David E. Lewis. 2018. "Elite Perceptions of Agency Ideology and Workforce Skill." *Journal of Politics* 80, no. 1 (January): 303–8.

Richman, Sheldon L. 1988. *The Reagan Record on Trade: Rhetoric vs. Reality*. Cato Institute Policy Analysis No. 107. Washington, DC: Cato Institute.

Richter, Brian Kelleher, Krislert Samphantharak, and Jeffrey F. Timmons. 2009. "Lobbying and Taxes." *American Journal of Political Science* 53, no. 4 (October): 893–909.

Riker, William H. 1961. "Voting and the Summation of Preferences: An Interpretive Bibliographic Review of Selected Developments in the Last Decade." *American Political Science Review* 55, no. 4 (December): 900–911.

Rissotto, Rodolfo Gonzalez, and Daniel Zovatto. 2008. "Direct Democracy in Uruguay." In IDEA, *Direct Democracy: The International IDEA Handbook*, 166–72. Stockholm: IDEA.

Rodrick, Dani. 2017. "Populism and the Economics of Globalization." Harvard Kennedy School Faculty Research Working Paper Series, June 2017.

Rogers, Todd, and Joel Middleton. 2015. "Are Ballot Initiative Outcomes Influenced by the Campaigns of Independent Groups? A Precinct-Randomized Field Experiment Showing that They Are." *Political Behavior* 37, no. 3 (September): 567–93.

Rogoff, Kenneth. 2016. "Britain's Democratic Failure." *Project Syndicate*, June 24, 2016. https://www.project-syndicate.org/commentary/brexit-democratic-failure-for-uk-by-kenneth-rogoff-2016-06?barrier=accesspaylog.

Romer, Thomas, and Howard Rosenthal. 1979. "The Elusive Median Voter." *Journal of Public Economics* 12, no. 2 (October): 143–70.

Roosevelt, Theodore. (1912) n.d. "A Charter of Democracy." Address before the Ohio Constitutional Convention, February 21, 1912. ehistory, The Ohio State University. Accessed August 13, 2019. https://ehistory.osu.edu/exhibitions/1912/1912documents/Charter of Democracy.

———. (1912) 2018. "The Right of the People to Rule." Speech at Carnegie Hall in New York City, March 20, 1912. American Rhetoric Online Speech Bank. June 21, 2018. https://americanrhetoric.com/speeches/teddyrooseveltrightpeoplerule.htm.

Roy, Denny. 2003. *Taiwan: A Political History*. Ithaca, NY: Cornell University Press.

Rush, Benjamin. (1789) n.d. "To John Adams from Benjamin Rush, July 21, 1789." Founders Online, National Archives. Accessed August 9, 2019. https://founders.archives.gov/documents/Adams/99-02-02-0695.

Sabato, Larry J., Howard R. Ernst, and Bruce A. Larson, eds. 2001. *Dangerous Democracy?: The Battle over Ballot Initiatives in America*. Lanham, MD: Rowman and Littlefield.

Sasse, Ben. 2018. "Sasse on Kavanaugh Hearing: 'We Can and We Should Do Better than This.'" Ben Sasse's official website. Press release. September 4, 2018. https://www.sasse.senate.gov/public/index.cfm/2018/9/sasse-on-kavanaugh-hearing-we-can-and-we-should-do-better-than-this.

Schildkraut, Deborah J. 2001. "Official-English and the States: Influences on Declaring English the Official Language in the United States." *Political Research Quarterly* 54, no. 2 (June): 445–57.

Schmidt, David D. 1989. *Citizen Lawmakers: The Ballot Initiative Revolution*. Philadelphia: Temple University Press.

Schrag, Peter. 2004. *Paradise Lost: California's Experience, America's Future*. Rev. ed. Berkeley: University of California Press.

Schroeder, Larry D., and David L. Sjoquist. 1978. "The Rational Voter: An Analysis of Two Atlanta Referenda on Rapid Transit." *Public Choice* 33, no. 3: 27–44.

Seabrook, Nicholas R., Joshua J. Dyck, and Edward L. Lascher Jr. 2015. "Do Ballot Initiatives Increase General Political Knowledge?" *Political Behavior* 37, no. 2 (June): 279–307.

Seifter, Miriam. 2017. "Gubernatorial Administration." *Harvard Law Review* 131, no. 2 (December): 483–542.

Sheperd, George B. 1996. "Fierce Compromise: The Administrative Procedure Act Emerges from New Deal Politics." *Northwestern University Law Review* 90, no. 4: 1557–683.

Shipman, Tim. 2017. *All Out War: The Full Story of Brexit*. Rev. ed. London: William Collins.

Shlaes, Amity 2013. *Coolidge*. New York: HarperCollins.

Shor, Boris, and Nolan McCarty. 2011. "The Ideological Mapping of American Legislatures." *American Political Science Review* 105, no. 3 (August): 530–51.

Simonovits, Gabor, Andrew M. Guess, and Jonathan Nagler. 2019. "Responsiveness without Representation: Evidence from Minimum Wage Laws in U.S. States." *American Journal of Political Science* 62, no. 2 (April): 401–10.

Skelton, George. 1978. "Los Angeles Times Poll: No Regrets by Prop. 13 Backers Found." *Los Angeles Times*, July 9, 1978, A1.

Smith, Daniel A. 1998. *Tax Crusaders and the Politics of Direct Democracy*. New York: Routledge.

Smith, Daniel A., and Caroline J. Tolbert. 2004. *Educated by Initiative: The Effects of Direct Democracy on Citizens and Political Organizations in the American States*. Ann Arbor: University of Michigan Press.

Smith, Jean Edward. 2007. *FDR*. New York: Random House Trade Paperbacks.

Snyder, James M. Jr. 1991. "On Buying Legislatures." *Economics and Politics* 3, no. 2 (July): 93–109.

Song, Jason, and Howard Blume. 2009. "Anger over Budget Cuts Boils Over at L.A. Schools; Hundreds of Teachers Call in Sick and Hundreds of High School Students Walk Out of Classrooms." *Los Angeles Times*, May 16, 2009, A7.

Stigler, George J. 1971. "The Theory of Economic Regulation." *Bell Journal of Economics and Management Science* 2, no. 1 (Spring): 3–21.

Stokes, Bruce. 2016. *Euroskepticism Beyond Brexit: Significant Opposition in Key European Countries to an Ever Closer EU*. Washington, DC: Pew Research Center.

Storing, Herbert J., ed. 1985. *The Anti-Federalist: An Abridgement, by Murray Dry, of the Complete Anti-Federalist*. Chicago: University of Chicago Press.

Stratmann, Thomas. 1992. "Are Contributors Rational? Untangling Strategies of Political Action Committees." *Journal of Political Economy* 100, no. 3 (June): 647–64.

———. 1998. "The Market for Congressional Votes: Is Timing of Contributions Everything?" *Journal of Law and Economics* 41, no. 1 (April): 85–114.

———. 2002. "Can Special Interests Buy Congressional Votes? Evidence from Financial Services Legislation." *Journal of Law and Economics* 45, no. 2 (October): 345–73.

———. 2006. "Is Spending More Potent For or Against a Proposition? Evidence from Ballot Measures." *American Journal of Political Science* 50, no. 3 (July): 788–801.

Strauss, Peter L. 1984. "The Place of Agencies in Government: Separation of Powers and the Fourth Branch." *Columbia Law Review* 84, no. 3 (April): 573–669.

Sullivan, Andrew. 2016. "Democracies End When They Are Too Democratic." *New Yorker*, May 1, 2016.

———. 2017. "The Reactionary Temptation." *New York Magazine*, May 1, 2017.

Taft, William Howard. (1911) n.d. *Special Message of the President of the United States Returning without Approval House Joint Resolution No. 14*. Online facsimile; originally published by [Government Printing Office] (Washington). Hathi Trust Digital Library. Accessed August 14, 2019. https://babel.hathitrust.org/cgi/pt?id=uc2.ark:/13960/t6154mw41&view=1up&seq=2.

Taiwan Foundation for Democracy. 2004. *Direct Democracy Practices in Taiwan and Asia-Pacific: The Taiwan Referendum Act, Reports, and Analysis*. Taipei: Taiwan Foundation for Democracy.

Tarr, G. Allen. 2002. "For the People: Direct Democracy and the State Constitutional Tradition." Chapter 6 in *Democracy: How Direct? Views from the Found Era and the Polling Era*, edited by Elliott Abrams. Lanham, MD: Rowman and Littlefield.

Thernstrom, Stephan, and Abigail Thernstrom. 1997. *America in Black and White: One Nation, Indivisible*. New York: Simon and Schuster.

Topaloff, Liubomir. 2017. "Elite Strategy or Populist Weapon?" *Journal of Democracy* 28, no. 3 (July): 127–40.

Truman, David B. 1951. *The Governmental Process: Political Interests and Public Opinion*. New York: Alfred A. Knopf.

Tucker, Paul. 2018. *Unelected Power: The Quest for Legitimacy in Central Banking and the Regulatory State*. Princeton, NJ: Princeton University Press.

Tyler, Tom R. 2004. "Procedural Justice." Chapter 23 in *The Blackwell Companion to Law and Society*, edited by Austin Sarat. Oxford: Blackwell.

UKPol. 2016. "Nigel Farage—2016 Speech to European Parliament." UKPol Political Speech Archive, June 28, 2016. http://www.ukpol.co.uk/nigel-farage-2016-speech-to-european-parliament/.

Urban, Wayne J., and Jennings I. Wagoner Jr. 2014. *American Education: A History*. 5th ed. New York: Routledge.

Vermeule, Adrian. 2015. "The Administrative State: Law, Democracy, and Knowledge." Chapter 13 in *Oxford Handbook of the U.S. Constitution*, edited by Mark Tushnet, Mark A. Graber, and Sanford Levinson. New York: Oxford University Press.

Versteeg, Mila, and Emily Zackin. 2014. "American Constitutional Exceptionalism Revisited." *University of Chicago Law Review* 81, no. 4 (Fall): 1641–707.

Wallach, Philip. 2016. *The Administrative State's Legitimacy Crisis*. Washington, DC: Center for Effective Public Management at Brookings.

Waters, M. Dane. 2003. *Initiative and Referendum Almanac*. Durham, NC: Carolina Academic.

Webster, Noah. (1787) n.d. *A Citizen of America: An Examination into the Leading Principles of America*. Online transcript of edition published by Prichard and Hall (Philadelphia). Internet Archive. Accessed August 14, 2019. https://archive.org/stream/examinationintoloowebs/examinationintoloowebs_djvu.txt.

Weingast, Barry R., Kenneth A. Shepsle, and Christopher Johnsen. 1981. "The Political Economy of Benefits and Costs: A Neoclassical Approach to Distribute Politics." *Journal of Political Economy* 89, no. 4 (August): 642–64.

Weiss, Debra Cassens. 2012. "Justice Ginsburg: Roe v. Wade Decision Came Too Soon." *ABA Journal Daily News*. February 13, 2012. http://www.abajournal.com/news/article/justice_ginsburg_roe_v._wade_decision_came_too_soon.

Wheeler, Russell. 2010. "Changing Backgrounds of U.S. District Judges: Likely Causes and Possible Implications." *Judicature* 93, no. 4 (January–February): 140–49.

White, Richard. 2017. *The Republic for Which It Stands: The United States during Reconstruction and the Gilded Age, 1865–1896*. New York: Oxford University Press.

White House. n.d. "We Can't Wait." White House (President Barack Obama). Accessed August 9, 2019. https://obamawhitehouse.archives.gov/economy/jobs/we-cant-wait.

Wike, Richard, Janell Fetterolf, and Moira Fagan. 2019. "Europeans Credit EU with Promoting Peace and Prosperity, but Say Brussels Is Out of Touch with Its Citizens." Pew Research Center. March 19, 2019. https://www.pewresearch.org/global/2019/03/19/europeans-credit-eu-with-promoting-peace-and-prosperity-but-say-brussels-is-out-of-touch-with-its-citizens/.

Wike, Richard, Katie Simmons, Bruce Stokes, and Janell Fetterolf. 2017. "Globally, Broad Support for Representative and Direct Democracy." Pew Research Center. October 2017. https://www.pewresearch.org/global/2017/10/16/globally-broad-support-for-representative-and-direct-democracy/.

Wilentz, Sean. 2005a. *The Rise of American Democracy: Jefferson to Lincoln*. New York: W. W. Norton.

———. 2005b. *Andrew Jackson*. New York: Times Books.

Wilson, James. (1787) 2009. "James Wilson Speech: Pennsylvania Ratifying Convention, 24 November 1787: Version of Wilson's Speech by Thomas Lloyd." In *The Documentary History of the Ratification of the Constitution*, digital ed., edited by John P. Kaminski, Gaspare J. Saladino, Richard Leffler, Charles H. Schoenleber, and Margaret A. Hogan. Charlottesville: University of Virginia Press. http://rotunda.upress.virginia.edu/founders/RNCN-02-02-02-0003-0002-0005-0004.

Wilson, Woodrow. 1912. "The Issues of Reform." Chapter 3 in *The Initiative, Referendum and Recall*, edited by William Bennet Munro. New York: D. Appleton.

Wood, Gordon S. (1969) 1998. *The Creation of the American Republic 1776–1787*. Chapel Hill: University of North Carolina Press.

———. 2009. *Empire of Liberty: A History of the Early Republic, 1789–1815*. New York: Oxford University Press.

Woodward, C. Vann. (1955) 2001. *The Strange Career of Jim Crow*. Commemorative Ed. New York: Oxford University Press.

Yates, Robert. (1787) n.d. "Robert Yates's Version, [18 June 1787]." Founders Online, National Archives. Accessed August 12, 2019. https://founders.archives.gov/documents/Hamilton/01-04-02-0098-0004.

Young, Samantha. 2009. "Gov. Schwarzenegger to Sign Budget-Balancing Bill." *San Diego Union-Tribune*, February 19, 2009.

Zapryanova, Galina, and Anders Christiansen. 2017. "Hope, Trust Deficits May Help Fuel Populism." *Gallup News*, April 7, 2017. https://news.gallup.com/poll/207674/hope-trust-deficits-may-help-fuel-populism.aspx.

Zingales, Luigi. 2012. *A Capitalism for the People: Recapturing the Lost Genius of American Prosperity*. New York: Basic Books.

INDEX

Abe, Shinzo, 93, 241n10

abortion: American policy path to unending conflict, 7–9; European approaches to, 9–10; public opinion on (*see* public opinion); as self-inflicted wound in the U.S., 163–64

abrogativo referendum. *See* petition referendum

accountability, factors undermining, 29–30

Adams, Anthony, 258n9

Adams, John, 100–101, 111–12

Adams, John Quincy, 254n20

Administrative Procedure Act (APA) of 1946, 20, 31–32, 242n7

administrative state, the, 17–18; advisory referendums on rules and regulations, proposal for, 132–33; business competition regulated by, 23–24; capture by interest groups, challenge of, 31–32; controlling, challenge of, 28–31; environmental regulation by, 21–23; in Europe, 80; ideological orientations of executive agencies, 30; international trade regulated by, 24–26; national parks, creation of, 26–27; origins of, 5, 18–20; overview and examples of the current, 21–28. *See also* technocrats

advisory referendum: called by Congress, proposal for, 130–31; called by petition, proposal for, 131–33; definition of, 62–63; initiatives and, differing impact of, 155; mandatory on specific issues, proposal

for, 133–34; mandatory referendums and, differing impact of, 155. *See also* binding referendum

Aera Energy, 195

African Americans: civil rights movement, 123–24; constitutional protections of, failures of, 206–7; disenfranchisement of, 123

Alito, Samuel, 17, 38

amendments: Asian constitutions, 93–94; city charters, 71–73; European constitutions, 83–88; South American constitutions, 95–96; state constitutions, 6, 12, 63, 67, 70–71, 125, 151, 233–34. *See also* Constitution, United States

American democracy, historical evolution of, 109, 124–25; the age of Jackson, conflict and change in, 114–18; democratizing movements of the 1950s-1970s, 123–24; the early republic, conflict and change in, 111–14; the industrial age, conflict and change in, 118–23; popular participation, the Founders' hostility to, 99–100 (*see also* United States, distrust of the common man by the Founders); the populist roots, 110; representative democracy, origin of, 105–7

American National Election Studies (ANES), 2, 53

Antiquities Act of 1906, 26–27

antitrust policy, 23–24, 33

Frankfurter, Felix, 39
Friedman, Milton, 142
Funk, Patricia, 262n24

Gailmard, Sean, 30
Gallup poll, 2, 165, 241n9, 249n16, 265n13
Gann, Paul, 141, 144
Garland, Merrick, 35
Gathmann, Christina, 262n24
Gephardt, Dick, 130
Gerber, Elisabeth, 200, 212–13
Germany, 83–84
Gilens, Martin, 55
Ginsburg, Ruth Bader, 8–9
Goebel, Thomas, 263n3
Gorsuch, Neil, 35
government, disaffection with. See
   disconnection between citizens and
   government
Great Railroad Strike, 119
Greene, Leroy, 143

Hajnal, Zoltan, 212–13
Hamilton, Alexander, 102, 111, 179
Hanssen, Andrew, 252n19–20
Hasen, Richard, 260n29
Hayakawa, S. I., 210
Hayek, F. A., 226
Hayes, Rutherford, 119
Hindenberg, Paul von, 84
Hitler, Adolf, 83–85
Howell, William G., 242n18
Huntington, Samuel P., 244n43

ideology: ideological orientations of
   executive agencies, 30; voting behavior of
   legislators and, 46–47, 50
immigration and trade, the best process for
   making a decision on, 222–23
impossibility theorems, 225–26, 267n10
information: informative elections despite
   uninformed voters, 171–74; rational
   ignorance, 171; technical and preference,
   distinction between, 218

information aggregation: Condorcet jury
   theorem, 165, 259n22; "law of large
   numbers"/"wisdom of crowds," 165, 174
information "shortcuts"/"cues"/"heuristics":
   required by voters in a referendum,
   219–20, 229–30; shortcuts, 172–74, 176–79,
   229–30, 261n19
initiatives: advisory referendums and,
   differing impact of, 155; approval rate,
   76–77; business groups/interests and,
   188–92; business groups/interests in
   California and, 192–99; cities with,
   72–73; definition of, 62–63; in Europe, 81;
   initiative and petition referendum, 70–71,
   122; national initiative process as
   unrealistic, 136; process of, a close look
   at, 71–77; prominent topics of, 75–76;
   spending by states with and without,
   180–81; spending on by interest groups,
   limited impact of, 199–201; states with,
   72, 74–75; threat to minority rights posed
   by, 207–11. See also referendum;
   referendum design
interest groups, 187–88, 244n40; business
   interests, success and failure in initiatives
   in California by, 192–99; business
   interests and initiatives, 188–92; capture
   of regulatory agencies by, 31–32; direct
   democracy as a tool to control the
   influence of, 201–2; Proposition 13 and,
   141–44; spending on initiatives, limited
   impact of, 199–201
Interstate Commerce Act of 1887, 242n5
Interstate Commerce Commission (ICC),
   18–19, 32
Iran Nuclear Agreement, 26
Ireland, 88, 134
Issacharoff, Samuel, 238
Italy, 9, 87–88, 163

Jackson, Andrew, 115–16, 118
Japan, 93, 241n10, 250n6–7
Japanese Americans, internment of, 206
Jarvis, Howard, 141–42, 167

A NOTE ON THE TYPE

This book has been composed in Arno, an Old-style serif typeface in the classic Venetian tradition, designed by Robert Slimbach at Adobe.